Lane Memorial Library

Hampton, N.H. 03842

Telephone 926-3368

P9-DHI-303

3 4509 00120385 0

Sharing Parenthood
After Divorce

Ciji Ware

Sharing Parenthood
After Divorce

An Enlightened Custody Guide
for Mothers, Fathers, and Kids

THE VIKING PRESS   NEW YORK

Copyright © 1979, 1982 by Ciji Ware
All rights reserved
First published in 1982 by The Viking Press
625 Madison Avenue, New York, N.Y. 10022
Published simultaneously in Canada by
Penguin Books Canada Limited

A selection from this book appeared originally in *New West* magazine.

LIBRARY OF CONGRESS CATALOGING IN PUBLICATION DATA
Ware, Ciji.
    Sharing parenthood after divorce.
    Includes index.
    1. Joint custody of children—United States.
I. Title.
KF547.W37   346.7301'7   81-69926 ✓
ISBN 0-670-40858-1   347.30617   AACR2

Grateful acknowledgment is made to the following for permission to
reprint copyrighted material:

Association of Family and Conciliation Courts: "Check the Pressure
Quiz," adapted from "Children and Divorce—Twenty Questions
Divorcing Parents Ask," Association of Family and Conciliation
Courts Pamphlet. Used by permission of authors Florence Bienen-
feld, Elayne Kardner, and Meyer Elkin, Consultant, 1981, and the
Association of Family and Conciliation Courts.

The Divorce Mediation Research Project: "Divorce Mediation
Sources" from *The Divorce Mediation Resource Book,* A Project of
the Divorce Mediation Research Project, the Association of Family
and Conciliation Courts, c/o Nova University Law Center, 3100 S.W.
Ninth Avenue, Fort Lauderdale, Florida 33315, Anne L. Milne,
ACSW, Editor.

Dr. John M. Haynes: "Household Budget" and the budget forms
appearing in this book have been adapted from the pamphlet
"Divorce Mediation: A Less Painful Path." Copyright © 1978
by John M. Haynes, Ph.D., Huntington, New York. Used by
permission.

Printed in the United States of America
Set in Video Times Roman

This book is dedicated
to Jamie,
who taught us all so much.

Preface

Please read this book before you hire a lawyer.

If you are already in the middle of a divorce, read this book before you make final any more decisions regarding the custody arrangements for your children.

If your divorce is final, but your life remains in turmoil, read this book for ways in which you and your former spouse can renegotiate your postdivorce relationships. You and your children do not have to suffer because of a child custody system that brutalizes families.

If anyone had told me back in 1973, when I was divorcing and facing a custody fight over my small son, that there are ways former spouses can be parents together—separately—after the divorce, I would have referred them angrily to my lawyer. How can two people who are angry enough to end a marriage, I would have demanded, ever be able to work together toward a cooperative custody arrangement that suits both of them and their children as well? How utterly idiotic! In fact, as a mother, I had particularly strong fears that any gesture of cooperation I might show toward my child's father would be interpreted as a sign of weakness and be used against me if our custody battle went on to a trial.

It was shattering to think that every divorced woman I knew automatically got custody and I might not. For me, as for many women, not getting custody of my son meant being judged before the world as an "unfit" mother. I realized only much later that, for my former husband, not getting custody meant losing his child. And now, nearly a decade later, I feel compelled to tell other mothers and fathers that there *is* a way out of the confusion that divorcing families face. Yes, finding one's way through the bewildering American custody system isn't easy. Indeed, changes in our attitudes about the roles men and women can play in child care and custody come about slowly. But *we parents,* in our frustration and agony, are seeking new solutions and structures for the changing family. And not a moment too soon.

The 1970s produced a startling one-million-plus divorces a year, two thirds of them involving children under fourteen years of age. Millions of parents are attempting to cope with a child custody system that almost always places the entire burden of child rearing on the single mother, while simultaneously depriving the father of access to his offspring. Now that nearly 79 percent of divorced mothers work, most do not have the luxury of staying home to care for their children. The children are either in the charge of a baby-sitter, or in school all day, or left to fend for themselves.

Many youngsters these days suffer more than ever from divorce because they see *both* parents less. Millions of children are growing up without the loving, nurturing, stabilizing, socializing influence that two parents can provide. Partly as a result of the social upheaval caused by a divorce, we have already seen increases in youthful crime, school vandalism, alcoholism, suicide, and drug abuse. Traditional sole custody is creating a generation of children who are being psychologically damaged by losing both parents when there is a divorce. For some children, traditional custody agreements result in a form of psychological child abuse.

The family-court system can be blamed, in part, for the suffering that children endure when their parents divorce. Even in states with no-fault divorce laws, the adversary legal system often escalates, not mitigates, the conflict between mothers and fathers. Too many courts, lawyers, and child specialists pit mothers against fathers in order to establish which is the "better" parent—a process often resulting in a traumatic "amputation" of one parent from the child's life—all in the name of "the best interests of the child." As Frank Williams, a psychiatrist and director of the Thalians Community Mental Health Center in Los Angeles, commented to his colleagues at a 1980 meeting on the changing family, "You would never consider performing an appendectomy on a child without anesthetic, but we do 'parent-ectomies' on kids every day."

There are no set formulas for resolving custody conflicts. There are, however, a number of options that many divorcing parents may not be exposed to, given the win-lose custody resolution prevalent in the courts. Divorcing spouses should know that it is possible to go outside the legal adversary system and to devise their *own* plan for continuing to be parents. They must realize it is within their power, as well as within the power of judges, attorneys, and mental health professionals, to determine what the eventual reorganization of their family will be. Regardless of how repressive or antiquated a state's custody statutes may be, there is no law in any state that says two parents cannot choose to practice cooperation on their own, despite what their official custody decree may say. The difficulty, of course, is for angry parents to realize that it is in their interest, ultimately, to agree to a cooperative rather than a competitive solution for raising their children.

Divorcing parents face a simple choice: let perfect strangers within the adversary legal system declare one parent the "winner" and dictate to both the details of their custody arrangement, or create a custody arrangement of their own design that takes into consideration both their own needs and their children's needs.

A cooperative partnership cannot be created quickly, and not without some conflict between natural parents, jealousies between old and new spouses, tension among children and stepparents and stepsiblings, and criticism from grandparents and former in-laws. But, ultimately, sharing parenthood when marriages dissolve can be one solution to the divorce war. It offers the hope that no one has to lose, especially not the children.

Which brings me back to 1973 and my son, Jamie. That was the year I was crazy. So was his father. We were both crazy with the grief and loss and disappointment of a marriage that hadn't worked for either of us. At that time we each thought the other was the source of our mutual pain, and we looked to our two-year-old child as the most precious, salvageable thing left in our lives.

Jamie. At two, he was a perfect little California surfer: blond, blue-eyed, and so adorable he caused traffic jams in the aisles at the supermarket. At birth, however, Jamie had looked as though he'd been in a prizefight with Muhammad Ali—and lost. He'd taken thirty hours of hard work to produce, and his father and I had struggled together mightily, according to Lamaze directives, to bring him forth. His dad had personally wheeled Jamie's plastic bassinet from the delivery room to the nursery at three a.m., in triumph. He'd stood for hours, sometimes with tears streaming, gazing through the nursery window at his baby—the kid with the squished nose and pointy head and forceps marks on his temples.

"To lose Jamie after the divorce was inconceivable," his father told me years later. But we almost did lose him. We *both* almost lost him. We nearly lost him to a system that institutionalizes single parenthood and child abandonment.

In 1973 no one had heard of *Kramer vs. Kramer.* In 1973 few men wanted to change diapers or minister to sick babies in the middle of the night. Attorneys and the courts were of the opinion that when a marriage dissolved, women, because of their biology, were the proper custodians of underage children. I, frankly, was basically of the same persuasion, despite women's consciousness-raising. And I was surprised when Jamie's father established from the very beginning of our separation a

regular and frequent schedule for being with our son, who was
then still in diapers.

As many couples do, we felt a tremendous amount of anger
while we labored to get a no-fault divorce. We no longer could
vent our fury in arguments over who was to blame for our "irreconcilable differences." The only arenas left in which to act
out all that rage were those of community finances and child
custody. As a reporter, I was working longer hours than my
husband, who was a TV producer. What, he demanded, was to
prevent him from challenging me for full custody? What, I re-
torted with fear and rage, was to prevent me from claiming 50
percent of all his future earnings from programs he had in development during our marriage? None of our various attorneys
detected that all the saber rattling sprang from deep and primitive motivations: both of us were terrified we would lose the
one we loved most in the world, our son.

Just as we seemed destined for Department 2 of Los Angeles
Superior Court, where custody battles are fought, my husband's latest legal warrior suggested we see a court-appointed
psychiatrist for advice on the potential impact of our divorce
on so small a child. I was afraid it was a trap to detect my defi-
ciencies as a working mother, but finally I agreed to go to one
meeting only.

The doctor told us several very important things that I wish
every parent headed for divorce could hear. "Your son will
survive the trauma of the divorce if he continues to have access
to both of you," he said. He never mentioned the word "custody" or such hideous terms as "visitation," "awards," "fit and
unfit," and the other jargon used whether one is talking about
divorce or criminals. "Your son has the capacity for loving as
many people as he's allowed to love," the doctor continued,
"as long as neither one of you makes him feel guilty." If he
loved his dad and spent time with him, it didn't mean he
wouldn't have enough love left for his mom. Obvious information for most people, perhaps, but Jamie's mother and dad had

had their common sense distorted. It wasn't the divorce, per se, that could harm Jamie, said the doctor. It was how we as parents conducted ourselves *after* the divorce that would determine the positive or negative impact on our son's psychological health.

The choice was ours, the doctor explained. We could fight over custody, with one of us coming out the loser, and risk whatever the protracted battle did to our boy, or we could work out a plan *ourselves* whereby we both continued to exercise rights and responsibilities as parents. The question was: How?

In 1973 no one used the terms "shared custody," "joint custody," or even "coparenting," but the court-appointed psychiatrist hammered home to two frightened and bewildered parents the idea that we could learn to cooperate instead of compete, that we could learn to be parents together—separately—after our divorce if we tried and if we truly had the best interests of our child at heart.

Learning to cooperate at that stage seemed an impossible assignment, but we managed an uneasy truce, with Jamie, who was just two years old, spending two early evenings during the week and every Saturday with his dad, always returning to my house to sleep. Father and son eventually exhausted Disneyland and the pony rides at Griffith Park, and finally settled into a routine of simply being together as parent and child.

When I realized I had begun to look forward to my time alone, without the demands of a toddler, I began to wonder if perhaps I really *was* the selfish, hard-driving career woman I felt my former husband thought me to be. I made sure, therefore, that Jamie's father clearly understood it was merely through the kindness of my heart that he had regular access to a child of such tender years. After all, the official court documents stated in typical fashion that I had sole legal and physical custody of Jamie and was in charge of administering "reasonable visitation." Although we had avoided an expensive and destructive custody fight, sharing Jamie in those days was an agony for everybody involved.

It's not hard to find precisely when we began to evolve a co-operative custody arrangement, sharing on a partnership basis the agonies and ecstasies of parenthood. It was that awful moment when we saw the tiny, ominous, peanut-shaped shadow on an X ray of Jamie's left leg, and heard the doctor recommend an operation.

Jamie's roommate the night before his surgery was a four-year-old who had just had his leg amputated because of a melanoma. At six a.m. Jamie's father and I stood together in the hospital corridor, frightened and helpless, as we watched the orderly wheel our own boy, who was by then three and a half, into the elevator that would take him to surgery. When the door slid shut, we led each other away, sobbing, to the waiting room. In fifteen minutes the surgeon came out of the operating room and approached us with some news. As he spoke, my former husband and I became sane again. We didn't want to be together, but we wanted to be *parents* together. We had just learned that Jamie would be all right and that we would have a child to parent.

All the jealousies and hurts and fears that one of us would be shortchanged if our son loved the other parent "too much" had been defused. As parents, we'd had our priorities straightened out by a cancer scare. It dawned on us that we were still a family—but a restructured one. And my former spouse and I began to negotiate with each other a more equal and cooperative sharing of responsibilities for the day-to-day care of our child.

The process by which we—and thousands of divorced parents like us across the country—were able to come up with a custody arrangement acceptable to all parties forms the substance of this book. That process takes time, it takes work, and often it takes help from others who understand the methods by which custody conflicts can be resolved through the science—

and art—of negotiation, mediation, and conciliation.

As happens in any compromise settlement, there have been days when I wished I could cancel the deal and take full control again. There have been times, I am sure, when Jamie's father wished he could scoop up his son, move to Tahiti, and have his child all to himself. And despite warnings from friends and some "experts" that we would confuse our son and split his loyalties because "he won't know who he belongs to," our own common sense tells us that sharing rights and responsibilities as parents is the right choice for us, for Jamie, and for other families who have chosen cooperation over competition.

Our formula for cooperative custody allows Jamie to spend a nearly equal amount of time with each of us. But not all former spouses can stay geographically close after a divorce. In these cases, shared custody takes on a different form. But however far apart a divorced couple may live, it is possible for them to share responsibility for their children. In a positive, supportive way, the parents can consult on important issues regarding schooling, medical problems, and vacation times, even if the logistics dictate that one parent assumes the major portion of physical care. It is also possible for divorced couples who remain furious at each other to learn through negotiation, mediation, and conciliation how to cooperate as parents. As long as they build enough respect for each other as parents, and neither is psychologically destructive or physically abusive toward the children, they can learn to forge a new relationship based on their common goal of wanting to provide a positive environment for their youngsters.

The logistics of day-to-day arrangements are the second phase of any cooperative custody negotiation. Phase One requires a reordering of the conventional wisdom about child custody; it requires acceptance of the idea that parents divorce each other, not their children. However it is accomplished physically, shared custody institutes in actual fact as well as in theory that favorite aphorism of family-law specialists: "Parents are forever."

I mentioned earlier that arriving at a negotiated shared custody settlement takes work, it takes time, and often it takes the help of a third party skilled in the art of mediation. Angry and hurting couples may have difficulty shifting the focus, by themselves, from their own feelings of loss or guilt to the specific task of working out how the children are to be cared for in the years following the divorce. Domestic mediators and court conciliators are trained to guide couples toward solutions. Progressive family courts around the country are offering mediation to parents *prior* to a child custody trial. In a few courts, divorcing parents fighting over the children are required to agree to try negotiating all custody and visitation conflicts before they're given a court date. But unfortunately there are few such courts. Until divorce mediators and conciliation courts are as available as divorce attorneys, books like mine will have to fill the gap for divorcing parents interested in exploring the option of sharing custody.

I am grateful to the court-appointed psychiatrist who, in one painful session, served as mediator during my divorce (and whose name I have blocked forever from my consciousness). I wish to thank him and all the people too numerous to mention by name who have contributed their time, their knowledge, and their extraordinary concern for children toward my efforts in the pages to follow. Special thanks go to Hugh McIsaac, director of Conciliation Court, a division of Los Angeles Superior Court, who never doubted that a nonlawyer, nontherapist could write a book for divorcing parents. And to Simone Katz-Savlov, a licensed marriage, family, and child counselor—and a joint custody parent—who asked me to help her launch Custody Options Workshops in Los Angeles, a series of seminars for parents in which we tested many of this book's prescriptions for working out shared custody agreements. Thanks, too, to my editor, Steve Gelman, whose unerring judgment and perceptive "third eye" kept this project on track and on time.

I would like to acknowledge my gratitude also, of course, to the people who opened their lives to me when I researched this book. Some of them told me their stories with a request that their real names not be used, and I note in the book those instances where I have changed names. To further disguise certain of them and their families, I have also altered geographical locations and other identifying characteristics.

All joint custody parents, present and future, owe a debt of gratitude to the two "fathers" of joint custody: Dr. Mel Roman, author of *The Disposable Parent: The Case for Joint Custody,* and James A. Cook, the tireless advocate of the California Joint Custody Law, the first in the nation to declare shared parenting the *public policy* of a state.

And, finally, my deepest thanks and admiration for the two parents who have taught me more about sharing custody than all the experts combined: my son's father and stepfather. These men, pioneers in a sense, redefined their conventional roles as males and forged new and nurturing ways of connecting with a little boy named Jamie.

In researching this book, I also spoke to many experts in the field of domestic law and child psychology who complained that all the talk about divorce mediation and shared custody arrangements had been drummed up merely for the convenience of parents and to lighten the burdens on judges. Shared custody, they declared, is actually detrimental to the child. These critics charged that two parents whose conflicts are serious enough to end their marriages are constitutionally unable to put their differences aside and cooperate in the future care of their children. Eventually, they claimed, the children will be ripped apart. Rarely, however, have these critics spent much time with the real experts: the couples and the children of the couples who are practicing two-parent custody under all sorts of conditions. This is a book about the *practice* of coparenting after a divorce. Its purpose is to show parents how to stop fighting over their offspring and negotiate a sharing arrangement that provides for the physical and emotional well-being of children.

In my own case, by the time Jamie was six, he was doing

extremely well by any of the usual yardsticks. He understood clearly that he lived in two houses; he loved school; he could read *Babar the Elephant* all by himself; he ate with gusto most of what was placed on his plate; he slept through the night without disturbance; he had lots of friends and a couple of special pals; he had a lively sense of humor; and, most important, he expressed love freely to the various significant adults in his life.

One evening, after a supper of steamed clams, Jamie was busily lining up empty shells on his place mat, unnoticed by myself, my second husband, Tony, and several other adults, who happened to be deep in conversation. Suddenly his happy voice piped up. "Here's the daddy clam, here's the mommy clam, here's the Jamie clam"—he paused for a second and reached back for the biggest clam left in the discard pile—"and here's the Tony clam!"

His stepfather, our guests, and I roared with laughter, but I had tears in my eyes.

It is my fervent hope that sharing parenthood after divorce works as well for mothers and fathers who read this book as it has for the family of my son, Jamie.

Los Angeles, California
February 1982

Contents

Part One

Why You Should Choose Shared Custody

Chapter 1
Sharing Custody
How Could It Possibly Work?

Learning to understand the lawyers' bias. The effects of the adversary legal system. The true cost of Don and Sarah Gilbert's $38,000 custody fight. Opposing views to sharing custody. Sexism and custody. Sole custody as a tradition in American family law. Pre-1900 fathers as sole custodians. Post-1900 mothers as sole custodians. Recent research on the impact on children who lose one parent through divorce. Challenges to conventional wisdom concerning child custody. Repercussions of fathers' rights and women's rights movements on traditional custody arrangements. The new role of mediation in child custody disputes. Shifting from competition to cooperation after divorce. Custody options defined. What are the "best interests" of the child?

There are periods in the lives of normal people when they are crazy—certifiably, verifiably wacko. Times when characteristic good sense and judgment depart, and all that is left is bizarre behavior—and pain. Divorce is one of those times. With all its attendant disruptions, the dissolution of a marriage can cause a kind of temporary insanity, a diminished capacity to cope with problems at the very moment parents are asked to make decisions that will affect them and their children for years to come.

At a time when it is agonizing even to talk rationally to each other, a divorcing couple is asked to sit down, feeling totally disoriented, to try to negotiate solutions for issues that run from high finance to who gets the wedding silver, the pet goldfish, the family photos, and the most precious products of any marriage: the children. The notion of *cooperating* with the one person who represents the source of all that pain is almost unthinkable. "You expect me to do *anything* for that bitch/bastard?" is a typical attitude. "You must be out of your mind!" Perhaps the only "solution" most divorcing parents seek during the initial upheaval of separation is an end to its accompanying torture. They want the divorce to be over, done with, put in the past. "If only someone or something would swoop down and take this awful burden off my back, maybe I could get on with my life!"

Usually that "someone" is an attorney, a person trained as a legal warrior with sparring skills honed in the adversarial arena of the court system of the United States. "We're trained to be tigers," chuckled one family-law specialist when asked how he saw his role as a top child custody attorney. Robert Mnookin, a professor of law at Stanford University, is deeply concerned that "the behavior of lawyers can *create* disputes" that often escalate and prolong the very misery they've been hired to abate. There is a desperate need, Mnookin believes, to examine the role lawyers play in the settlement of marital disputes, especially those involving children. "Some lawyers make things worse and heat up the battle," he notes. And the battle can have grave consequences with which the parents and children will have to contend long after the lawyers have collected their fees.

The adversary legal system itself, through which custody fights are supposedly settled, attempts to apply a legal solution to what is essentially a highly charged emotional problem: Who gets the kids? And emotions are felt by *people*. Waging a custody fight in court may satisfy a need to retaliate. But for most parents the exhilaration of fighting and "winning" a custody battle is short-lived—and often disastrous for the entire family, as it was for Don and Sarah Gilbert, pseudonyms for a couple I have come to know very well.

Don is a professor of history at a California college. Sarah, a former high-school teacher, is now a computer consultant. Don is thirteen years older, and they began dating when Sarah was an undergraduate and Don was studying for his doctorate. They married in 1967. Their son, Ronnie, was born in 1969 and their daughter, Penny, in 1970. When they divorced in 1975, these highly motivated, middle-income parents fought a two-and-a-half-year custody war that resulted in attorneys' fees amounting to $38,000 and the kind of heartache no family should endure.

In the beginning, Don had not asked for sole custody. "I felt that the children needed both parents. I just didn't want to lose my position as a parent." For a while Don and Sarah were able to work out a time-sharing plan under which both of them took care of the children on an alternating basis. "I was willing to let Don have the children physically half the time," says Sarah, "but I wanted legal custody to be mine. I felt then that the children needed one home base." Don, on the other hand, was concerned that Sarah would leave the state, as she had threatened to do, taking the children with her.

Sarah also acknowledges now that she was feeling rejected and abandoned at the time of the divorce. "The divorce was Don's idea. I felt devastated. I had lost my husband to another woman and I was leaving my home as well. I couldn't bear the thought of losing custody of my children, too. I needed the respect given a mother with custody." Don, for his part, felt there had been basic problems with their relationship for years and maintained that the issue of custody should be kept separate from the failure of the marriage. He insisted he wanted to share the children on a legal as well as physical basis and wanted them for the same number of school days as Sarah. Sarah refused to agree to that and, through her lawyer, filed for sole custody; so Don and his own lawyer, a well-known Beverly Hills family-law attorney, countersued for sole custody.

"For a father to win custody in most states," says one cynical family-law specialist, "the mother must be shown to the court to be a drug addict *and* a streetwalker. Nothing less will do." In line with the tactics devised by attorneys in many such custody cases, the Gilberts began lining up the heavy artillery. Don "borrowed" a diary in which Sarah had written some of her doubts about her relationship with their son, Ronnie, during the difficult time following the separation. In pretrial depositions, Sarah brought up Don's relationships with other women as purported evidence of his lack of commitment to his children. Don countered with an attack on Sarah for her involvement in the religious group Nichiren Shoshu, asserting that "she would chant for hours a day, and she was neglecting the children." Sarah, in turn, denounced Don's signing up as "room parent" at the children's school as a cynical attempt to enlist the faculty to support his side at the trial. Each accused the other of mental and emotional instability, since both had sought psychological help during the breakup.

The thirty-two-month battle left them and the children in emotional collapse. Don's second wife, Lucy, still chokes up when recalling what the children suffered during the fight in and out of court. "Besides the hostile way they acted toward us and each other, they had headaches, stomachaches, and a fear of going to sleep at night." Ronnie, who was very close to his father, became "manipulative," all the adults now agree. "I was afraid to discipline the children when they were with me," Sarah says, "because I was afraid if I yelled or punished them, someone would hear me and report it to Don. I even felt like the kids were spies and I was walking on eggs all the time. I had to be the 'perfect parent' every moment, and I was afraid that if I did anything the children didn't like, they'd report it to Don and it would be brought up in court." Don's fear was that, in spite of his close relationship with his two children, "because of the tradition of the court that the mother always gets custody of the kids" he would lose access to his children. The fear that motivated each parent was "I might lose custody."

And that was the name of the legal game: Who would receive custody? As the Gilberts entered their third year of psychiatric evaluations, frantic phone calls to attorneys, financial declarations, escalating lawyers' fees, interrogations by attorneys and social welfare workers, a very fortunate thing happened: the court-appointed investigator, after interviewing both parents and the children, refused to make a recommendation to the judge in Superior Court as to which parent should prevail, saying that both Sarah and Don were good parents. The judge looked up from the bench in surprise as the investigator suggested the couple be referred to Conciliation Court, a division of Los Angeles Superior Court, for a process known as mediation. The judge agreed.

"When I walked into the first session," Sarah remembers, "I had no intention of coming to an agreement with Don." Sarah saw Conciliation Court as one more delay before the custody trial. "For the first three sessions," she recalls, "our counselor, Hugh McIsaac, provided a place where we could express our hostility and get out the hatred that had been building up for all those years." By this time, the two parents absolutely despised each other. "The whole legal system, in terms of family law," Don insists now, "is designed to bring out the worst in parents, not the best. Before I realized it, I had gotten myself entrapped into saying awful things about my former wife and her family," he says, "things which I absolutely didn't believe."

When the Gilberts began the mediation process, both were emotionally exhausted. "We were broke; we'd gone through one trying experience after another," recalls Sarah. "I, especially, did a lot of attacking, finally getting my feelings out." At the time of the third session she began to feel better when Don acknowledged that he understood Sarah's feelings of rage concerning his own attempts to prove that he was the better parent. However, Don added softly, he still didn't want to be a weekend parent.

"I had been hearing him say that for two and a half years," says Sarah, "but when he said it that day, I *felt* it. I didn't just hear it, I felt it. I realized that I didn't want to be a weekend parent, either." It was at this crucial point, with a neutral third party helping them focus on the issues they had in common, that the Gilberts could conceive of coming to some sort of agreement. "For the next seven sessions we started talking about things we would want to put in an agreement *if* we could make an agreement." Through the process of mediation, the former couple had agreed to agree to try being parents together—separately. They had agreed to give cooperative custody another try.

Their counselor, Hugh McIsaac, the director of Conciliation Court, acted as mediator during those ten one-and-a-half-hour sessions. He operated from the premise that the parents' divorce was not the end of the Gilbert family, it merely marked the beginning of a reorganization of that family into two separate units. "Their act of agreeing to *try* to come up with a plan was as important as the contract they ultimately worked out," McIsaac says. He explains that the process of "contracting" in mediation consists of setting goals for the family, confronting fears each parent may have about the other's actions, and hammering out a compromise that has good things in it for the parents as well as for the children. "Mediation can be in and of itself a therapeutic process as well as a practical way of settling conflicts. It can set in motion a healing process, providing a way of focusing in a healthy, rather than destructive, way on the needs of the children within a context that is also good for the parents themselves."

Ultimately the Gilberts agreed to joint legal and physical custody. They agreed to share equal rights and responsibilities regarding the welfare of Ronnie and Penny, who by then were eight and six years old. For two successive Mondays, the children were picked up after school by Sarah, and they stayed with her through the week. On the following two Fridays, Don picked them up after school and they spent the weekend with him and his second wife, Lucy. Then Don brought them back to school on Monday. Every two weeks, the schedule was reversed, so that each parent had two full school weeks and two full weekends a month with the children. The children could call either parent on the telephone any time.

In addition to the logistics, the agreement stipulated that Don would not take Lucy to school functions and that he would not run for office on the parents' board. Sarah agreed that TV watching would be limited to an hour and a half a day in each home and that Ronnie would be taken to the same barber by each parent in turn so as "not to get involved in a power struggle." Don assumed the responsibility of taking the children to their dental exams and Sarah was to take them to their medical exams. Each parent was to inform the other of results, needs, and problems. Each parent agreed in writing to support the other's role as "parent." Don, Sarah, Lucy, and Sarah's father all signed the document, which was later approved by the judge.

"We found the agreement worked out beautifully," says Don. "The kids are tops in their classes; socially, the other kids love them, and they love themselves." No more stomachaches, no more nightmares. All the adults and the Gilbert children meet once a month for breakfast to discuss any problems. Sarah insists that "before, it was impossible to be a parent to the children. Now that we're cooperating, I think we're both doing a really good job with the kids." Don agrees.

In the beginning, implementing the plan wasn't easy, even though the agreement was in writing. "I could finally communicate with Don," Sarah says, "but I really didn't like him after all we'd been through, and he didn't have good feelings toward me, either. It was only after we started to put the agreement into practice that our relationship with each other began to change." The couple at first managed to take only baby steps in the slow process of building up trust in each other as parents. Sarah told Don of one or two problems she'd had disciplining Ronnie, and Don acknowledged he'd encountered similar snags. The couple began to work on presenting a united front, which not only produced improvement in their son's behavior but also gave them confidence they could trust each other on specific issues. In time the results were dramatic. "Before," says Sarah, "the children were miserable with us fighting over them; now they know we love them and we're all involved in their lives. I'm positive they are happier now."

But even a war that ends with a signed peace treaty is bound to leave scars. The Gilberts still owed several thousand dollars in past-due attorneys' fees three years after their final divorce decree. And tensions still surface occasionally between Don and his former in-laws, between the children and their grandparents, and even among Don, Lucy, and Sarah. When a problem becomes too severe, they return to their Conciliation Court counselor to talk things over. "Mediated shared custody may not work in every case," admits Sarah, "but for us it's right."

Despite successes such as the Gilberts', there are formidable mental health and legal experts who insist that, under any circumstances, sharing custody is dangerous. The criticism begins with opposition to mates' continuing to maintain a relationship, a bond viewed by some as a kind of incest. Margaret Mead once remarked, "Once divorced, [former spouses] have been declared by the law to be sexually inaccessible to each other; the aura of past sexual relations makes any further relationship incriminating."

There is also the criticism that a child who is "shuttled" back and forth will have no sense of home or continuity, and will suffer psychological damage bound to surface in the future. No one in our mobile society speaks of "shuttling" children to visit Grandma, or to sleep over at a friend's, or to spend a month at camp in the mountains. But children who alternate between the homes of divorced parents are automatically condemned by some health professionals to become victims of a "Ping-Pong Syndrome."

But, mostly, criticism of shared custody is based on the American cultural tradition, which has held for decades that women are the proper custodians of underage children. Because of this tradition, sole custody is granted to the mother in more than 90 percent of cases. Yet the courts did not begin to exalt women as the crucial influence in the upbringing of children until the Industrial Revolution left Mother in the house to raise the kids so Dad could work in the factories and in commerce. ·

Up to the turn of the century, American *fathers* had always been granted sole custody, regardless of the circumstances, in the nation's infrequent divorce cases. After all, women and children were chattels, owned and controlled by men. But in postindustrial society, when Father was no longer around the farm, and therefore unavailable to baby-sit occasionally while Mama fed the chickens, it was good-bye Daddy, and men began to buy the notion that they were inept as parents. They rarely practiced their skills as parents anymore, at least not before Junior was old enough to throw a baseball on a Saturday afternoon or to go swimming during summer vacation.

Particularly from the 1920s onward, male judges and lawyers began to condemn their divorcing brethren to absentee parenting. Fathers were allowed to "visit" their children at the convenience of the mother. In a stunning evolutionary reversal, fathers had lost the knack of nurturing youngsters into adulthood. It became a psychological truism that *mothers* bonded more meaningfully with their offspring.

The next major development in courtroom philosophy came with the publication in 1973 of *Beyond the Best Interests of the Child,* which became the Bible for most experts in family law. Written by three academic heavyweights—Joseph Goldstein, a law professor at Yale; Anna Freud, a renowned child psychoanalyst; and Albert Solnit, a child psychiatrist and the director of the Yale University Child Study Center—the book strongly recommends that *one* parent, mother *or* father, have total management and control of custody. The other parent, say the authors, should have no legally enforceable right to see the child unless so allowed by the custodial "psychological" parent. This, they say, is to provide consistency and stability in the child's life. For these authors, what was beneficial for children when their parents were living together—that is, two parents acting as positive role models—is no longer good for them psychologically once the parents have ended their marriage because, according to the authors, divorced couples are too angry to cooperate with regard to their children's needs. Therefore, a child having equal access to both parents will automatically be faced with conflicting loyalties, guaranteed to produce devastating consequences over time.

Goldstein, Solnit, and Freud cite no scientific studies on family interaction to prove that parents are constitutionally unable to put the needs of their children above their anger at each other. In fact, the authors ignore substantial evidence to the contrary. Nor do these experts offer much more than opinion to support their thesis that sole custody is, de facto, the best solution for most children of divorce. However, the prestige of the authors effectively silenced any dissenters until recently.

Long-term studies, completed in the 1970s and early 1980s, began to reveal the problems of children who have been deprived of, or abandoned by, one of their parents. One such five-year study was completed in 1979 by Dr. Judith Wallerstein, lecturer at the School of Social Welfare of the University of California, Berkeley, and her colleague, Dr. Joan Kelly. The authors concluded that "the children [131 in the study] who were not visited by the absent parent frequently showed diminished self-esteem, except where the relationship with that parent was psychologically destructive to the child." Dr. Wallerstein voices alarm for these children, whom she considers to be emotionally "at risk." Although she does not believe that joint custody will work in every case, she says, "What makes for a good adjustment after a divorce is an arrangement in which the child maintains contact with both parents."

Wallerstein and Kelly's findings are in agreement with other new studies that refute many of the assumptions upon which custody decisions were based during the last century. In a paper presented at the 1978 meeting of the American Orthopsychiatric Association, Judith Brown Greif, chief social worker of the Division of Child/Adolescent Psychiatry at New York's Albert Einstein College of Medicine, wrote that research has made it "abundantly clear that with few exceptions, the trauma of divorce can be minimized by the child's continuous open and easy access to both parents." Greif believes that standards for what is in their "best interests" are the same for children of divorce as for children from intact families. "Rather than support the imposition of legal visitation restrictions," she says, "we should do everything in our power to maximize contact between the child and both parents. One clear way is through joint custody arrangements."

Perhaps the most public challenge to Goldstein et al has come from Dr. Mel Roman, director of family studies at Bronx Municipal Hospital Center and professor of psychiatry at the Albert Einstein College of Medicine. In *The Disposable Parent: The Case for Joint Custody,* Dr. Roman concludes from his study of forty joint custody families that cooperative custody arrangements are in the best interests of the majority of children and should be so presumed under law unless there are compelling reaons to the contrary. "Our evidence suggests that [joint custody] should be increasingly the pragmatic, and hence American choice."

In 1980 the Jewish Family Service completed two years of observing twenty-four joint custody families living in and around the San Francisco area. Project director Susan Steinman noted that a significant trait shared by this group was the low level of hostility between the fathers and mothers two years after the original separation. "They kept the hostility well contained and constrained," she says, a feat the authors of *Beyond the Best Interests of the Child* claimed was nearly impossible for divorcing parents. "These children really do have a sense of both parents being devoted to them and loving them," says Dr. Steinman. "Most were not burdened with conflicts of parents fighting about them and most of the kids in our study were doing well [with the cooperative custody arrangement]. They were moving along in their lives."

In the long run, American parents themselves will bring about the most meaningful changes. There are some eighty-five militant fathers' rights groups around the country whose members refuse to accept any longer society's notion that fathers are "disposable." The present system of sole custody, usually granted to the mother, doesn't work for them. It's lonely, it's depressing, and it's unfair, they say, that they and their children should be deprived of their basic civil right of access to one another. And although women are understandably reluctant to give up their only power base in the custody and divorce game, they are beginning to sense that this power has carried a terrible price. By 1980, 68.1 percent of divorced women with children under six were working outside the home in order to survive economically. The burdens of being mother, breadwinner, plus chief cook, bottle-washer, chauffeur, homework adviser, and psychological cheerleader, are clearly beginning to take their toll in mental and physical stress among these women.

To the benefit of shared custody also, a growing number of family-law experts are starting to encourage mediated, not litigated, custody solutions in order to try to unclog the courts, which are jammed with parents (and especially fathers) who refuse to accept meekly the old custody formula. Mediated cooperative custody arrangements not only free up courts for other civil procedures; they have proved to be cheaper for taxpayers as well as clients than custody fights, and more equitable for all concerned. In Los Angeles County alone, where 60,000 divorces are filed each year, every case settled out of court saves thousands of dollars. And less than 16 percent of mediated joint custody cases ever return to court, whereas nearly 31 percent of sole custody cases tried in court do. In a Dane County, Wisconsin, study, only 10 percent of custody conflicts negotiated in Conciliation Court resulted in subsequent problems, while 34.2 percent of cases decided through the adversary process ended up back in court.

Clearly the arguments in favor of mediated joint custody are growing stronger. Nevertheless, there is still a great deal of deep resistance to shifting our thinking from *competitive* to *cooperative* solutions. The very terms "joint custody," "alternating custody," "divided custody," "split custody," "shared custody," and "coparenting" are controversial and, like most phrases that have become code words, hold different meanings for different people. Among judges, lawyers, child specialists, and many parents who have never bothered to learn the definitions of such terms, they set off alarm bells and anxiety. In order for parents to begin to understand their options, they must know the definitions.

Joint (or *shared*) *custody*. There are three kinds of joint custody: joint *legal* custody, joint *physical* custody, and joint *legal and physical* custody. Joint legal custody means both parents retain and share the legal responsibility and authority for the management and control of the child. If Johnny becomes a juvenile delinquent and robs the five-and-dime, both parents are responsible. If Allison runs up debts at the record shop, both parents have to pay. Theoretically, parents with joint legal custody share equally in all decisions concerning the child's welfare: what school he or she attends; what religious training he or she has or doesn't have; where he or she spends Christmas or Hanukkah. But in America, *possession* is nine tenths of the law. So if the parents have joint legal custody but one has sole physical custody, the other can end up legally responsible for a child and yet be prevented from actually guiding or influencing the child. Sharing legal custody with an "uncooperative" parent who has sole physical custody is the worst of both worlds.

Joint legal custody is more meaningful if the physical custody is shared by the parents in such a way as to assure the child frequent and continuing contact with both parents.

There are also thousands of joint custody arrangements in which a couple shares the *physical* care of a child on a fairly even basis, but not the legal custody. One parent, usually the mother, retains the legal rights over the child according to the legal order filed originally with the court at the time of divorce.

In the best of all possible worlds, cooperative custody means joint legal *and* physical custody with a time-sharing formula devised to benefit and accommodate both the children and the parents. Joint legal and physical custody is also referred to as *shared custody, cocustody,* or *coparenting after the divorce.*

Divided or *alternating custody* may sound like joint custody but is actually sole custody for each parent part of a year or in alternating years. For example, Susie is with Mom in California for the school year and spends the summers with Dad in upstate New York. When Susie is with her, Mom has the sole legal and physical responsibility for the girl. When Susie is with him, Dad has sole responsibility. Unless the parents also agree to make all major decisions about the child together, regardless of which parent she happens to reside with at the time, this arrangement is not joint custody.

Split custody is an arrangement whereby one child lives permanently with Mom while the brother or sister lives permanently with Dad. Under most split custody agreements, each child "visits" the parent and sibling he or she does not live with. Again, unless the parents agree to make all important decisions regarding the children together and accept jointly all responsibility for the children's actions, split custody is not joint custody.

Sole custody is an award of custody to one parent with the other maintaining rights to see the child from time to time. The sole custodial parent is legally responsible for the child's activities, conduct, and well-being. She or he is also the administrator of the custody and therefore, in reality, controls the child's access to the parent with whom the youngster does not live. The final court document may state that Dad has the right to see his children on alternating weekends and every Wednesday night for supper, but if Mom moves from Chicago to Colorado, as she is free under many orders to do, she effectively negates whatever theoretical rights Dad thought he had under the law. Also, there is nothing in a sole custody agreement which guarantees that the parent without custody will exercise his or her right to spend time with the children. The custodial parent may (and frequently does) find that an uninvolved parent will simply bow out, leaving the "winner" with the entire financial, physical, and emotional burden of rearing the children.

Genuine shared custody is any time-sharing formula that has, as an *operating premise,* the commitment of both parents to continue to be involved in all important decision-making regarding the children, and to maintain as much frequent and continuing physical contact as circumstances and geography allow.

How are angry, disappointed, grieving, even "slightly insane" former marriage partners able, eventually, to learn to work together? Don and Sarah Gilbert and thousands of shared custody pioneers did. And it is within your power to make shared custody work for your family, too. The rest of this book will tell you how. The first step is one of the most difficult: you must *redefine* your relationship with your former spouse. You may be divorcing the other parent, but you are not divorcing your children. You and your spouse are no longer in the *marriage* business together; you're in the business of being *parents* together—separately—for life.

Chapter 2
The *"Kinder"* Connection
A Tie That Binds

The Simons' story: redefining their relationship as parents. You're still Mom and Dad: the link that divorced parents cannot break. Long-term payoffs from the cooperative approach to shared parenting. Evan and the price of escalating warfare during divorce. Getting simultaneous divorces: legal, emotional, and social. Why separating from even a hated spouse is so hard. Recognizing the Ten Levels of Divorce. Parents' needs, children's needs, and separating the two. Problems of being out-of-sync during the divorcing process. The "successful divorce." Your Individual Divorce Analysis (questionnaire).

One quiet rainy afternoon in 1979 I sat sipping sherry and nibbling pâté with a couple whose real names I cannot use, but whom I will call Jill and Ted Simon. The Simons were in the process of filing for divorce; Ted had his misery under careful control, although there were times in our conversation when his sentences remained unfinished because of the lump in his throat.

When the Simons told their three children of the decision to split, fifteen-year-old Jonathan cried, "You can't *do* this to me!" Jill and Ted immediately assured the children they wouldn't be forced to choose between their parents. The one thing the couple agreed on, the Simons told the kids tearfully, is that they loved the kids very much and would both take care of them in the years to come—though not in the same house.

The Simons had been married for seventeen years and had agreed, even before they filed the dissolution papers, that they would share the legal and physical custody of Jonathan, twelve-year-old Amanda, and sixteen-year-old Kimberly until the youngest child was at least eighteen years old. Both parents are computer programmers and had agreed to share financial responsibilities for the kids on a 3:2 ratio, based on the amount of their respective salaries. The couple had agreed to live in the same school district, close enough so that the children could go from one residence to the other on foot or by bicycle. The time sharing would be close to fifty-fifty, with the children living with one parent for a month and then switching. "Of course, they can see or talk to the other parent whenever they want," said Jill. "It means a lot to us not having every single detail spelled out." The Simons viewed their children as very self-sufficient. "Teenagers need you when they want you," the two parents agreed.

But could two people who had differences serious enough to end a seventeen-year marriage continue to agree so totally on what would be best for their children in the years to come? When I asked that question, the Simons sat silently, each waiting for the other to answer. Ted ventured first. "Well," he said softly, self-conscious about the emotion in his voice, "we shared in bringing them up so far."

Jill nodded emphatically. "There are major things that aren't working between us as a couple," she said, "but we're *both* good parents and we've always been with our kids." As Jill set down her glass of sherry, she added in a small, sad voice, "Besides, we promised the children they wouldn't have to choose."

The Simons had faced a reality that many divorcing couples

refuse to confront for a long time after they separate, and that some perhaps never do. There is one bond they cannot break: the children they bore together link them forever. Most divorced parents eventually rupture all legal, financial, emotional, sexual, and social connections, but, noted a divorced friend of mine, calling forth his rudimentary German, "You cannot forget the '*Kinder* Connection'! You know, ya got your *Kinder;* ya got your kindergarten; and you got your *connection!* You're still Mom and Dad."

Harriet Whitman Lee, a lawyer who is working toward a Ph.D. in psychology, was divorced in 1971. She recognized very soon afterward that one tie with her former husband could not be severed without harming the emotional development of the couple's two daughters, who were then eight and ten. "People with children think when they get divorced, 'I'm gonna get free,'" she explains, "but let me tell you that, with kids, there ain't no freedom—ever! That's a hard thing to accept, but it's a fact."

Lee, who was one of the early supporters of shared custody and family dispute mediation in the San Francisco Bay Area— she was a cofounder of Berkeley's Family Counseling Services—believes that as long as there are children in a marriage, divorce never completely ends the relationship between the parents. "There is never a total putting away of that other parent out of your life. You have to accept the reality of that whether you like it or not. You are *tied* to that person, so you'd better invest something in making that new parental relationship *work*." The returns from that investment, Lee declares, are enormous: smoother times at family occasions such as holidays, weddings, funerals, graduations, parents' night at school, music recitals, and Little League games. She believes that divorced couples who are able to build a decent, businesslike relationship with regard to their offspring will be paid off tenfold with happy, well-adjusted children who "are not going to bring either parent an inordinate amount of grief as the years go by." The more parents invest at the outset of their divorce in making cooperative parenting work, she says, the higher the dividends down the road.

Ted and Jill Simon had instinctively acknowledged the *Kinder* Connection. They decided to invest a lot of effort in a cooperative parenting relationship even though they were in the painful process of ending their relationship as spouses. Because of their long and positive history of mutual involvement in the lives of their three children, the Simons had, perhaps, an easier time of it than many divorcing parents. They were able to separate their problems as husband and wife from their responsibilities as parents. Understandably, some people are able to do that only with a little help from a divorce counselor.

The director of a conciliation court in one Western city tells the story of a couple who had been referred to a therapist for counseling because they had nearly destroyed each other and their eight-year-old boy in a battle over his custody. The intense rage they continued to display toward each other, said a court investigator's report, had made "a basket case of the child." The counselor took the parents aside and told them, "I want you to pretend that Evan is sick. That he has leukemia. What would you two do then?" The parents stared back at her wordlessly. The counselor continued with greater emphasis, "I know what you would do; you would stop this fighting and start asking me, 'Where's the best clinic? The best doctor? What can we do to help Evan in this crisis?' " Having jolted them into thinking about their son's needs, the counselor quickly went on to assure the parents that divorce is a process that takes perhaps two years to complete psychologically, and that it is normal to have angry feelings. "But at some point," she insisted, "you have to start helping Evan through what is a crisis for him as well." She assured them that if they started focusing on what was a good parenting arrangement for Evan, things would start to get better for all of them. "But if things don't get better, if you do not scale down this warfare to a much lesser degree, leukemia is going to look *good* to Evan, compared to the hell he's going through with you two."

It was probably a revelation to this couple, as it is to many, to discover that they were not merely getting *legally* divorced from each other; they were also breaking apart *emotionally.* The Emotional Divorce of Evan's parents had obviously not coincided with the filing of the couple's final dissolution papers.

An increasing number of divorce experts agree that the aftermath of separation will probably follow a course of symptoms as identifiable as a bout of the chicken pox. The severity of the reaction varies. After the initial onset of symptoms, there is usually *denial* ("Oh, no, this can't be happening to me!"). Then comes the *fever* (anger: "I hate you for hurting me so!"), and sometimes the fever, if it's severe, turns into *delirium,* causing hallucinations and the diminished capacity of temporary insanity ("My ex is a monster! I'd like to kill that bitch/bastard!"). With time, the patient often suffers *depression* ("I feel awful; will I always feel this awful?"). This is often followed by *mourning* one's lost health ("What I *had* felt better than what I'm faced with now"). Finally, the sufferer simply *accepts* the situation ("At least I don't have to put up with the bad stuff anymore"), and gradually comes the *recovery* ("I've survived and life looks good again!").

This cycle, say mental health experts, is apparently triggered by some very primitive emotions in most of us. The adult form of "separation anxiety" caused by the pulling away from one's mate re-creates for many the same feelings we experienced in childhood, when, for example, our mother was dangerously ill in a hospital, or our parents shipped us to summer camp before we felt comfortable being away from home. People report that the pain and anxiety they experienced during their divorce literally made them feel like hurt and defenseless children again. One woman told me, "I felt, genuinely, as if I were a four-year-old for much of that first year after George packed his bags and moved out." The woman said that years later she realized that her father had died when she was exactly four years old. "I cried and cowered during the years following my separation *just as I had after my dad's funeral.*" Apparently the actual process of separation has a way of recalling those painful times in childhood when we felt helpless and abandoned.

However, divorced people *are* able to survive the pulling-away process and discover that they are *not* children, and that, unlike children, they have untapped resources and strengths with which they can cope and nurture and take care of themselves.

There are those in the divorce field who contend that people go through separation not merely on two levels—emotional and legal—but on three, five, some say even *ten* levels of divorce simultaneously. In most states the legal wrangles can be completed in six months to a year, but some former spouses can remain connected on various psychological levels for many years, even though their official divorce decree is on the books. "I've had parents who were separated twelve years," says psychologist Linda Campbell, director of the Family Divorce Counseling Service at San Francisco Children's Hospital, "and when I ask the people about the issues still causing them problems, their angry answers sound as if they'd parted twelve *days* ago!"

Harriet Whitman Lee has had similar experiences with her clients and believes that, as soon as they decide to separate, couples need to be informed that divorce is not an event but a *process,* and that within that process they are parting in numerous ways. Lee breaks it down like this:

Legal Divorce	Consists of breaking the legal contract of marriage, filing papers, appearing in court.
Economic Divorce	Requires a shift to two economic units from one. The property settlement may still leave those units financially connected in some ways (for example, alimony, tenants-in-common in terms of ownership of the family home), but the eventual financial relationship is legally spelled out and neither is responsible for the other's debts.

Physical Divorce	The family unit shifts physically from one residence to two.
Emotional Divorce	Refers to what is happening to the individual spouses within the relationship that is dissolving. The parents must reconstitute their relationship from one of dependence to one of independence, or interdependence if both are participating actively in child rearing.
Psychic Divorce	Refers to how the individual parent going through a divorce feels inside about himself or herself in terms of the various roles played in life (parent, worker, lover, and so on).
Sexual Divorce	The two parents are no longer engaging in sexual relations—not even flirting or indulging in "unconscious" come-ons.
Social Divorce	Consists of each parent's accepting the notion of "singlehood"; seeing himself or herself as separate in society.
Family Divorce	Refers to each parent's accepting his or her changed status within family groups, especially with in-laws.
Coparental Divorce	Refers to each parent's seeing the other as a separate but equally important figure in the lives of the children they bore together.
Community Divorce	Refers to each parent's feeling comfortable about his or her changed status within the community, including dealing with priests, ministers, rabbis, school principals.

The key to completing each level of divorce is a process known as *separation:* one unit, consisting of two parents, is dividing into two units, each consisting of one parent. On a psychological level, the two parents not only must eventually see themselves as separate entities; they must see their children as separate, too. Parents who do not have the capacity to separate their children's needs from their own, says Linda Campbell, of San Francisco's Children's Hospital, continually involve their youngsters in unresolved disputes with the former mate. "These parents can only see themselves and *their* needs and *their* hurts," she says. "They truly cannot see their child as *separate* from them."

This is what happened with the parents of little Evan until the counselor introduced the image of leukemia. "The parents had been too busy putting themselves back together with Scotch tape to be able to help Evan in those days," recalls their counselor. "When they left my office, I asked them just to try to think about what I said. *'Think about Evan,'* I told them. And you know," the counselor adds, "they came back about a year later to talk about changing some aspect of their custody agreement and they told me Evan was flourishing because he was no longer a part of their conflicts." By shifting their focus to concentrate on what Evan needed from each of them, they began to give him permission for the thing *he* needed most of all: to be able to feel it was all right to love *both* his parents.

Harriet Whitman Lee did not handle Evan's case, but she counsels comparably difficult custody disputes. She believes that it is of great help for couples to be informed of the levels of divorce, and to be reassured that people proceed through these levels at various speeds. A couple, she explains, may have agreed on a division of the property, but the wife hasn't taken steps, such as finding a job, to become financially self-sufficient, causing a lot of arguments over how long alimony payments should continue, and thereby postponing the Economic Divorce. "There are tasks to be performed to get through each stage of each level of divorce," Lee explains. "A person cannot get on to the next stage, to complete the Emotional Divorce, for instance, if he or she hasn't worked through the sense of grief and loss that ending a fifteen-year marriage can churn up."

Delays and obstacles can occur, blocking the completion of any of the ten levels of divorce, and so making it difficult for the adults to proceed with the task of learning to be parents together—separately. "One spouse may be way ahead of the other in some departments and retarded in others," Lee notes, "and this can cause even more confusion and misery." A typical example of this is when one of the partners (often the spouse who called it quits first) emerges safely from the Emotional Divorce long before the other partner can accept the fact that the emotional and sexual relationships are truly finished. Being "out of sync" on any of the levels of divorce can stir up additional conflict between the adults and thereby create more problems for the children caught in the middle. "I am continually amazed by the complexity of the divorce process itself," comments Lee. "Imagine a child trying to comprehend that there are all these things happening at all these different levels at any number of speeds for the individuals involved." No wonder it takes at least two years to sort everything out.

But Lee and many other experts are developing new approaches and new methods for coping. Dotted around the country are a few counseling centers with staffs trained in various disciplines. The centers have certified public accountants to help with the Economic Divorce, lawyers to handle the legal side, counselors trained in mediation and family-systems work who can help couples complete their Emotional Divorce, therapists who work well "one-to-one" with people who need self-esteem restored to complete the Psychic Divorce, and child specialists who can assist with the Coparental Divorce.

This "one-stop shop" divorce service center will likely have wide impact in the future. For the present, most divorcing couples will seek out lawyers. If they are lucky, a well-trained, sensitized family-law specialist will refer them to professionals who can help them deal with the multiple problems of divorce, so that ultimately, in the words of one conciliation court brochure, the couple can "close the book gently" on the marriage, while learning to cooperate in their new relationship as single coparents.

The feat of redefining a relationship from one of spouses-in-a-marriage to one of parents-in-common demands some extremely complicated psychological footwork on the part of everyone in the divorcing family. Former spouses must, on the one hand, *cement* their relationship as parents while, on the other, simultaneously *severing* all other ties that previously existed between them. The children must come to accept the fact that the marriage of their parents has *ended* but that their parents' roles as mother and father *continue.* "Pretty tricky stuff," sympathizes Harriet Whitman Lee, but for those who can accomplish this formidable psychological shift, the eventual payoff is a relatively tension-free environment for both the children and the adults.

A chart blending the concepts of such family specialists as Dr. Paul Bohannan, Dr. Alice Aslin, Harriet Whitman Lee, and Dr. Campbell, who have all contributed greatly to our understanding of a "successful divorce," would look something like this:

THE MAKING OF A SUCCESSFUL DIVORCE

Redefining the Relationship

Level of Divorce	As Former Spouses	As Parents
1. Legal Divorce	no connection	equal responsibility for well-being of mutual children
2. Economic Divorce	independent or interdependent financially; self-directed and skilled	equitably defined financial responsibilities for care of children
3. Physical Divorce	no connection	living in two separate residences
4. Emotional Divorce	tolerance and/or respect for each other as adults; emotionally mature and self-directed functioning	tolerance and/or respect for each other as parents; loving bond to children

Redefining the Relationship

Level of Divorce	As Former Spouses	As Parents
5. Psychic Divorce	respect for oneself as a functioning adult; adequate self-esteem	respect for oneself as competent parent; adequate self-esteem
6. Sexual Divorce	no sexual connection between former spouses	each parent a positive role model for children
7. Social Divorce	separate members of society	single parents engaged in a cooperative enterprise: child rearing
8. Family Divorce	each adult part of restructured family	divorced parents of mutual children in parental partnership, encouraging supportive contact with extended-family members
9. Coparental Divorce	needs of adults seen as separate from needs of children	parents attending cooperatively to needs of mutual children
10. Community Divorce	unmarried colleagues raising children together—separately—within the community	joint custodians of mutual children, recognized as such within the community

Achieving success at each level of divorce demands a great deal of concentrated effort, even for parents as conscientious as Jill and Ted Simon. Eighteen months after they ended their seventeen-year marriage and launched their new relationship as parents-in-common, I asked them in separate interviews to evaluate how far they felt they had come in terms of the various stages of the divorcing process. Ted and Jill both agreed that their Legal, Economic, and Physical divorces appeared to be complete. "We're still splitting the kids' expenses on a three-to-two ratio, according to our ability to pay," Ted reported. "And when people hear our entire divorce cost four hundred and fifty dollars in lawyers' fees, I get incredulous looks," he added, laughing. Each parent lived in a house and each took care of his or her own bills.

As far as the sexual aspect of their divorce was concerned, they had severed all connections at the time of the breakup. Socially, they saw themselves as single parents; as coparents, they clearly recognized that the children's needs to maintain strong contact with both parents were separate from their personal needs not to live together anymore.

They still hadn't completed the Emotional, Psychic, Family, and Community aspects of their divorce. Both acknowledged that there was less tension over many of the issues that used to cause friction before their breakup. However, Jill said that even after eighteen months she was experiencing tension of a new kind. "Sometimes I feel that I'm walking on eggs when I talk to Ted. He still acts cold toward me; he doesn't look at me directly when we talk face-to-face, and he never calls me about arrangements—he lets the kids tell me what's up."

Jill had left the marriage first. She suspected that, emotionally, Ted hadn't got past his hurt and angry feelings. As a consequence, she believed a lot of feelings of anger on Ted's part and guilt on her side were still "stirring up the pot." As evidence that Ted hadn't made a complete break with the past on an emotional level, Jill pointed out that it had been months before he told his mother about the breakup. However, when the families did get the news, members on both sides had been reasonably sympathetic and supportive. Jill had been dating a man since she moved out of the family home, a factor that, she believed, helped trigger the tension she felt when she had contact with Ted about the children.

As for their Psychic Divorce, both Ted and Jill reported feeling better about themselves as individuals than they had eighteen months before, during our initial interview. Jill had sought counseling before she decided to leave her marriage, and felt that the support of her therapist and friends since the separation had helped her tremendously. Lately, she said happily, she had been playing the piano again and writing articles that had been published in local newspapers. "Now I know that I'm capable of doing things on my own which make me feel good."

Ted, too, had a sense that he was adjusting pretty well to single life, saying proudly, "I've always liked to cook, and now I've taught myself to make pasta from scratch and manufacture my own yogurt!" Both felt they'd made good adjustments within their community, where they live only three miles apart. "We notified the school of our joint custody agreement, and all our friends tell us they think our sharing arrangements and the fact there's no fighting about the kids is wonderful," says Ted.

But there are many aspects of divorce that certainly are not "wonderful." I asked each of them, "What has been the toughest part for you and the kids about the past eighteen months?" Ted hesitated before answering, choosing his words carefully. "I suppose what's evolved has probably worked out the best it could for everyone concerned, given the negative fact we split up. The kids seem just the same to me. Sometimes, though, we have to prod them to exchange houses after a month or so. I don't think they like moving." Ted sighed. "I don't spend a lot of time thinking about it."

When I asked Jill what she found to be the most difficult part of the new sharing arrangement, she immediately blurted out, "Holidays!" She felt she'd made a mistake accepting an invitation to Thanksgiving dinner from her former mother-in-law. "Everybody meant well by it, but I was sorry I went."

The three Simon children, now fourteen, sixteen, and eighteen, pretty much set their own schedule as to whom they lived with and when. "All three never seem to be in the same place at the same time anymore," said Ted. "They see each other at school and band practice, and that's got to be a big change in their lives." Fourteen-year-old Amanda, who has an extremely close relationship with Jill, lived one school year entirely with

Ted because Jill's job at an aerospace firm required her to be at work by seven-fifteen in the morning. Jill couldn't drive her daughter to school that early, so the only solution seemed to be that Amanda make her headquarters at her father's until she started junior high, which is within walking distance of her mother's new house. "That year was hard on all of us," admitted Jill, "but it was a growing experience for everybody." However, both Jill and Ted agreed that all three children had matured tremendously and had taken a remarkable amount of responsibility for themselves. Both parents had found that coparenting allowed them time to develop much deeper relationships with the children individually. "We're closer than ever with the kids," Jill said proudly. "I have the only sixteen-year-old son in town who will still give a hug to his mom." She paused. "Of course, the kids would rather we still all were together in one house, but they've accepted the divorce and they tell us they understand." All three were cheerful, doing well in school, and were involved in numerous musical activities on and off campus.

Asked for an overall evaluation of the restructured family compared to the last time we had talked, Jill said she couldn't honestly report that in eighteen months she and Ted, despite their conscientious planning and goodwill, had completely achieved a so-called "successful divorce." On an emotional level, there was still a certain amount of unfinished business to clear up at some point. "We're definitely not marriage partners anymore," Jill said. After I reminded her that many divorce experts estimate it takes about two years, and often longer, to complete the separating process, Jill said, "We've broken a lot of those important ties. . . ." Then she stared straight ahead silently for a few moments. "Our communication needs to be worked on, and I don't feel I'm in a true partnership with Ted about the kids," she said finally. She wasn't satisfied with the fact that each parent operated in a separate orbit around the kids—not crashing into each other, but not communicating clearly, either. Suddenly her voice had a hopeful note to it.

"But I *know* we both love those kids, and we've both stayed committed to taking care of them since the divorce, so maybe, in a way, we're *getting* there."

"Getting there," when it comes to resolving divorce and custody problems, is not "half the fun" (as the old cruise-ship ads used to say), but it is an opportunity to work out some of the problems that may have been bothering you for years in an unhappy marriage. To redefine your relationship with a former spouse, you must first acknowledge, as the Simons did, that as long as you and your ex-spouse have underage children in common, you have a bond: the *Kinder* Connection. Next, as Ted and Jill did for me, you might want to assess how far you've come with your various "divorces." Once you can locate the trouble spots, you can start working on them from your side, with the ultimate goal of removing any obstacles that you have put in the way of a cooperative, relatively stress-free, effective, shared-parenting arrangement. For the moment, forget about the "uncooperative" other parent. It's time to take a good look at who *you* are.

INDIVIDUAL DIVORCE ANALYSIS
Where Are You Now? (and Where Have You Been?)

Level of Divorce	As Former Spouses	As Parents
Check the boxes that apply to your past or current situation in order to assess how many levels of divorce you have completed.		
1. Legal Divorce	☐ have met with lawyer and/or mediator ☐ case filed ☐ papers served ☐ court appearance(s)	☐ custody options discussed ☐ impact of divorce on children researched, (in books, articles, etc.)

☐ settlement conference(s)

☐ interlocutory decree

☐ final divorce decree

☐ counseling sought as to needs of children and reactions to divorce

☐ written custody plan developed

☐ final custody agreement signed by judge

2. Economic Divorce

☐ financial situation assessed

☐ expert financial advice sought (if needed)

☐ detailed budget drawn up for each new household

☐ steps taken by both spouses toward financial independence (jobs, training, etc.)

☐ assets rearranged (if required)

☐ final financial settlement reached and executed

☐ budget for children's present and long-term needs drawn up

☐ each parent's financial responsibility for children defined

☐ written plan for children's financial future developed and incorporated in final financial settlement

3. Physical Divorce

☐ all personal possessions separated

☐ two separate living residences established

☐ living space arranged for children in each residence

4. Emotional Divorce

☐ denial stage

☐ anger stage

☐ divorce discussed with children on level they can understand

Level of Divorce	As Former Spouses	As Parents
	☐ depression stage ☐ mourning end of marriage ☐ acceptance of divorce ☐ recovery, allowing for respect for (or at least tolerance of) other parent as adult	☐ children reassured both parents love them and will care for them ☐ professional help sought (if problems have developed) ☐ trust and respect developed for ex-spouse as parent
5. Psychic Divorce	☐ feelings of loss ☐ feelings of rage ☐ feelings of abandonment ☐ fear for individual survival ☐ severe loneliness ☐ meeting(s) with counselor (if necessary) to work toward dealing with loss ☐ feelings of accomplishment ☐ feelings of adequate self-esteem	☐ feelings of guilt for putting children through pain of divorce ☐ feelings of inadequacy as single parent ☐ outside help sought in acquiring parenting skills (Parent Effectiveness Training, etc.) ☐ feelings of competence as parent
6. Sexual Divorce	☐ sporadic sex with former spouse ☐ flirtatious "come-ons" to former spouse	☐ child put in role of absent parent as "little dad" or "little mom" ☐ child put in role of "messenger" between parents

☐ mixed sexual messages to former spouse

☐ going through "second adolescence" sexually after separation

☐ clear messages sent to former spouse to end sexual ties

☐ enjoying sex with new partner(s)

☐ no sexual connections of any kind with former spouse

☐ acting as positive role model for child

7. Social Divorce

☐ misfit in world of couples

☐ disapproved of by society

☐ ill-at-ease with other singles

☐ not happy in the social scene, but surviving

☐ some new relationships established

☐ alone, but not desperately lonely

☐ seeing self as separate, surviving member of society

☐ feeling accepted as divorced member of society

☐ feeling part of "broken home"

☐ embarrassed to be single parent

☐ progress made in coping with role as single parent

☐ seeing self as competent single parent, ideally in cooperative enterprise of raising child with former spouse

Level of Divorce	As Former Spouses	As Parents
8. Family Divorce	☐ judged negatively by family members ☐ pressured to conform to wishes of family members ☐ feeling family has been destroyed by divorce ☐ notion accepted of family restructured into two units	☐ seeing children as victims of "broken home" ☐ children's contact with other parent discouraged sometimes (or often) ☐ contact with other parent and his/her family painful ☐ sense of deepening relationship with children ☐ need acknowledged for continuing contact with child's extended family, and same encouraged
9. Coparental Divorce	☐ at times seeking to punish ex-spouse for hurtful things he/she did ☐ disrespect for other parent ☐ need of other parent to have contact with children disregarded ☐ need of other parent to maintain contact with children acknowledged	☐ determined to "win" custody dispute ☐ seeing other parent as disruptive to children's well-being ☐ lack of respect for other parent's role in children's lives ☐ acknowledgment that other parent may have some contribution to make to children's lives

☐ jealous of other parent's appeal to children

☐ acknowledgment that some needs of children are separate from needs of adults

☐ mostly at ease with coparenting arrangements

☐ children's need of access to both parents acknowledged, if neither parent psychologically destructive toward children

☐ willingness to attend cooperatively to children's needs

☐ feeling other parent is reasonably cooperative

10. Community Divorce

☐ feeling outcast in community of happy couples

☐ rejected by institutions of community (church, temple, social organizations)

☐ uncomfortable as parents-in-common within the community

☐ feeling divorced life-style disapproved of by minister, priest, rabbi

☐ feeling accepted regarding divorced life-style within community

☐ feeling uncomfortable at church, school functions

☐ disapproved of as single parent within community

☐ judged negatively by arbiters of community standards (rabbis, ministers, teachers, etc.) in role as single parent

☐ support sought as single parent within community (Parents Without Partners, organization, etc.)

Level of Divorce	*As Former Spouses*	*As Parents*
	☐ feeling comfortable as unmarried colleagues raising children together— separately—within community	☐ feeling accepted as cocustodian of mutual children within community

Use the results of your Individual Divorce Analysis to pinpoint trouble spots and to draw up a personalized blueprint for redefining your relationship from that of spouses to parents-in-common of your children.

Levels completed (a level is considered completed if you checked the last box in each section):

Legal Divorce ☐
Economic Divorce ☐
Physical Divorce ☐
Emotional Divorce ☐
Psychic Divorce ☐
Sexual Divorce ☐
Social Divorce ☐
Family Divorce ☐
Coparental Divorce ☐
Community Divorce ☐

Number of levels of divorce completed: _____
Levels still to be completed: _____

Levels where I need to concentrate the most: _____

Imagining you are your ex-spouse, try to respond to the individual divorce analysis from his/her perspective. What levels would you guess he/she still has to complete? _____

What levels do you think are causing the most problems for him/her?

Levels that both you and your ex-spouse have yet to complete (your levels-in-common): _____

Chapter 3
Mom Power

What Parents Need to Know About Mothers and Custody

Lauren's story. Fears and fantasies of losing custody. The connection between a woman's self-esteem and custody. The realities of being a single mother: some statistics. Mom Power and the Motherhood Mystique. Role stress and the demands of children during the initial separation period. The cruel and unusual punishment of twenty-four-hour custody. Custody, the women's movement, and single-mother martyrdom. Building trust between divorced mothers and fathers. Jo Ann looking back. Mom-Power Quotient (quiz).

"I feel that I am going absolutely insane," said the mother of two-year-old Judy while absently comforting the child sobbing in her lap. Neither she nor the visitor curled up on one of the matching plush white corduroy couches in the living room of her bungalow would allow the youngster to play with the tape recorder sitting on the coffee table. Little Judy was reacting with a toddler's righteous indignation. Her mother sympathetically patted the child's trembling shoulders while trying to explain the turmoil in her life. "Ever since David and I split up, I am confronted with so many decisions and I'm not ready to make any of them!"

Lauren Michaels (not her real name) and her estranged husband had recently been through counseling on "custody options," a program that explored custody options and attempted to introduce the concept of shared parenting to them. Lauren had been persuaded to attend by Judy's father, who had been insisting since their official separation that he wanted to share custody of the child. If she proved unwilling to "do joint custody," he had told her, then he would consider going to court to ask for full custody of their daughter.

"I know this is a difficult time and this confusion I'm feeling is a normal thing," Lauren said, scattering kisses atop Judy's head, "but it's just that I'm afraid if I agree now to joint custody, I'll be forced to make decisions that I'll have to live with later that may not *work* for me later."

Lauren diverted Judy from the tape recorder by reminding her of the new Star Tracker toy in her bedroom. Soon Judy was happily showing the guest her space-age tricycle. And before long the adults were free to talk in privacy.

As Lauren settled into a couch, she began to speak hesitantly. "I find that I really resent David's wanting joint custody *now*. It infuriates me that he suddenly wants 'his half.' " Her eyes began to glitter. "From the day Judy was born, I breast-fed her; I took care of her night and day those months she was colicky; I got up at three a.m. with her when she had those awful, endless sieges of bronchitis last winter." Lauren's voice began to shake. "David *said* he'd get up for Judy—it was always an issue and an argument with us—but then he didn't because he knew I would always come through. He never did anything with Judy until the baby could walk and talk, and now that Judy is old enough to give something back, David suddenly steps in and wants her!"

Lauren clenched her fist and pounded the arm of the corduroy sofa. It was as if she were having an argument with David right there in the room. "Well, I gave up a career to stay home with an infant who cried a lot and was very demanding, and I completely gave of myself, and I didn't get much back until now—so, yes, I *do* feel possessive! I feel like yelling at David, 'You don't *deserve* to get Judy! You weren't there in the hard times! I earned the right to be with our daughter. I feel that I've proved myself and that I've earned the right of control." There were tears in her eyes. "Judy is more *my child!*"

Lauren was filled with many fears. Would agreeing to sharing custody mean that this man she no longer wanted to be married to would forever be intruding in her daily life, trying to control all her moves? Would Judy grow up bewildered and fragmented as a result of being caught between two parents with different notions about child rearing? How could Lauren be sure David knew enough about taking care of a child to ensure the little girl's safety? Would David strap Judy into her car seat *every time?* What if Lauren couldn't get back into her profession as a company newsletter editor and couldn't make ends meet where she was presently living? Would she have to give up Judy if she had to move to a job in another city? "I don't like the fact that maybe joint custody would force me to stay in the same locale as David—especially if sharing Judy with him is awful."

And then there were her fears of what would happen if she *didn't* agree to joint legal and physical custody. "I'll probably get custody if it comes to a court fight, but I think I'm a little bit afraid David could do something.

"I think there is something in me that wants to make everything okay and that fears a direct confrontation with David about custody. Maybe I'm afraid deep inside that I would lose Judy in some way through a confrontation." Lauren tried to put into words a certain "primitive connection" that she felt bonded her to her daughter. "That child is the most important person in the world to me, and any kind of threat is frightening."

Lauren's terror was not unusual. Many women speak of the fear and confusion and uncertainty and rage they've felt in similar circumstances. A challenge to a mother's desire for custody of a child strikes at the very foundation of so many women's sense of self. Who am I if I am not a good mother? What am I if I don't get full custody of my children?

The role playing that most couples fall into creates a situation in which a woman, to feel good about herself, must be the all-knowing, all-caring, all-doing, all-sacrificing Number One Mama. Even if she can't quite manage all that because of the competing demands of a career and homemaking, the "Motherhood Mystique" tells her she *ought* to be all those things society still says moms are made of. Lauren Michaels, as an example of this, acknowledged that ever since Judy's birth she felt she'd been reacting to an almost unconscious pressure to live up to her own idealized notion of "Mother." This pressure had prevented her from asking David directly for the help she needed in raising the child. "When I gave up a career to care for Judy, I guess I had to feel that being a mother was an important thing," Lauren remembered. "Maybe I didn't let David *in*. I kept sending him all those signals that I was so damned capable. Maybe I didn't *let* him become deeply involved when he showed no natural inclination to do so because of *my* need to feel important." In order to replace the good feelings about herself that she used to get from her writing job, Lauren had seized on "Mom Power." The Power of Being-a-Mom. The power of ruling the roost.

For decades, men, happy to be free of any requirements that might smack of "women's work," gladly bowed to Mom Power. For years Mom Power was about the only power women managed to get. Historically, women have been the silent partners in just about every endeavor in our society *except* the rearing of children. So, clinging to the notion that children need mothers *more* than fathers, some women find shared custody arrangements difficult to accept. And they face a tough choice. Should a mother opt out of a child custody system that says women should be totally in charge and thereby confront society's and her family's disapproval? Or should she accept sole custody and, as a result, be condemned to a single-family household, without the economic and emotional support another parent can provide?

At some point, divorcing parents must ask themselves this question: Hasn't acceptance of the protective, presumptive mantle of Mom Power sentenced entire families to years of unnecessary disruption and trauma when marriages end? That was the opinion of one matron in her forties who stood up before six hundred lawyers, judges, and family counselors at a national conference on family law in the 1980s. As she took the microphone (after she'd listened for an hour to a panel of parents explain how they had fought the legal system in various states to achieve joint custody), the woman's voice began to quaver.

She began timidly, "I really didn't come prepared to make a speech, but I am reacting very strongly to what I heard here today. I was awarded sole custody of four children fifteen years ago, and, looking back on it, it turned out to be some form of cruel and unusual punishment!" The audience tittered at what at first seemed to be her little joke. "I don't think *anybody* benefited—myself, the children, or their father." The room became silent as the woman's voice grew bolder. "We were victims of the current consciousness. It never occurred to me to fight for joint custody. I would have seen myself as less than an acceptable mother or woman. And, somehow, women coming to lawyers and counselors for divorce need to be told that it's okay to *share* the raising of children. We get stuck in the position of single parent, and the odds are tremendously against us raising children successfully by ourselves. We need to know that we're okay if women turn over half that responsibility when there's a divorce!"

Some shocks await nonworking wives who assume that their ex-husbands will continue to support them and the children they "won" after the divorce. Long-term alimony is, in many states, a condition of the past. According to the statistics of recent years, only 14 percent of divorced or separated women receive *any* alimony at all. The typical divorced woman does not sit home waiting for a support check; she gets a job. Three out of every four divorced women work, compared with one of every two married women.

For divorced *mothers,* the statistics are not much more reassuring: 78.2 percent of all divorced mothers have to find a job, regardless of the age of their children; 69.3 percent of divorced women with children never even receive child support from fathers. Divorced mothers under thirty who *do* get child support receive an average of $1,290 annually, and divorced mothers over thirty get around $2,060, according to the Bureau of the Census. Among fathers who start off paying child support, most stop sending the check within two years of the divorce and often ultimately abandon all parental roles.

By 1978, the typical annual income of a divorced woman receiving child support was only $8,940. If she was among the 69.3 percent who *never* received child support, her income, on the average, was $6,216. Clearly, mothers who win sole custody have managed a rather dubious victory. As one mother with five years' experience as a successful joint custody parent put it, "Women should be told at the time they're getting a divorce that there are tremendous *personal* bonuses down the road to sharing custody—not to mention the emotional benefits to the children to still have that continuing contact with their father. If they only knew, those women would tell their lawyers, 'Cut the crap; just make sure the custody agreement has Harry signed up for his share of driving the car pool and taking the kids to his place every other weekend and Wednesday nights for supper!' "

Because one income can seldom support two households, a mother who did not work before her divorce is generally forced to enter the job market with few skills, little earning capacity, and minor or nonexistent support from her former husband. The father, officially relegated to the status of "visitor," has less and less incentive to participate in the long-term economic and emotional survival of the family. Therefore, mothers like Lauren Michaels not only find themselves with all the Mom Power; they discover that they have unwittingly inherited the Pop Power as well. The burden of serving as mother *and* father can leave divorced women bitter and exhausted, with few resources to be the generous, loving, nurturing parents they would like to be.

Ironically, some feminist organizations are encouraging single-mother martyrdom. Some of these groups, in the name of helping and supporting divorced mothers, publicly oppose joint custody legislation, urging women not to "give up their power base." They counsel women to use child custody as a means of gaining leverage in fights with their former husbands about money or control, or as a means of revenge. And many women are understandably suspicious that joint custody may be merely another trick by men who either want to pay less child support or who would like to grab the one area of power women have traditionally held.

Fathers who ask for shared custody should keep in mind the decades of programming that have gone into the creation of Mom Power. And they must then try to understand what it *feels* like to be a mother in the last decades of the twentieth century. Fathers have to try to comprehend the complicated, contrary, sometimes ambivalent connections that bond most mothers to their children at this point in our history. For a mother, most of the rules are changing, and her life may feel very fragmented because of all the demands placed on her. Fathers who ask to share custody need to acknowledge the almost primitive link women like Lauren Michaels feel regarding their children. Every mother did, after all, carry her baby inside her body. She experienced physically pushing that infant into the world. Most mothers put their own needs aside in order to guarantee the physical survival of their children during the first years of life. This primal connection between most mothers and their children has forced an extraordinary bond between them, and any perceived threat to it can provoke a fierce response. If a divorced father's request to share the children is interpreted by the mother as a threat to punish her by trying to take away her youngsters—or if depriving her of the children is actually what an angry father has in mind—there is major trouble ahead.

A father who sincerely wants to *participate* must have an appreciation of the fears divorcing mothers experience. If he doesn't, he will probably not be very successful in securing his ex-wife's voluntary cooperation. He must assure her in the clearest language possible that his motives are *not* to take the children away from her. He must assure her that wanting a shared custody arrangement does not mean he thinks she is an incompetent parent. As part of any discussion about custody plans, he should fully and specifically acknowledge her achievements as a mother and her contributions as a caring parent. Naturally, there will be areas in which he is bound to be critical of her as a mother, but he should tell her—if, indeed, he genuinely wants his children to have the benefit of two parents—that he deeply believes that both fathers and mothers are crucial to the well-being of children, especially following divorce.

A father must also let the mother know that he understands her uncertainty about whether she will be doing the "right thing" for the children by agreeing to share custody. He must be aware that she may be receiving criticism of the idea from parents, friends, colleagues, lawyers, or psychologists. He must allay her fears so that she can take the next step and view joint custody as being in the best interests of her children and, ultimately, in her own best interests as well.

Lauren Michaels's fear of taking that next step reminded me of another woman I had met several years before. Jo Ann Bohanan is of Choctaw and Cherokee Indian descent. "Mothering was very, very heavily embedded in me because of my own upbringing," she told me. "When Conrad said he wanted custody of Dana, all of a sudden there was this threat I might lose her. I've never been so frightened. I was a wreck. I had stomachaches. I couldn't sleep, and I was full of fear."

Jo Ann's daughter, Dana Knudsen, was five when her parents split up. About a year before the separation, her father, Conrad, then forty-one, suffered a heart attack. When divorce proceedings began, he threatened Jo Ann with a court battle for sole custody if she did not agree to share formal joint physical care of their daughter. "I didn't want to put Dana through a fight like that," said Jo Ann, looking back, "and I was worried about Con and furious with him at the same time. But on the other hand, I felt Dana should be with me. If I lost her, I would have gone nuts. I felt damned if I did and damned if I didn't." In the beginning, Jo Ann didn't see any way she and Con could work something out. "I thought it was either going to be a horrible court battle or I would have to do everything by Con's rules. I hadn't even heard of joint custody."

Jo Ann acknowledged that at the time she and Con were splitting up, her perception of motherhood was very different from what it is now. What Con was proposing, joint legal and physical custody, sounded "very Marin County" to her, and she doubted it would be a good way to rear Dana. "I had been raised in a traditional way, where mothers did everything for their children. When the breakup happened, I just wanted to clutch Dana to me and not have to deal with all the anger Con felt because I had left him. I simply wanted to be in charge and administer how the custody would go. I wanted to be in control and watch over Dana like I thought I was supposed to, to make sure she was safe."

Like Lauren Michaels, Jo Ann wasn't convinced that her former husband could completely give their child the necessary care. At the time of the breakup Jo Ann thought Con was merely trying to get back at her for the hurt he was feeling, and she wasn't at all sure she could trust him. "I tend to be more precise than Con about where Dana is and what she's doing. He's looser and more relaxed."

As their arguments heated up, it was hard for Jo Ann to see a lot of the good things Con had to offer Dana. "I felt *I* was the best nurturer. I didn't feel he had been doing it for long enough, and he had faded out for six months after we separated and hardly saw Dana during that time, since he was so mad at me. I felt then that I was the more consistent parent."

They became so furious with each other that they could not even sit in the same room. "I was especially angry over Con's threats to take Dana and his failure to cope with the end of the marriage. In fact, I was probably angry about a whole bunch of things that had happened during the marriage which I just hadn't dealt with."

It was Jo Ann's lawyer who suggested custody counseling. The family therapist saw both Jo Ann and Con individually and then with Dana. At the third session the couple wrote out a custody contract. "It all sounds easier than it was," Jo Ann told me. "But in the presence of the counselor we were able to talk together and get some of the fury out. I told him how angry and scared I was about his threats to take Dana away, and he told me how frightened he was he'd lose her. I was able to tell him that I knew and appreciated the fact he was a good father, and since I knew he thought I was a good mother, supporting each other as parents seemed to take away a portion of the battleground we'd been using against one another." Con started to let go of some of his anger, and Jo Ann began to relinquish her "smother-mother" image. "I said to Con, 'Okay, I'm going to let Dana live with you half of her life even though it's a killer for me.' I know now that if I hadn't done that, Con's feelings of deprivation would have fed those fires for years and it would have been awful for everyone."

Slowly, in the first weeks of their shared custody arrangement, they began to test out what might work for all of them and what might not. At first Dana thought she wanted to live a week at her mother's house and a week at her dad's apartment, three blocks away. Soon Dana said it seemed too long a time before she saw the other parent, so the routine became Thursday evenings through Sundays with Conrad and Mondays through Thursday mornings with Jo Ann, who worked on the weekends. Both parents agreed to live in the same general area and told Dana about it. "Basically, I guess what we had going for us was that, deep down, *somewhere,* we had respect for each other as parents. I still feel protective of Dana and don't leave myself open because there's always the fear Con might take advantage, but I'm polite. It's easier for me to talk to Con on the phone. I want our arrangement to be businesslike, and it is."

Jo Ann said she believed that if she and her ex-husband hadn't worked out sharing Dana physically as well as legally, Con would never have accepted losing his daughter and the bad feelings would never have been allowed to die. "With joint custody, those feelings have really just faded away as time has gone by. A lot of my possessiveness as a mother has largely disappeared. At first I was totally panicked about how sharing Dana would work out—especially for *Dana.* I was worried Con might disparage me in front of Dana because I was involved with another man before he was involved with other women. I was also worried about shuffling Dana back and forth, but the benefits have far outweighed the negatives involved in shared parenting."

Jo Ann found, in fact, that not supervising Dana's every move was good for both of them. "I think Dana is better off having some part of her life separate from mine." At the time of the divorce, the five-year-old would cling to her and "be a perfect little girl, afraid to speak her mind." Now, said Jo Ann, Dana is able to tell her, "I don't want to do so-and-so," and her school work, which suffered during the first year of the separation, has improved, and both parents have grown able to relax the schedule to accommodate changes of plans. "If something special comes up and I want to take Dana with me, I check with Con to see if he's planned anything. If not, we go!" An added benefit, Jo Ann said, was that she and the new man in her life have time to spend with each other without the restrictions children can impose.

The hardest part for Jo Ann was redefining her role as a mother. "I had *never* been alone in my whole life. I had never spent time alone with *myself*!" At first, on the days Dana was with Conrad, Jo Ann filled up her time by visiting friends and constantly going places. She often got the blues and sometimes felt an almost physical gnawing inside. "I finally got tired of running all over the place, so I'd stay home and watch TV to fill the empty hours. Then, finally, I learned I could just *be.* Most mothers I know never experience what that feels like. I didn't have to entertain or be entertained. I started really learning about myself, and it's allowed me to grow more as a person." Jo Ann smiled as she described the changes in herself. "I've become stronger as a person *and* as a mother." Before sharing her role as parent with Con she felt, as do many women, that her entire identity was as a mother. "It's wonderful to be a mother, but that's not all of me—it's just one part, and I had never faced up to that." Sharing custody, she said, "gave me *time:* time for myself, time for work, time for play, and a special kind of time with Dana. I've had time to find out what it's like to *be with me!*"

As a result, Jo Ann began to explore her "Indian-ness" and eventually took Dana back to Oklahoma to meet all her Cherokee and Choctaw relatives. "I go to powwows now and teach Dana about her heritage. I know now what it means to be Indian, and I might never have had this if it hadn't been for Con and sharing Dana."

What was most surprising to Jo Ann was that the hostility she and Conrad felt for each other had virtually disappeared. "I can't believe it! I think that's the part of this thing that is truly miraculous." She believed her relationship with Con felt "totally finished" except for the good things they still shared through Dana. "In a major sense now I am able to feel happy that I was married to Con because we produced Dana and she's such a wonderful, happy child. It doesn't feel like we made this horrible mistake anymore. Now I'm able to think about that marriage and myself as a mother in positive instead of negative terms, and that's made it easier for both Con and me to concentrate on what is best for Dana."

Sitting with Lauren Michaels, I wished she could talk with Jo Ann Bohanan; Jo Ann could ease Lauren's fear of losing Judy. I also wished David Michaels could meet Conrad Knudsen so that, father to father, Con could explain that support for the other parent, not threats, offers the best chance for initiating a shared parenting arrangement. And I wished more parents understood how to respect and cushion the fearsome impact of Mom Power.

MOM-POWER QUOTIENT

Estimate your own/your former spouse's "MPQ"

1. As a mother, I feel/she feels most comfortable with: (CHECK ONE)

   mother administering custody; father not participating ☐

   mother administering custody; father participating according to her plan ☐

   father administering custody; mother not participating ☐

   father administering custody; mother participating according to his plan ☐

   mother and father jointly administering custody and participating according to ability and circumstances ☐

2. As a mother, I feel/she feels that I, the mother/he, the father/both parents make the best (MARK: M, F, or BP)

   nurturer ____

   physical-care giver ____

   empathizer regarding children's problems ____

   recreational companion ____

   chauffeur ____

   nurse ____

   cook ____

home-maintenance worker   ____

academic tutor   ____

housekeeper   ____

budget keeper   ____

religious counselor   ____

career counselor   ____

audience for school, music, or dance recitals   ____

team fan   ____

moral guide   ____

sports coach   ____

school-lunch maker   ____

attendee at parents' night at school   ____

disciplinarian   ____

scout leader   ____

3. As a mother, I feel/she feels the children's father *should* make these contributions:
(CHECK THOSE THAT APPLY)

give financial aid   ____

spend a substantial amount of time with children   ____

participate in educational planning for children   ____

participate in some school activities (parents' night, parent-teacher conferences, etc.)   ____

provide a positive physical environment when the children are with him   ____

provide a positive emotional environment when the children are with him   ____

chauffeur the children to some of their activities   ____

participate in some extracurricular activities with the children (sports, music lessons, scouting)   ____

participate in some hobby activities (model building, shell collecting, etc.)   ____

provide an acceptable moral environment   ____

SCORING:
Section 1

Give 4 points for Answer 1 ____
Give 3 points for Answer 2 ____
Give 0 points for Answer 3 ____
Give 1 point for Answer 4 ____
Give 2 points for Answer 5 ____
TOTAL: ____

Section 2

Give 4 points for every M ____
Give 2 points for every BP ____
Give 1 point for every F ____
TOTAL: ____

Section 3

Give 4 points for every important contribution *not* credited to the father.

TOTAL: _____

Sections 1, 2, 3, TOTAL: _____

POINTS:

90–132   Scores between 90 and 132 show an extremely high Mom-Power Quotient. A high MPQ type wants to keep control of the children to herself; she does not acknowledge many significant contributions by the father. Mothers who deny their children access to fathers who have something to offer tend to score high MPQs and are themselves potentially damaging to their children. However, keep in mind that mothers who believe (and in some cases, they may be right) that their ex-husbands are physically or psychologically destructive to their children could tally a high MPQ due to their determination to shield the children from danger.

50–89   A high MPQ. These mothers would like to be the final arbiters, although some may be willing to share a portion of the child-rearing responsibilities along traditional lines of sex-role assignments.

23–49   This MPQ score indicates the mother has accepted the importance of the father's role in the lives of the children and has balanced this with an understanding of her own contribution in fulfilling the needs of her children. In terms of sharing custody, this score bodes well as far as chances of working out a successful cooperative parenting arrangement with the mother are concerned.

below 23   Very low MPQ. In fact, this score indicates the parent has very little interest in mothering at all. In these cases the father may be the primary—or only—parent involved.

Chapter 4
Back-Seat Daddies

What Parents Need to Know About Fathers and Custody

Grant Treadwell and the Fatherhood Mystique. Getting past the "Feeling-Crazy Syndrome." Financial and emotional truths about divorce and fathers. Loss of family and the realities of being a "visiting" father. Learning to become nurturer as well as a provider. Developing untapped skills as a role model for children. Climbing out of the back seat: how fathers can help themselves and their children after divorce. Fighting the flak of the antifather bureaucracies. How mothers can build trust with their former spouses regarding the children. Back-Seat Daddy (quiz).

May in the Rockies at eight thousand feet. A season full of promise. Chilly air in the early mornings, and by midday enough warmth to melt another couple of inches of snow and coax out the tiny leaves of the Rocky Mountain aspen. But for a thirty-four-year-old man I shall call Grant Treadwell, who worked as a stockbroker in Denver, May in the Rockies in 1976 brought with it a terrible sadness.

The last several years of his twelve-year marriage to Linda had been unsatisfying for both of them. They had been teenage sweethearts in California, their parents had been friends, and, says Grant, "Ours was the original 'jailbreak marriage.' We dated each other exclusively for four years before we were married, and, basically, I think the two of us were escaping from our parents." Grant witnessed the birth of both sons: Todd, born in 1968, and Matthew, delivered two years later.

For a while, Grant worked at his father's firm, a company manufacturing parts for agricultural machinery. Joining it as a young bridegroom, Grant summoned up images of the film *The Graduate,* in which an adult gravely confided to Dustin Hoffman that the secret of the future was "Plastics!" "My dad actually *had* a plastics company and just assumed I would go into the business with him, but I lasted there less than a year." Following several other disappointing jobs in California, Grant and Linda moved to the quieter, rural suburbs outside Denver.

Through the years, both Linda and Grant Treadwell admit now, they never learned to talk to each other frankly about the conflicts in their marriage. In the twelfth year, when Linda attempted to bring out some of the submerged feelings, Grant would simply withdraw. If she wanted a "deep talker," he would tell her, she should have married a philosopher. "I look back on that with embarrassment," he says now.

Grant looks back on their twelve years together with a new understanding of how he contributed to the failure of the marriage. He sees the roots of that failure as follows. Growing up, he had difficulties as a shy middle child with a vivacious older sister and a younger brother who seemed closer to his parents than Grant. "I grew up feeling I was a golf orphan. I saw my parents between the last hole on Saturday afternoon and their cocktail parties Saturday night. I know now my parents loved all three of us very much, and I don't think they should be blamed for that lack of closeness any more than any other upper-middle-class parents of that generation. But I hated school and grew up thinking I was dumb and couldn't do the work. I had a lousy self-concept."

His sense of himself did not change in marriage. "I felt Linda was the smart one," says Grant, "that she was the one that was always right about the house or the kids or where we should live and what we should do." Grant Treadwell was in the grip of the "Fatherhood Mystique," which dictated that he was supposed to be the provider, leaving the nurturing functions of parenthood up to his wife. He went along grudgingly, even when her plans for them to build a house in the mountain town of Evergreen caused him concern. Although disturbed that the home would force upon him an hour commute to his job in Denver and would drain their capital, well, he thought, two kids, a wife, and a house in the suburbs was, after all, the American Way and who was he to oppose that? "There was a lot of passive resistance on both our parts as the house went up," he says. "I felt she had become a taskmaster and our sex life was zero." Linda, on the other hand, felt Grant lacked direction professionally and was uncommunicative and withdrawn. "We were both right," he says glumly.

Soon, Grant reached a decision after an unsuccessful attempt to get Linda's commitment to work on their problems through therapy: he wanted out of the marriage. One morning in May 1976 they asked their two boys to come into the living room of their newly completed natural-cedar dream house. "The toughest part of the whole thing was telling them we were going to split up," Grant says. "I remember it was mostly me talking. The kids had seen us fighting—no violent things, but they had heard us arguing. I told them that their mother and I had talked it over and we'd decided that the best thing to do was to split up, that the situation was making all of us unhappy." The two children, eight and six, kept absolutely still, staring out the picture window at the spectacular Rocky Mountain skyline. They didn't cry and they didn't ask any questions.

Within a week, Grant had moved into a bachelor apartment in Denver, close to his job at the brokerage house. Linda stayed in the house, close to her job as a dental technician. She began receiving reports that eight-year-old Todd was suddenly losing his temper and hitting children who were his special friends. At home Todd was abusive toward Linda as well.

During their initial separation, Grant made a point of having the boys with him nearly every weekend. "Linda was suddenly very social, coming into Denver Friday night, dropping the boys at my place, and then picking them up on Sunday," he recalls. Soon, both parents declared they wanted custody of the children.

Grant's attorney discouraged him from claiming full custody, since Linda was apparently a competent mother and well thought of in the community. Grant was torn about what to do next. "What I *really* wanted was an equal say in how the kids were raised," he says. "I didn't want her to be able to pull up and leave town." Linda had started to date a man who was involved in acting and drama. "I started thinking that Denver was a small town for that sort of thing and the most likely move for a guy like that was LA or New York and, if Linda was with him, there would go the kids. It made me feel like my children were being taken away from me without my having anything to say about it."

Grant read about joint custody in a book called *The $27 Divorce,* but since he and Linda lived forty-five minutes from each other, he dismissed the idea as impractical. Still, accustomed to the notion of "either/or" sole custody, he instructed his attorney to resist Linda's demand for full custody. The matter was referred by the family court to the welfare department for an investigation. "The 'investigation' consisted of a forty-five-minute interview by a woman I had never met and have never seen since," Grant says. "It was a joke."

The welfare worker's report stated that she saw no reason for changing the custody of the children from what it had been in the temporary order: "sole custody to the mother; liberal visitation to the father." However, Grant still persisted, insisting to both attorneys that he wanted full custody. He was driven by one fear: "I thought, 'Hey, maybe I'm going to lose the boys.' Now I look back and realize how much *I* needed *them.*"

Alone in his sparsely furnished apartment during the week, working at a stockbroker's job he had grown to hate in order to support a life-style he no longer enjoyed, and discouraged, he felt, by a custody system that automatically favored mothers over fathers, Grant felt the helplessness and isolation common to many divorcing fathers. According to therapist Nancy Weston, the fathers she works with at the Divorcing Family Clinic in Los Angeles suffer feelings of deprivation for years after the divorce when mothers get sole custody and refuse them access to their children. Weston recalls a young man's telling her that the only way he survived the emotional upheaval and sense of dislocation was by talking into a tape recorder every day for three months. "He had hours of tapes, and my guess is that what was on them was his despair, loneliness, fear, and hostility toward his ex-wife and the legal system which seemed to be depriving him of everything important in his life."

In therapy, divorcing men have described a shocking sense of isolation when they move out of the house, leaving their children behind. "Some men," says Weston, "*if* they're lucky, have two or three men friends they can talk to, but often they'll talk about baseball averages instead of the agony they're going through." Many separated men are also afraid to level with their employers about the internal chaos going on in their lives. One father, a salesman in a high-pressure job in Honolulu, never mentioned to his boss for more than a year that his marriage had broken up, despite the fact he was having trouble concentrating at work and his formerly impressive sales records were slumping. "My boss wouldn't have cared," the salesman insisted. "He would have simply got rid of me and hired someone else to do the job."

Men seem to have a perception that they do not, or *ought not,* endure the same wrenching dislocations that women experience when the family breaks up. Divorced men are often viewed as having superhuman powers of recuperation, of having the capacity to plunge happily into a carefree existence with no worries or responsibilities. What is more often the case, however, is that they quickly discover it takes an estimated 25 to 35 percent more income to support two households, and that it is the man's income that will most likely be tapped for the difference. In addition, they find that some courts allow ex-wives, under certain circumstances, to share a husband's pension benefits acquired during the marriage and even share in his *future* earnings from projects conceived or executed during the marriage. With the average divorce costing upwards of $3,000, the husband is often required to pay not only his own attorney's fees but his wife's as well. And if divorce litigation results in a full custody fight, the bill could run another $5,000 to $10,000 and up.

Even those fathers without financial problems often have no idea how to rebuild social and personal connections or how to create a pleasing new environment on their own. Often the divorced father will find himself with only a six-pack of beer in the refrigerator and an unkempt, depressing environment, minus his kids and any sense of "home." "A newly divorced man feels cut off physically and emotionally," therapist Weston maintains, "and in a very real sense, he *is* cut off from his former world. Some men have told me they actually feel in a state of panic as soon as their kids walk out the door to return to the mother." Grant Treadwell remembers getting stuck in the "Feeling-Crazy Syndrome." "Sunday nights were by far the worst time of the weekend for me for four years!"

Linda had been the only person Grant had ever opened up to, even a little bit. "There is something in our culture that discourages men from connecting with their feelings or from having really close friends with whom they share what's truly going on with them," says Weston. "And that's sad." Grant, as an example of this, had few single friends. "I didn't know very many unmarried men," he says, noting that most of Linda's and his married friends had been people Linda had met through work. As happens with many couples, Linda had got "custody" of their social life.

Weston has observed that men who feel isolated and afraid to acknowledge their feelings to others find that anger and hostility toward their ex-wives, lawyers, and the court become their only outlets for hurt and rage. Often these men will engage in a flurry of "dating" to try to replace the missing pieces of their lives, and will attempt to substitute *something* in the outside world for the loss of home and wife and kids and sex. Others will remarry quickly, and 50 percent of *those* marriages will be failures. Their former wives, in turn, sometimes view such activity as a callous and unfeeling reaction to the marriage breakup, and pass this view along to their children. "Your father certainly doesn't care much about you kids or the family. Look how he's behaving!"

Eventually, for a lot of men like Grant, who himself spent the first few months prowling singles spots in Denver, the freedom to find a different woman every night becomes wearing. "Every night [bar-hopping] would be a disappointment and that got really old after a while," says Grant. "I felt I had to get out there and look for *somebody*. It took me a while to get over the bar-hopping routine and the notion that I was going to meet Miss Wonderful."

At some point the divorced father usually recognizes a reality: "I'd like to have a nice place with nice people and nice kids around." But as Grant learned in court, in regard to custody of his kids, the father will often be forced to take a back seat.

The legal system is not the only force pushing fathers into the position of Back-Seat Daddies. "In marriage as well as out of it, there are no support systems for men with kids who want to be involved parents, just as there are few support systems for women with kids who need or want to work outside the home," declares Lynn Littman, a mother and a stepmother as well in a joint custody situation. Littman has worked as a network television executive and film director, and it is her business to know what "plays in Peoria." She believes that Back-Seat Daddies are the accepted norm across the country because of the lack of value placed by people in general on efforts that are involved in the day-to-day parenting of children. "Remember what happened when Ted Kramer began to focus his attention on the needs of his small son after his wife left in *Kramer vs. Kramer?*" she says. "He got *fired!*"

Parenting is *inefficient* in the American economic scheme. In Littman's view, if men fully shared the responsibility for taking care of their children, they wouldn't be putting all their energies into their "real" work—work that is rewarded with bonuses, promotions, and gold watches for "years of devoted and loyal service." Littman holds that fathering "gets in the way of our most cherished national goal: turning out material goods at a fast, efficient clip."

It disturbs her that very little in our profit-oriented culture says to men and women that, as a country, we recognize and support the idea that doing a good job as an involved father is crucial to the well-being of our children and is valuable to the society as a whole. "There are few material payoffs or much public appreciation for being an Alan Alda, the Involved Dad, so there aren't a lot of Alan Alda types around," says Littman. Therefore, she contends, we don't see effective, participating fathers portrayed in much of our popular culture. By failing to acknowledge the importance of fathering, society licenses men to take a back seat in the care and nurturing of children. A divorced mother who bothers to see her child only two Sundays a month is considered not very attentive. A father who has dinner with his kids every other Wednesday evening is considered "consistent."

"My bosses told me that kids were taboo and that it was a drawback to admit on résumés that I had a greater than usual responsibility for my kids," says one father. "If those men in corporations had to take care of a child—I don't mean simply pay the bills—but actually had to deal with young humans and think about what they need ... they couldn't make the business decisions they do. ... Most jobs for men don't support being involved with kids."

So, when men like Grant Treadwell go into custody battles, they encounter all the instincts and resistance of a society that considers the back seat the proper place for a divorced father. In Treadwell vs. Treadwell, Grant lost his job at the brokerage firm a few weeks before the hearing was scheduled for both the property and custody settlement in his divorce. He continued voluntarily to pay $150-a-month child support, but since Linda had refused to put the mountain house on the market, he was "feeling the pressure."

At the stage when people are fighting over money and property, therapist Nancy Weston believes, it is even more important than ever for a father to continue to see the children on a regular basis. "If a man can continue to see his kids," she says, "he will feel less anxious about the way his life is going, and in many cases his anger toward his ex-wife—regardless of who ended the marriage or who's demanding what slice of the marital pie—will often abate, given some time." But if, as a weapon in an impending court fight, a father is not allowed to see his children or is hassled about visitation, he will tend to feel all the more enraged and victimized, Weston has observed, and his anger will be directed even more toward the children's mother. "The wife needs to understand that her ex-husband is feeling, 'Hey, I've got to have a connection to *something* and have some say about my kids or I'm gonna go bananas!' "

During the time leading up to the trial, Grant was going slightly "bananas." Fortunately, Linda was willing to let him continue to see Todd and Matthew nearly every weekend, but it was clear to Grant that she and her actor friend had developed a serious relationship. "I could see how this whole business could drive men to kidnap their children or encourage them to abandon their kids and say, 'To hell with it! I'm getting out of this deal,' " he says.

Because of his research on the Colorado family court system, where men get custody of their children less than 16 percent of the time, Grant knew he would probably lose on the issue of custody. So, resigned, he agreed the night before the trial to allow his lawyer to make the best possible deal out of court. In return for what he felt was a more equitable distribution of their mutual property than the court might have awarded, he accepted the uncomfortable and unsatisfying position of Back-Seat Daddy, agreeing to "sole custody to the mother; liberal visitation to the father." Linda would have the right to define how liberal the visitation would be, but basically both parents agreed they'd try to go along with what they'd already been practicing: Grant would take the children on weekends, for six weeks in the summer, and for a week at Christmas or Easter. The Treadwell divorce had concluded with the usual compromise—Money vs. Custody. Linda was definitely in charge of custody, and Grant—officially demoted to the status of "noncustodial parent"—would be required to negotiate the degree to which he could participate as a father. It would take Grant Treadwell a long time emotionally to climb out of that back seat.

In the months following the legal compromise about custody of Todd and Matthew, Grant knew he had to get his life into better order. He took a job teaching in high school and sought out adult classes on parenting and courses on the effects of divorce on children. The leaders of one program involving divorced parents and their children would not let him attend because he was the noncustodial parent. "The teacher said she felt that the course was for parents *with* custody because the children attended, too, and if both parents came, she felt the kids would play them off against each other. Here I was, trying to take an active part in my kids' lives and stay involved, and I was shut out!" It seemed to him that there ought to be a middle step between the extremes of sole custody to the mother or sole custody to the father. "I hated having to ask Linda all the time for permission to see my children."

Grant and the boys fell into a familiar routine on the weekends. They did the household chores together and then Grant dropped Todd and Matthew at their Saturday music lessons. Afterward, all of them would go to Matt's soccer game. Sundays they'd plan an outing or fool around with home computers.

Once or twice when the kids became sick at his house over the weekend, Grant was engulfed by a sense of being an inadequate parent. He either called Linda to ask what to do or requested she come and retrieve the ailing child. Therapist Nancy Weston has found such experiences common. "Lots of men don't even know how to run the washing machine or read a glass thermometer; they're afraid they might not have the patience to deal with children for hours at a time or take care of them when they're sick." And sometimes, says feminist Gloria Steinem, women gloat at the clumsiness of untutored fathers. "Sometimes we women like to be regarded as indispensable, and we are not. Nor are we the only people who can parent children or clean kitchens and make food. The thing we have to reconcile ourselves to is that if someone else does a particular task, it won't necessarily be done the way we want it."

Linda, Grant recalls, would sometimes express concern that the boys were staying up too late at his house, but when he bought an electric broiler so he could dish up easy menus of hamburgers or chicken on the weekend he was grateful that "she never criticized me that I was feeding them junk food all weekend. I felt that most of the time she was supporting me as a parent."

Nancy Weston urges the divorcing men she works with to learn to ask for advice and feel all right about it. "Men can read instruction sheets and cookbooks, but it's important they let learning these tasks be of value to them, not demeaning to them. Learning to run a washing machine is no great mystery, but it's an important skill to have if you don't want you and the kids to look like slobs." She also urges former wives and friends to offer to teach fathers some of these skills in an uncritical way, or at least to point the men toward sources of information where they can teach themselves. Gloria Steinem concurs: "It's important that children see their fathers changing diapers (and doing other household chores) to grow up knowing that men can be loving and nurturing people, too."

Grant discovered he was, in fact, far more capable of being a nurturing parent than he had suspected. He also grew more sensitive to his sons' reactions about his new women. If Grant had a date when the boys were with him, his companion was expected to fit into whatever he and his sons had planned—a movie, a trip to the hobby shop, a sail on Chatfield Reservoir. "Sometimes it was tough, always having the kids with me, but it was understood that whatever we did on the weekends would involve the boys." Grant also decided to be quite direct with the children about the women whom he saw steadily. "I told the kids, 'Hey, I'm not going to up and marry and get out, so don't get worried just because I'm dating so-and-so a lot.' "

He designed his life around his weekends with the boys. He began to feel closer to them than ever before. Slowly he had shifted roles from that of mere breadwinner to a parent who knew what to do when the flu struck at three a.m. or how to respond appropriately when his son played that first perfect scale on the clarinet. Grant began to experience a "father love" that tapped feelings he'd never sensed when married. He was connected to his sons in a way he had not known with his own father. He'd broken the cycle of father-son estrangement that he felt had been a theme in his family. The rewards of "hanging in there" after divorce more than balanced some of the sacrifices he'd had to make to be a full-time father every weekend.

During the week, Grant missed seeing the children and helping them with their homework, but his own experience on the weekends and occasional Wednesday afternoons taught him to realize that Linda had a hard job, too, having to be the "heavy" sometimes to make sure the boys completed assignments for school and to insist they keep their rooms at her house in decent order. "I guess I tended to run things looser than she does," Grant acknowledges, "but it was nothing drastic. I could see that, basically, we had the same philosophy about the kids."

In the period before their divorce decree became final, Linda took a job in Denver and drove the boys to school there each day rather than let them continue attending classes in Evergreen. "It really fried me that they were spending a total of three hours a day in the car for what I saw as her convenience," says Grant. "I talked to her about it, but she wouldn't listen." Not long after that, however, Linda sold the mountain house, moved into Denver, and enrolled the children in neighborhood schools. That argument, and its aftermath, made Grant realize he had some powers of persuasion, and he came away feeling that Linda was starting to respect him as a parent.

Both Linda and Grant made it a point to attend parents' night together, as did Linda's new man, Paul, who had taken an active interest in the two boys. Because the parents felt comfortable with the situation, the boys handled it well, too, even joking with their teachers about their "two fathers." Todd's outbursts against friends at school had stopped. "Both kids saw that even though I had physically left," says Grant, "I wasn't leaving *them*. They were spending a lot of time with me and they started relaxing." For help with Todd's outbursts, Linda and Grant had consulted a psychologist, who was also working with them on fine-tuning the parenting schedule. The psychologist pointed out that under Colorado law the custodial parent cannot leave the area without first going to court to ask permission. "And with that information," says Grant, "Linda began to acknowledge that I had some rights, too." He began to feel less resentful.

One evening after a scout meeting that Grant had attended, he and Linda sat down to chat. "Suddenly we started talking about the kids and how they were doing since the divorce, and it's the first time she and I opened up since we had *known* each other! She told me how much she liked her new guy and we ended up talking about how our marriage had gone sour. It was the first time I had felt comfortable in that kind of conversation and I think it was the same for Linda. She had said to me once, a long time ago before, that she couldn't be happy with me because I wasn't happy with myself. She had detected that I hadn't liked myself very much and she'd been right."

Grant realized after their conversation that he was feeling a lot better about himself, partly as a result of the good experience he was having with his boys. In his teaching job, though, the prescribed routine of the high-school classroom didn't seem to be ideal for him. He began to introduce innovative, experimental lessons, hoping to make math exciting for gifted students bored with the standard classwork or for students who hated school in much the same way he once had. Successful at it, he sensed he had much to offer professionally, but not in the conventional classroom setting. In 1980 he resigned from the school and founded a small educational consulting company. Soon he began to land contracts with city after-school programs, social groups, and parents both of gifted children and of those having trouble with schoolwork.

Although there are better opportunities in larger states for people in his business, Grant is determined to stay in Colorado "to see the boys through." He says, "I've got to admit that the thought has occurred to me about moving away from Denver—perhaps to California, where I have some friends and my brother lives and where there's about the greatest sailing in the world; but I'd never really consider it because of the kids—at least until they go to college, if they choose that."

Grant has come to regard himself as a de facto joint custody parent. The boys and he call back and forth on the telephone during the week. The schedules in both households are now fairly flexible. Even after Linda married Paul, and Grant had to get over his initial fear that her new husband would "lay his values on my boys," Linda and Grant's relations remained reasonably cordial. Grant has grown to like Paul and appreciates the stepfather's care and concern for his boys.

The year before Todd entered junior high, Linda and Grant jointly decided he would do better in private school, which they then selected together. They agreed to share the tuition expenses equally. Grant elected to be the parent who checked on what uniforms would be required and what supplies Todd would need for his first term. "I even educated them a little bit at the school about coparenting," says Grant. "There was no place on the school form for me, so I had to cross out all the stuff about change of address and write in my name, phone number, and address right on the sheet. On the bottom I wrote in big letters: 'FATHER TAKES AN ACTIVE PART IN LIVES OF HIS CHILDREN. PLEASE SEND ALL COMMUNICATIONS RE-GARDING CHILDREN TO BOTH PARENTS.' Now I stand up to the bureaucracies that don't have the right niche to put me in."

In 1979 Grant moved out of his original bachelor apartment. With the proceeds from his half of the mountain home, he bought a small house on the outskirts of Denver, half an hour from where Linda was living, and converted the basement for the boys' use. Grant says he no longer feels like a Back-Seat Daddy. But he still doesn't believe he has equal access to the "controls" of child custody. "People seem amazed that Linda's and my system works so well this way. Still, a lot of decisions are made between Linda and the boys and I hear about them afterward. I still would like to have an equal say in how they're raised and in all decisions regarding them, but"— Grant pauses—"I think I've finally got my life going in the direction I want. I see a lot of myself in the kids." He pauses again, and, with reference to his own trials growing up, says, "No one knows better than I do what the pain feels like if parenting is not done right."

Not all fathers are as willing as Grant Treadwell to try repeatedly to cooperate with their former wives in working out a shared custody plan, or as determined as he was to remain part of their children's lives. But according to psychologist Mel Roman, professor in the department of psychiatry at the Albert Einstein College of Medicine and pioneering researcher in the field of joint custody, "We've seen more and more men really wanting to be involved with their kids. The degree to which they want to, of course, varies. Some feel Sunday afternoons are enough, but many more want a greater involvement than that. I think this is really a function of our changing society."

Dr. Roman is concerned that a lot of men and women don't know that it is possible for fathers to stay meaningfully connected to their children after divorce. "I think, though, as men become aware of the possibilities, more and more will want joint custody." And perhaps more and more *women* will understand the need to continue to be with each other that both fathers and children feel after divorce.

In fact, a former wife can reduce some of the tension between her children's father and herself by communicating as soon as possible after separating (or even before) that she doesn't intend to deprive the father of parental access to their children. It will help fathers if their former wives acknowledge to them directly that the entire family—the father included—is going through a difficult period of adjustment. Many potential legal problems can be averted if former wives let their former husbands hear that, as mothers, they appreciate the importance to youngsters of a healthy father-child relationship as well as a good mother-child relationship.

It's reassuring for a father to hear something like "I realize this is hard for you, too, especially since you've moved to a new place and everything—and I want you to know I recognize how important the kids are to you and you to them."

If a father seems to show little interest in his children following separation, or is experiencing—in his wife's eyes—a second adolescence of frenetic dating, a mother might do some objective fact-finding before concluding that her former mate no longer cares about the welfare of their youngsters. Has the current situation made him feel hopelessly cut off from his kids? Has the conflict between spouses made seeing the children too painful or, in his view, too damaging for the children?

Mothers can underscore to their former spouses how much children need and want to see their fathers, especially during the crisis phase of the separation, and can describe to the men how children react when their fathers disappoint them by not showing up as promised. On the positive side, a mother can tell her former husband how much the youngsters look forward to spending time with him (if they do), or how crucial she thinks it will be for the children's long-term benefit that they and their father develop a good relationship in the coming years.

Says Dr. Roman, "Men and women must come to some understanding of their own responsibility for what has happened to bring about the divorce, and gain an awareness of what might happen to their children following divorce if the adults continue to put those children in the middle of their conflicts." Instead of having to shoulder needless blame for "messed-up kids," Dr. Roman hopes parents will seek a solution of sharing that will work for their children's growing-up years.

Perhaps we have come to a time when, unless there are compelling reasons to the contrary, asking for *anything less* than shared custody will be considered a form of child abandonment, and asking for anything more than shared custody, a form of child abuse.

For Grant Treadwell, the official language of his custody agreement does not adequately describe the role he plays in the lives of Todd and Matthew. "No doubt I'd feel a lot of guilt if I bailed out and moved away from Denver, but anyway, being with the boys is what I want to do," he says. He thinks about that and smiles. "Or maybe," he adds, "I just haven't given myself enough credit for sticking around."

Considering the odds against most fathers, maybe he hasn't.

BACK-SEAT DADDY

Fathers: assess yourself.
Mothers: assess your former spouse.

Before I separated from my wife, I participated
    (M) much of the time
    (S) some of the time
    (R) rarely
    (N) never

in preparing for the birth of the children (child-birth and child-care classes, etc.)   ————

in the physical care of the children when they were infants and toddlers (changing diapers, clothes, etc.)   ————

in planning extracurricular activities for the children (soccer, ballet, music lessons, etc.)   ————

in taking the children to extracurricular activities   ————

in driving a car pool or arranging for transportation for the children   ————

in planning the educational program for the children   ————

in overseeing and helping with homework   ————

in attending parents' night at school   ————

in attending parent-teacher conferences   ————

in making school lunches or doling out lunch money each day   ————

in disciplining the children   ————

in supervising the amount of television the children watch   ————

in reading to (or with) the children   ————

in taking part in or watching the children's puppet and talent shows   ————

in planning family outings half of the time (at least)   ————

in attending family outings half of the time (at least) ＿＿

in spending time alone with each child ＿＿

in planning vacation trips with the children ＿＿

in taking family vacation trips ＿＿

in showing the children where I work and where I "play" (golf course, gym, etc.) ＿＿

in paying the children their allowance or rewarding them in some way for good behavior ＿＿

in assigning them household chores ＿＿

in taking the children to the doctor or dentist for checkups and for emergency visits ＿＿

in caring for the children when they're sick during the week (night or day) ＿＿

in mediating arguments between siblings or between children and their friends ＿＿

in working on projects specifically intended for children (making models, building blocks, playing board games, practicing sports skills, etc.) with the children ＿＿

in working together on family projects (vegetable gardens, tree houses, yard work, painting the apartment, etc.) ＿＿

in scouting or playgrounds or other community activities organized for children ＿＿

in working with other parents in child-oriented projects (paper drives, school carnivals, etc.) ＿＿

in taking the children trick-or-treating on Halloween ＿＿

in helping plan and carry out the children's birthday parties ＿＿

in planning with the children what to get Mom for her birthday, Christmas, or Hanukkah ＿＿

in playing sports with the children (tennis, basketball, peek-a-boo, etc.) ＿＿

in talking over problems the children may have at school, with friends, or within the family _____

in talking with the children about the separation and/or divorce on a level they can understand _____

SCORING:

Give 1 point for every M _____
Give 2 points for every S _____
Give 3 points for every R _____
Give 4 points for every N _____
TOTAL: _____

POINTS:

108–144	virtually an absent father during the marriage
72–107	a genuine Back-Seat Daddy
37–71	an involved father
36 and under	a sharing, cooperative parent

The *higher* the score, the more the term Back-Seat Daddy may describe certain fathers during their marriages. Many fathers score in the "absent father" or "Back-Seat Daddy" range *after* their separation if they don't achieve liberal visitation or coparenting arrangements regarding their children. Fathers who are sharing child-care responsibilities (some, perhaps, for the first time) after separating from their wives may find they score in the "involved father" or even "sharing, cooperative parent" range if they take this quiz as single fathers a year or so after their breakup. Fathers who wish to become *more* involved as parents can use this quiz to pinpoint the areas where they want to be more active in the lives of their children. Mothers can use this quiz to determine areas they would like to encourage their former spouses to participate in to a greater extent.

Chapter 5
Suffer the Little Children
The Impact of Divorce on Youngsters

What parents need to know about the effects of divorce and continued parental conflict on their children: immediate, long-term. The California Children of Divorce Project. The Loneliness Project at New York University. Which children survive divorce best—and why? The Wallerstein and Kelly study's 131 children. Real-life dramas: the impact of divorce at various ages and stages. Why shared custody: Mark's story. The San Francisco Joint Custody Project: shared custody kids and how some fared. Check the Pressure (quiz).

"Everyone oughta know that divorce isn't healthy for kids and other living things!" exclaimed a friend of mine one day. We were watching our sons at soccer practice in the park. Or, rather, I was watching my son; she was there to pick up her stepson. My friend was reacting to the apparently endless struggle between her husband and his first wife. The first wife had been back to court many times in a fruitless and damaging effort to establish who was the "better" parent. And my friend was concerned that the nine-year-old son seemed to grow more withdrawn and sullen every day.

In 1978, studies were released in England detailing the damage such unrelenting anger between former spouses can do to youngsters. The research concluded that children of divorce experience more depression and illness, have a shorter life expectancy, leave school earlier, and have a 66 percent greater chance of committing suicide as teenagers than children from homes where the parents remained married. Another study, conducted by New York University researchers Phillip Shaver and Carin Rubenstein, has found that adults whose parents were divorced are lonelier than those from intact families and that the younger the person was when the parents broke up, the lower the person's self-esteem and the more lonely he or she is likely to be as an adult. My friend shook her head sadly as she watched her stepson glumly approach us from across the field. "I hope we don't look back on this period of easy divorce as a holocaust for kids," she said.

But is it the divorce itself that causes these severe effects? Or is it the way in which most divorces are handled by the parents? Is it possible for mothers and fathers to learn new ways to deal with their own fears and angers while ending a marriage so as to avoid inflicting more hurt than their children may already be suffering? To answer these questions, parents need to take a look at what is known about the impact of divorce on children.

In the California Children of Divorce Project, a major five-year study that surveyed immediate and long-range effects of divorce on youngsters in America, Judith Wallerstein, a professor of social work, and Joan Kelly, a psychologist, found that a child's adjustment depended more on what happened *after* the divorce than on conditions in the family beforehand. In *Surviving the Breakup: How Children and Parents Cope with Divorce,* a book that details their findings, Wallerstein and Kelly say, "Over one half [of the 131 children studied] did not regard the divorced family as an improvement over their predivorced family," say the authors. Even among those youngsters who had seemingly adjusted well to their parents' breakup, "all had the sense of having sustained a difficult and unhappy time in their lives which had cast a shadow over their childhood or their adolescence. . . . A significant part of their childhood or adolescence had been a sad and frightening time" because of their parents' decision to divorce and the intense conflict it created within the family.

Upon completing their study in 1979, Wallerstein and Kelly concluded that "where [parents] have made arrangements to maintain good parent-child relationships with both parents— then those children are not likely to suffer developmental interference or enduring psychological distress as a consequence of the divorce." On the other hand (and the italics are my own), "if the divorce is undertaken primarily as a unilateral decision which humiliates, angers, or grieves the other partner and these feelings *continue to dominate the postdivorce relationship* . . . [and] if the children are poorly supported and poorly informed or co-opted as allies or fought over in the continuing battle . . . [and] if the relationship with one or both parents is impoverished or disrupted . . . *then the most likely outcome for the children is developmental interference and depression.*" In other words, how well the children come through the trauma of the family breakup is primarily determined by *the way in which the parents behave following their separation.* Children caught in a long-lasting divorce war may end up suffering throughout their lives for the "sins" of their parents.

As an example, one woman I met while I was researching this book told me how her dad left home for another woman in the early 1950s, leaving her to be brought up by her mother, who drove a school bus to earn a living. There is pain in the woman's voice as she remembers, "My mother told me she said to my father that she'd take no alimony if he'd agree never to see me. He didn't care about me and now I don't care about him!" She remembers writing letters to her father when she was six. "My mother would find them in my drawer and beat me." As an adult this abandoned child married an older man, whom she described to friends as "the perfect father for me."

But still, she says, she was not happy. Several years of psychological counseling did not help her determine "what's wrong," and early in 1980 she left her husband for another older man.

In contrast, Bill Robertson, a writer friend of mine who reviews books for a Florida daily newspaper, expresses a remarkable affection for both his parents, who divorced when he was two years old. "My dad was always involved in my life. I saw him regularly and was allowed to take trips with him. My parents consulted jointly about me and I think I had a much better childhood than most kids in my situation." Bill's mother remarried when he was eleven, but he continued as a teenager to have a sense that "both Mom and Dad loved me and didn't put me in the middle." Bill himself has recently married. "I consider myself one of the lucky ones," he says. "I wasn't caught in the middle of a power struggle."

But what about the unlucky children? What is it that happens to well-meaning mothers and fathers during their divorces that puts such stress on children?

First of all, parents rarely offer their children an explanation about what has happened to the family. In the Wallerstein and Kelly study, 80 percent of the children not only weren't provided with an adequate explanation; they were not given assurances that both parents would continue to love and care for them, either. For about one third of the youngsters in the study, the split came as a complete shock; the children had no idea their parents were unhappy together, and simply woke up one morning to discover that one parent had vanished. "What children need and often don't get early on," says Florence Bienenfeld, senior marriage and family counselor in Los Angeles County's Conciliation Court, "is a simple explanation about the divorce without blaming anyone. Something like 'Mommy and Daddy will be living in two separate houses from now on' will do fine and let the children know that they will be cared for by both parents even though they won't be living together anymore." When news of an impending divorce comes without warning, children are traumatized. In some cases children may blame themselves for causing the divorce because of the way they may have behaved in the past. Many are never told directly that the divorce is *not* their fault and that both parents love *them* even if the adults no longer love each other.

Virtually all the children in the Wallerstein and Kelly study reported that the initial breakup was the most stressful period of their lives. At the very time they most needed love and reassurance from both parents, the parents seemed unwilling or unable to put their own turmoil aside to provide it. In fact, half of the 131 children in the study felt their fathers were entirely insensitive to what they were going through, and nearly a third felt their mothers became less caring about them.

Nearly two thirds of the children surveyed became "difficult to manage"—understandable considering the stresses they experienced: 50 percent witnessed the parents being extremely abusive to each other; another 15 percent were confronted with the threat of having to go to court and choose between parents; 25 percent were aware of physical abuse between parents; and almost all had been used as "hostile messengers" between the parents. Two thirds of all the divorcing parents had openly competed for the children's love and loyalty, an action that the youngsters said they heartily disliked.

The Wallerstein and Kelly research reveals that not long after the initial separation of the parents many children begin to respond negatively to pressures to side with one adult or the other. Numerous other researchers have also chronicled reactions that are almost predictable among certain age groups of boys and girls put under this kind of stress. "It's a good idea for parents to educate themselves about normal child development," urges Elayne Kardner, a Los Angeles marriage, family, and child counselor, "so as not to confuse divorce-related stress with the natural ups and downs kids go through as they grow up." Parents who know something about what's predictable for youngsters at particular ages and stages, she says, don't make "mountains out of molehills." But there is also certain behavior that seems directly related to divorce.

Infants, Toddlers, and Preschoolers

Nursery-school teachers will tell you it's easy to pick out the children whose parents are in the process of a tumultuous divorce. Look for the three-to-five-year-old clinging to a parent in panic when brought to school. Many little ones can't stop crying once the parent has left and seem convinced their mothers or dads will not return at the end of the day. Children who were able to use the toilet before their parents' separation will suddenly be messing their pants and wetting their beds. Many will acquire an intense fear of the dark or will insist on sleeping with the remaining parent once the other has left home. Other youngsters will attach themselves, like Linus, and perhaps for the first time, to a special blanket or toy.

Since these little ones feel they have "lost" one parent, they fear, logically enough, that they may lose the second. Very young children have a sense of time that makes a single day seem as long as a week would to an adult; they need frequent contact with *both* parents, especially during the postdivorce phase of readjustment. Even very short periods with the parent who has left home can be comforting. And at the same time, children under five need continuity of routine and of caring people around them—parents, grandparents, relatives, baby-sitters, and teachers. If small children are given both *contact* and *continuity* and are allowed to adapt to the changes in their lives gradually, most, say the experts, will be able to regain their equilibrium.

Early-Elementary-School-Age Children: Six-to-Eight-Year-Olds

There can be especially difficult adjustments for these children, particularly young boys whose fathers leave the family home. Researchers Wallerstein and Kelly were struck by the pervasive sadness they encountered among six-to-eight-year-olds.

Many of these youngsters were afraid they would lose their families and perhaps be sent to live with strangers.

After his parents separated in 1978, Adam Wheeler, a young friend of mine, whose name I have changed, became almost a textbook case of the grief and sadness experienced by many children his age. An only child, he hadn't seen much of his father in the year leading up to the divorce; his dad had moved from Chicago to California in an effort to find work. Finally, Adam and his mother were brought West and discovered that Harlan Wheeler was living with another woman. He had enticed his family to California by hinting at a reconciliation, but in fact he wanted them there so he could get a divorce under the state's no-fault-divorce system. The day Susan and Adam arrived in California, Harlan picked them up at the airport, handed them the keys to a used car and the key to a house they had never seen, and announced that he was terribly sorry but the marriage was over.

In the weeks that followed, Adam began to express an unrelenting rage toward his *mother* and started to stutter painfully between clenched teeth. Rage, the psychologists say, is a "stage two" emotion, often covering up an even deeper feeling of helplessness. These feelings often surface in children, especially six-to-eleven-year-old boys, who keenly fear the collapse of their families and experience an almost physical longing for the absent parent, whether or not they were close before the separation. Six to eight is the age of burgeoning sexual identification, and without the father's presence many little boys become anxious and angry. Often their mothers are the most convenient target. So it is not uncommon for boys six to eight, who feel great hurt at the loss of their fathers, to accuse their mothers, directly or indirectly through their rage, of having driven their fathers away.

As do preschoolers, early-elementary-school-age children often need special reassurance from both parents that they, the youngsters, didn't cause the divorce. They need a clear statement from both parents that it is all right to love both (regardless of who did what to whom). And they need to be allowed to express affection toward all the people in their lives who are good to them, including grandparents, relatives, and even Daddy or Mommy's "friend," if that adult acts considerately toward the child.

In the weeks following the Wheelers' split, Susan had an understandably difficult time coping with her own sense of grief and betrayal. Although she tried not to explode in front of Adam, she was clearly and justifiably upset. Meanwhile, the physical proximity of his family now brought home to Harlan Wheeler the reality of his actions. He became very unreliable as a visiting parent, alternating between feelings of guilt, remorse, and rage that his wife and child should be causing him such discomfort by living in the same town. His erratic behavior, of course, bewildered and upset Adam as much as the fact that "Daddy didn't love Mommy anymore." Adam was hurt by his father's indifference to promises to visit.

Susan Wheeler, struggling with a shattered marriage, a new city, no job, a child who was constantly tearful and could barely speak a sentence without his painful stutter, sought counseling. She was urged to separate the issues of the marriage from the issues concerning Adam. She encouraged him to keep contact with his father, no matter how unreliable Harlan was about keeping dates, because she could see that it was in her interest, as well as the child's, that Harlan stay involved with Adam's upbringing. As much as it enraged her that her former husband arrived late or changed plans at the last minute, and as much as her pride was in tatters when his new woman slammed down the phone any time Susan called to make arrangements for his visits, Harlan's access to his child was never shut off. "In the long run I could see it would be better for all of us if he stayed in the picture, even though it nearly killed me to be so 'noble,' " Susan says.

When she was alone with the few friends she'd made in California, Susan would "yell and scream and cry and complain" about Harlan's treatment of her, but she would not demean him in front of her son.

It took nearly two years for the Wheeler family to calm down. Eventually Harlan became more dependable as a coparent. He and Susan also decided on sharing custody. "Adam's stuttering is my barometer as to how we're all doing," says Susan, "and when he starts to stammer, I pay attention to what's going on with all of us."

She has not yet lost her angry feelings toward her former husband. But because she was able to keep those emotions separate from Adam's needs, her son has not been hurt as much as he might have been. Adam still bears scars, but he did eventually get the care and reassurance he needed from his mother and his father, and "that has made all the difference," says Susan.

Recently Harlan Wheeler remarried, but the new Mrs. Wheeler does not hang up on the first Mrs. Wheeler. Susan found a job she's happy with and has started to date. "It's been quite a struggle," she says, sighing, but she feels proud that she and Harlan are now both involved in Adam's education and day-to-day activities.

Preteens: Nine-to-Twelve-Year-Olds

Divorce can turn all children, but especially preteen youngsters, into cover-up artists. Unfortunately, divorce in the family of nine-to-twelve-year-olds comes precisely at a time when these children—if they are feeling lonely, frightened, deprived, or despairing—are embarrassed to express these emotions. Their friends pressure them to "be cool" about life in general. Crying "like a three-year-old" or saying "I'm afraid" within earshot of a preteen contemporary can have mortifying consequences. The burden of keeping their feelings private is added to the weight they are already carrying about the family breakup.

One eleven-year-old I know appeared nonchalant and even jaunty following the announcement that his parents' marriage of thirteen years had ended. He whizzed by on his skateboard with an offhand wave and responded with a shrug when friends expressed their concern. A month or so later, one close family friend got a call at around six in the evening. The youngster was fighting tears. Apparently his mother had gone out, thinking his father would pick him up for dinner, but the parents had somehow mixed up the dates. "There's nothing to eat in the house," the youngster wailed angrily, "and I don't know what to do! Can I come over to your house?" Gone was his savoir faire; behind the mask of a budding teenager was an eleven-year-old *child* who still needed the care of his parents.

The anger these preteens sometimes feel toward their parents is usually apportioned equally: half of this group will be angry at their mothers, half at their fathers—and some will be equally angry at both. In fact, preteens in general seem to have an inherent "fairness quotient" by which they judge people and events in their lives. In the Wallerstein and Kelly study, the nine-to-twelve-year-olds showed a remarkable sense of loyalty and an alarming capacity for moral outrage. Many had a disquieting inclination to side with the parent he or she felt (or was told) had been "wronged." In the first year after the separation, many of these children were sympathetic to the father who no longer could enjoy the home. Later, mothers, especially those who remained bitter toward their ex-spouses, were often successful in wooing sons to their side. After the first year, children in this group tended to remain allies of the parent in whose house they lived. Having lost one parent, these nine-to-eleven-year-olds weren't going to risk losing the other.

Preteens want to know what, *exactly,* to expect from their postdivorce situation. They long to belong *somewhere* and feel very threatened when the divorce makes them stand out in the crowd, or when they seem in danger of losing the identity of *their* school, *their* neighborhood, or *their* family.

According to child-development specialists, the major assignment for children of this age is sexual identification, and the need is great for a competent adult model of the same sex. If the father is rarely or erratically around as a model for nine-to-twelve-year-old boys, or if the mother is in such bad shape as to be emotionally unavailable for preteen girls, the mix of divorce and preadolescence can mean future trouble. It can also bring on physical symptoms of distress: stomachaches, headaches, and an unwillingness to go to school because "I don't feel good."

According to Dorothy Corkille Briggs, a school psychologist and marriage, family, and child counselor for more than twenty-five years, both parents, by staying involved and giving children permission to be loyal to both mother *and* father, can provide the structure preadolescents need as they strive toward independence. Briggs suggests that both parents encourage preteens to join constructive groups such as the Boy or Girl Scouts, soccer teams, or gymnastic clubs, and that the adults participate in those activities. She urges parents to offer their youngsters the chance to develop skills with "no strings attached." If the children like building models with Dad, both parents should encourage that; if they want to learn to play the tuba and Mom happens to teach music, both parents should give the okay to try the tuba.

Although children living with divorced parents are often asked for more help around the house than other youngsters, preteens shouldn't be given so many chores that there is no time for playing with pals. In fact, Briggs says, fathers and mothers of nine-to-twelve-year-olds ought to plan some activities that include their children's friends.

The most ominous development to guard against, particularly with this age group, is an alignment with one parent against the other. The idea that "It's us against him/her" can have long-range repercussions regarding sexual identification and instill an inappropriate sense of power in preteens; the mother of a budding adolescent may find that the mini-ally suddenly becomes a little tyrant. Preteens need to know the *parents* are in charge and responsible for decisions about the family. A parent who leans on a child for too much adultlike support may be shocked at the consequences of resentment and arrested development in the youngster.

The nine-to-twelve-year-old does best when the "who, what, where, when, and why" of postdivorce family life is clearly spelled out. As self-absorbed as it may seem, most youngsters are concerned with one central question when there is a divorce: Who is going to take care of *me?* Children of this age especially want to know who will drive them to swimming meets or help them with math. Not only are they afraid of abandonment; they want to know the particulars, the schedule, the routine of what life will be like under the new arrangements. Wallerstein and Kelly call it a need for a "protective structure"; Dorothy Corkille Briggs, in her book, *Your Child's Self-esteem,* defines it as "home as sanctuary." If the preteen's primary task between nine and twelve is to learn to define himself or herself according to the world *outside* the family, and if the reconstituted structure *within* the postdivorce family provides only stress and chaos, then that task of self-definition can be frightening indeed.

It is frightening, for instance, as my young friend discovered, for preadolescents to be home alone at night with no food in the refrigerator—no matter which parent is responsible for the oversight, and despite the fact that the child may be physically capable of riding a bike to the grocery store and making a sandwich for supper. It is inappropriate for even the most sophisticated preteen to be treated by preoccupied divorcing parents as if he or she were an adult. A child who is really well taken care of by both mother and father during the initial period following the parents' separation usually feels anxiety diminish as the pattern of good care is solidly established. In the words of one child psychologist, the well-cared-for youngster "can get on with the business of being a kid," and can emerge from a sensitively handled divorce feeling independent of the marital problems of the parents and headed toward adolescence with enough self-esteem to get through.

Teenagers: Thirteen-to-Eighteen-Year-Olds

Self-esteem is very much at stake for the adolescent youngster. The tricky psychological footwork required of teenagers becomes even more treacherous when the family structure, within which a lot of the experiments in independence are tried out, crumbles. How a teenager reacts to divorce depends primarily on the relationship that existed *before* the breakup and the quality of the relationship the young person develops with *each* parent following divorce.

To a sixteen-year-old from Minnesota whom I shall call Annie Cowan, it seemed both her parents were behaving like idiots. Annie had spent the past few years concentrating on school, cheerleading, and ballet, doing well in all three despite the tension she sensed between her mother and dad. For her fourteen-year-old brother, Peter, however, the highly charged atmosphere of the last few years had been depressing. No one seemed to have time to notice how unhappy he was at school or to do anything but criticize him about how much weight he had gained. He didn't like his father's drinking, nor did he think his mother had paid enough attention to his father, the house, or the kids since returning to work full-time.

After her husband was hospitalized overnight following an accident while driving drunk, Mrs. Cowan asked for a divorce. Her husband moved out, leaving her to tell the children of the decision. Annie and Peter took the news of their father's departure as if hearing that someone had died—not at all an unusual response among teenagers. They showed all the symptoms of deep mourning: tears, angry outbursts, an inability to concentrate, coupled with feelings of hopelessness and disturbing dreams at night. Annie's grades went from A's and B-pluses to C-minuses in one quarter. Peter, who hadn't been doing well in any subject except history, fell even further behind.

Annie was deeply upset by her father's condition and soon felt it was her duty to move in with him and look after him. Like many teenage girls, she was very angry with her mother for asking for the divorce. Peter grew to feel sorry for his mother and stayed with her. As their father and mother began dating new people and eventually became involved in romantic relationships, both children wondered what their world was coming to. Their parents seemed to be acting like adolescents, and the kids didn't like the role reversal at all.

The experiences of the Cowan youngsters provide a glimpse of what often happens when parents of teenagers divorce. For Peter and Annie, the normal levels of teenage anxiety—about identity, school, parents, and sex—were magnified. Wallerstein and Kelly found in their study that whether negative reactions prove to be temporary or long-term depends to a great extent upon how well the youngsters keep themselves separate from the conflict between the parents. Conflict at home can provide a powerful distraction from the teenager's psychological task of finding out, between the ages of thirteen and eighteen, "Who am I and where am I going?" If the parents continue a long-lasting battle, teenagers have little hope of finding a home base where they can get the nourishment (both physical and psychological) they need to continue their struggle toward independence.

In the case of the Cowan children, Annie's grades fell below those which were required for entrance to a four-year college. She took a job as a waitress, applied to a junior college, and was accepted. The second summer after her parents' divorce, she attended a six-week course in dance given in another city. Both her parents, despite their differences, encouraged her to go on to ballet school, which she realized was exactly what she wanted to do. When she returned to her dad's after the summer, Annie could see more clearly that the man had a severe drinking problem that she could do nothing about. Annie stopped riding in the car when her father was driving it while drunk, and no longer attempted to "rescue" her dad from the consequences of being a heavy alcohol user. She stopped trying to be a parent to her parents, and, belatedly, she understood some of the reasons why her mother had wanted out of the marriage.

Peter continued to stumble through high school, putting on pounds and finding companionship with other overweight teenage wallflowers. His unhealthy eating habits eventually produced intestinal problems. As he recovered, he observed the benefits his sister was receiving from an after-school job and he got a part-time job, too. It temporarily boosted his self-esteem.

Annie and Peter, like most teenage children of divorce, say that they wish their family were still one unit, but each youngster has come through the experience with a deeper understanding of adults. Annie increased in maturity and has developed confidence in her artistic talents and a sense of professional direction applauded by both her mother and her father. Peter eventually graduated from high school and married two months later. Neither bride nor groom had a job or money, and Peter's mother continues to be concerned about her son's future while wondering what actions could have been taken in the past that might have helped Peter cope better with his problems during the divorce and in its aftermath.

The key to the emotional survival of teenagers of divorce is, perhaps, the extent to which they can manage to distance themselves from the upheaval. The more the parents are aware of the particular needs of their teenage sons and daughters, the likelier the chances their youngsters will survive with a sense of self-worth.

For all children of divorce, regardless of age or stage, continued contact with both parents *coupled with* an absence, or at least an eventual reduction, of conflict between the parents seems to be the salient formula for future well-being. Parents considering divorce should learn of the potential impact upon their children. However, when they put their knowledge into practice, the problems can be very subtle, as I learned when I spoke to a "joint custody kid" approaching his fortieth birthday.

"I was sent to a school equidistant from New York and Washington, D.C., at age five and a half because neither my mother nor my father would agree which was to be the 'primary' parent and they each wanted their *half.*" The man telling me about his extraordinary upbringing spoke casually, almost as if talking about someone else. However, his courtly manner and slight British accent were significant clues to his past: he had lived in England for the last twenty years, thousands of miles from both the mother and father who designed what people these days would label a joint custody plan. I would label it *pseudo* joint custody, and so, I believe, would "Mark Kingston," the person who had to live with it.

"My parents never really discussed with me whether or not I liked their arrangement," Mark says without great bitterness. "It was simply understood that my going to this particular school halfway between New York and Washington was a necessity. One just had to accept it." At an extremely early age Mark also accepted the fact that his parents disliked each other intensely and could not seem to give up the perverse pleasure of hurting each other, however indirectly, through their young child. It didn't seem to help young Mark to know he was a loved child. "Part of my dilemma was that I knew how much each of them loved me and needed me and how jealous of my love for the other parent each was. They didn't actually want to deprive me of each other, but there was this constant competition and phenomenal tension."

The Kingstons had come to America after World War II. "Because my parents had been so displaced by what had hap-

pened to them during the war, they were emotionally dependent on me for their roots," Mark reflects. What he remembers
most distinctly of his early years as a "shared child" is the
sense of not having a home in either parent's house because of
the strain and commitment and obligation he felt to "help my
parents" survive their divorce. Mark's mother had left his father for another man. "I can remember my father trying to be
very stoic and sitting in his room in Washington in a chair,
crying. I remember seeing his misery and wondering at age five
what I could do to help."

When Mark visited his mother in New York, he felt guilty
about having supported his father when in Washington. "My
mother said she expected me to understand things from her
position and would say to me, 'Well, you know what Daddy is
like.' I felt like yelling at them so many times, 'Please don't do
this to me! Don't put me through this!' but instead, I became
an expert in 'shuttle diplomacy.'" Mark despised the fact that
he had to negotiate, that while loving the parent he was with,
he had to apologize for wanting to be with the other parent
when it came time to leave. What made the situation so difficult for Mark was the subtle, "civilized" way in which each
parent insidiously undermined the other. "Children need permission to love both parents freely," says family therapist
Elayne Kardner, noting that as a youngster Mark apparently
didn't get this from either mother or father. In fact, the supreme irony is that the Kingstons, Mark believes, thought they
had designed a reasonable solution to their own problems as
spouses by being "fair" and sharing their son—but fair to
whom? In their attempt to divide Mark's time between them,
they had overlooked the importance of sharing Mark's love.

Over the years, Mark's father continued to act the wronged
victim; his mother, the righteous wife. Each persisted in telling
and retelling the story of the other parent's failings by way of
veiled remarks and pointed "little jokes." Both continually demanded their son's unswerving loyalty. "To keep peace in the

valley, my time with each parent was precisely fifty-fifty. For nine months a year I was away at school; I'd spend fifty percent of the holidays with each parent and half the summer with one and half with the other. I always had this kind of longing that I could stay where I was at the time—and that could be either Washington or New York—but I knew I couldn't and I never stayed *anywhere* long enough to plead my case."

Mark's parents may have quietly congratulated themselves for devising a shared parenting arrangement years before anyone had heard of the term "joint custody," but one essential ingredient in a successful cocustody agreement was missing—a separation of the conflict between the parents from issues regarding the child. Neither adult adequately supported the other *as a parent;* they were too busy reminding their son through their cryptic comments how disappointed each remained with the other. Each parent loved Mark and kept in contact with him, but the other necessary part of the shared custody equation wasn't there—permission to love both parents *from* both parents. Loving a child of divorce simply isn't enough if successful joint custody is a goal; *sharing* that love is the key, and some divorcing parents can't quite accomplish this.

Even when Mark's mother remarried, the competition between his mother and father didn't diminish. Mark felt pressured to call his new stepfather "Mr. Crandell" in front of his own father so "Dad wouldn't think I'd grown too close to Mother's new husband." On the other hand, if Mark accepted an invitation from his father for an unplanned weekend in Washington, he dreaded having to tell his mother about it and having to justify his wish to spend time with his dad. "The negotiating process was exhausting," he remembers.

The result was that Mark took on the role of "parent" to his parents because of their inability to deal with each other face-to-face as divorced adults. As a growing youngster he became more and more unnerved every time he had to deal with conflict in any form. "I had a very repressed teenage experience because I felt such an obligation to both my parents to be kind and not upset things, and I fought down my natural inclination to revolt. I felt responsible for *their* happiness." Mark had what he now refers to laughingly as an "override switch" that he would flip on mentally in order to remain neutral when conflict between his parents flared up. "I'd take refuge psychologically in one house if things got tough in the other. I'd say to myself, 'The heck with you—you can do whatever you want,' and try to detach myself from both of them." He learned not to long for anything himself, because it might hurt his parents. Consequently, as he grew older, he rarely felt fiercely committed to anything or passionate about striving for what he believed in. As the product of what his parents would certainly call a "shared custody arrangement," Mark developed a remarkable empathy toward everyone, but he was rarely able, until he married and had children of his own, to take a stand for what was in *his own* interest.

Dr. Susan Steinman, a clinical social worker who headed one of the first major studies of shared custody, talked to children as well as adults in some twenty-five families whom she studied for two years in San Francisco in 1978 and 1979. She found that one of the most striking characteristics of the youngsters she interviewed was their very empathetic nature and their concern about their parents, traits that Mark Kingston certainly possessed. An equally striking characteristic, however, for some children in her study was their lack of assertiveness, spontaneity, and decisiveness at home with their parents. Others developed a kind of "hyperloyalty" both to their parents and to the joint custody arrangement itself. Some children seemed excessively worried about "siding with one parent and hurting the other," noted Dr. Steinman. "While empathy is certainly a highly valued character trait, the sense of responsibility for keeping things even and their parents happy was clearly burdensome."

In Mark's case, joint custody was arranged primarily for the convenience of the parents and without their declaring a truce. The war between the parents was burdensome and was probably just as stressful in many ways as an unsatisfactory sole custody arrangement would have been. Looking back over his years of commuting between the two camps in Washington and New York, Mark says, "My advice to parents—no matter *what* the custody arrangement—is to *lay off!* Don't talk badly about the other parent because you'll never convince a kid that Daddy is a bastard or Mommy is a tart." He adds with the wisdom of his thirty-five years, "I never felt that either parent didn't love me, and that was good, but they created a situation where I felt responsible for their happiness as my parents. All of a sudden I realized, not too long ago, after having negotiated between them for decades, that they were screwing up my life by acting as they did." Showing anger for the first time during a discussion that had gone far into the night, Mark said, "I deeply resented both of them for doing it."

As Mark Kingston matured, he began to rebel against always playing the diplomat. When Mark was in his mid-thirties, his father remarried and transferred a lot of the dependency for his emotional support from Mark to the new wife, a much younger woman. "At first I felt disconcerted that my father switched allegiance so quickly after all those years of needing me so badly," Mark reflects. "Then I felt phenomenally relieved—joyous, in fact." His mother, however, more than twenty years after the divorce, still did not have a charitable word to say about Mr. Kingston or his new bride. Mark remembers each side's stepped-up demands of loyalty. "I thought one day, 'My God, I've had thirty-five years of practicing playing the negotiator ... *what do you people think you're doing?* Fight your little fights from now on *without* me!"

If parents want to reduce the impact of divorce on their children and make shared custody work most successfully, that advice from Mark Kingston should become their motto.

CHECK THE PRESSURE*

Fathers and mothers should try to be as honest as possible in answering questions regarding their relations with their children since the parents' separation.

	YES	NO
1. Have I done anything directly or indirectly to discourage my children from loving, being with, or making contact with the other parent in person or via telephone or letter?	☐	☐
2. Have I ever implied to my children that I will withhold my love for them if they express a liking or affection for a new stepparent or other adult who is kind to them?	☐	☐
3. Have I ever directly or indirectly threatened to send the children away or to leave them if they don't behave in the manner I demand?	☐	☐
4. Have I directly or indirectly used the children to carry angry or subtly hostile messages back and forth?	☐	☐
5. Have I ever told or implied to my children that the other parent is bad, shiftless, uncaring, indifferent, greedy, selfish, immoral?	☐	☐
6. Have I ever accused my children of being "just like your father/mother" when I was angry or irritated with them?	☐	☐
7. Have I ever given the impression that I will withhold my love for them if they express affection or longing for the other parent?	☐	☐
8. Have I ever made a substantial change in the family routine without preparing the children beforehand (such as moving, changing the chil-		

*Adapted from "Children and Divorce: Twenty Questions Divorcing Parents Ask," Association of Family and Conciliation Courts Pamphlet. Used by permission.

                                                                    YES   NO

dren's schools, planning medical treatment,
remarrying or moving in with another adult, or
unilaterally shifting the time the children are to
spend with the other parent)?   ☐   ☐

9. Have I ever burdened the children with problems
   of dire financial difficulties, legal matters, suicid-
   al thoughts, personal or sexual hang-ups?   ☐   ☐

10. Have I expected my children to comfort me, in-
    stead of seeking adult companionship or profes-
    sional therapy?   ☐   ☐

11. Have I continued to have verbal and physical
    battles in person or on the telephone with the
    other parent in front of the children?   ☐   ☐

SCORING:

Answering "Yes" to *any* of these questions can mean parents are
acting in ways especially damaging for children. Mothers and fathers can use each question as a means of pinpointing areas in
which they will strive to remove their children from the crossfire
of postdivorce conflict.

Part Two
How You Can Work Out a Shared Custody Arrangement

Chapter 6
Negotiate, Don't Litigate!

Custody Mediation and How It Works

*A day at Conciliation Court. Negotiation, mediation, concili-
ation, and arbitration defined. Lawyers who mediate instead
of litigate. Mediation of issues other than child custody:
property-settlement and support questions. How will things
turn out in mediating versus litigating child custody questions? Creating your own "law" in mediation. Basic rules of
mediation. Tony and Nina: an "impossible case" sent to mediation. Am I Willing to Mediate? (quiz). Am I Ready to
Mediate? (quiz). Questions to ask a (potential) attorney.
Questions to ask a (potential) divorce counselor or mediator.*

It was February 14, Valentine's Day. Business as usual in the
crowded halls of the Superior Court of the County of Los Angeles, where some sixty thousand divorce actions are filed annually (more than double the number, incidentally, filed in all
of Australia each year). Tense groups of adults huddled
around attorneys who were giving last-minute instructions to
clients. Children sat hunched on oak benches, waiting to find
out which parent they would lose as a result of the custody trials about to begin.

Inside the "holding" area of Room 241, parents waited for the conciliation counseling sessions judges had ordered them to attend. Most of the parents were under the misapprehension that they had been sent to this special division of the court to "get reconciled." Although part of the purpose of some conciliation courts in several states is to offer marriage counseling, mainly they exist to help mothers and fathers resolve the conflicts surrounding their divorce. Particularly, they aim to teach parents to determine custody by conciliating—settling—their differences, rather than by fighting them out in a win-lose adversary court. The process of settling these differences is known as mediation, although other techniques for resolving family conflicts can include negotiation and arbitration. To understand how these alternatives to litigation can help families arrive at coparenting agreements, it is necessary first to define the terms.

Negotiation involves two or more people who try, through a process of give-and-take—of compromise and old-fashioned "horse trading"—to resolve their conflicts outside of court. Negotiating is the act of proposing and counterproposing solutions to a problem. The solution both parties can agree to becomes the settlement. The husband and wife can negotiate directly or they can have their representatives do it.

Mediation is the process of asking a neutral third person to enter into the negotiations. The mediator does not decide the solution to problems, as a judge would. Rather, the mediator helps the two sides define what is at issue and examine what alternatives are possible so that they can come up with solutions of their own design. By proposing basic ground rules that both parties agree to observe, the mediator helps keep the husband and wife "on task"—helps them stay focused on what it is they're trying to decide. The mediator wants them to look toward a parenting plan that will be in their children's best interests, and not to remain bogged down in arguments about conflicts of the past.

Conciliation Court mediators are skilled at exploring with

the husband and wife the various options of caring for children after divorce. The ground rules both parents adopt during their mediation may include an agreement to keep what takes place confidential—even from other family members—and to keep a rein on anger. In order to build trust during the negotiations, most couples agree to disclose all financial information that may be relevant to the issues of spouse or child support. If the mediation is to help resolve property questions as well as child custody, this agreement is absolutely essential.

An important commitment both sides must get from their mediator is that he or she will never endorse a settlement that isn't essentially fair to both husband and wife, even if both sides have agreed to it. (Some people who feel guilty or angry may bargain away future rights in an effort to "get it all over with.") Also, both sides should agree, if the mediation fails, that nothing disclosed there will be used later in court, that the mediator will not be called upon to testify in court, and that all records and notes of the mediation process will remain confidential.

A typical child custody mediation takes four to six sessions. If other issues, such as property and spouse support, are involved, the process may average eight to twelve sessions, each lasting an hour to an hour and a half.

There are a variety of ways in which trained mediators operate. Some work only when both parties are present. Others will begin the mediation with both sides in the same room, then see each parent individually (and sometimes the children as well) in separate rooms, and occasionally use "shuttle diplomacy," alternating between rooms to discuss proposals. Some mediators work alone, some in teams, and others work only within a specific area of expertise. There are mediators who work for public agencies, and others in private practice. At some mediation clinics, a therapist and a lawyer may work together and refer the family to specialists, for example to a certified public accountant for financial counseling.

The Family Mediation Association, based in Bethesda,

Md., is a nonprofit professional organization coordinating research, training, and mediation services around the country. It publishes a directory of mediators who have trained in accredited programs. (The FMA's address, as well as information for contacting other potential sources of qualified family mediators—including the American Arbitration Association, the Association of Family Conciliation Courts, the Family Service Association, and a number of state agencies—will be found in Appendix A.)

Conciliation is a form of mediation and, according to Hugh McIsaac, director of Los Angeles County's Conciliation Court, is "mediation—plus." The "plus" is that the conciliator—who is neutral, as is the mediator—will suggest options for the husband and wife to consider, exploring with them the pros and cons, helping them to develop negotiating skills of their own, so that they can select a solution to which they both can agree. Since most conciliators have solid backgrounds in the behavioral sciences, they are trained to be alert to underlying emotional issues that may be overwhelming the practical issues. Conciliators often suspend mediation in such cases to work on whatever psychological problem has surfaced.

In California and a few other states, cases involving child custody disputes are automatically referred to Conciliation Court for a possible mediated solution before being dispatched to a formal trial proceeding. Most conciliation counselors have at least a 50 percent success rate in assisting mediated settlements. Some report that 90 percent of their cases result in cooperative parenting plans that families themselves design and agree to in writing. In the West Los Angeles District, Commissioner John Alexander found that of 138 joint custody cases negotiated between September 1978 and September 1980, only 16 percent came back to court because of further disputes. Nearly twice as many—32 percent—of the sole custody awards made in that same period had to be dealt with again in court. "These are statistics family courts across the country should take a look at," says Commissioner Alexander. "Solutions that the couples design themselves are clearly more likely to stick," adds Conciliation Court Director Hugh McIsaac.

Arbitration involves a neutral third party hearing a case, but the arbitrator, unlike a mediator, usually has the power to decide custody or property-settlement issues. People who consent to *binding arbitration* agree to abide by the arbitrator's determination, and in most states there is no appeal after that decision has been rendered. *Advisory arbitration* allows the couple to accept or reject the arbitrator's ruling; if it is rejected, the case then goes to trial, as happens when settlement efforts fail in Conciliation Court.

There are several advantages to choosing arbitration over a courtroom trial. Unlike a judge, who is assigned by the court, the arbitrator is selected jointly by the husband and wife. Also, the arbitrator hears one case at a time and usually has far more time to consider the case than busy court agendas allow a judge. Arbitration is an adversarial process and in most cases both sides are represented by lawyers. But the process is more informal than a courtroom trial; meetings are held in private, affidavits are not required, and witnesses are not expected to be advocates for one side. The best-known source for arbitrators specializing in divorce matters is the American Arbitration Association, a group that has set up family-dispute services in many major cities around the country.

Attorney/mediators are rare, mostly because the American Bar Association's code of legal ethics holds that a lawyer must represent one client only. When agreeing to mediate for a husband *and* wife concerning the unresolved issues in their divorce, a lawyer risks the wrath and possibly the disciplinary action of colleagues. But Bonnie Neuman, a certified family-law attorney in Los Angeles who serves on the Family Law Advisory Commission of the California State Bar Association, believes that the adversarial approach in family law could and should be modified to allow properly trained attorneys to me-

diate. "I tell couples that I will serve as an impartial third party to try to help them resolve their differences over the
children," she says. "They sign an agreement with me that
they understand that, should our negotiations break down, I
will not represent either one of them in any future actions."
O. J. Coogler, formerly a practicing attorney and the first director of the Family Mediation Association's Training Division in Fort Lauderdale, Florida, thinks that mediation will be
an accepted legal specialty by the end of the 1980s. "Mediation
is *mediation*," he says, "and an attorney properly trained in
this field is not violating any code of ethics."

Perhaps the most difficult part of determining a plan for the
children following divorce is that so many other issues become
entangled: property settlements; cash settlements; who gets the
antique clock; who is going to pay what bills. Can mediation
help sort out these other issues as well? O. J. Coogler thinks it
can, with these cautions: "A mediator must know enough
about taxation and the law to guide the couple through the
particular problems facing them. But in my training program I
tell my mediators I'm not going to teach them how to be a lawyer or decide on tax problems, but rather how to recognize
what problems exist and to know when the mediator needs to
call on competent specialists for help or refer the couple to
them." The average cost of a *mediated* custody and divorce
settlement runs to about $400. If tax specialists or child psy-
chologists are consulted, the process could cost $900 to $1,000.
The average *contested* divorce runs $3,000 and up.
     What Coogler sees as the key to the success of mediation is
that the couple *keeps control of how things will ultimately turn
out.* "Couples always ask me, 'How will I come out using mediation as compared with how I will come out if I go to court?'
I tell them that the difference is, with mediation you *both* are
in control of how things turn out. You'll only end up with
what you *mutually* agree to in mediation. In court, you don't

know how you're going to come out. In most states, it depends on the judge you get, what mood he or she is in that day, what was the last case the judge tried, and what the judge's biases are, going into your case." As one lawyer says bluntly, "Basically, divorce court is a crapshoot."

A major difficulty for couples who go to court is the vagueness of the laws. The rules for property division, spousal support, child support, and child custody are subject to vast differences in interpretation, even within the same courthouse in the same county or state. In private mediation, says Coogler, a husband and wife can, in a sense, create their own laws.

The mediator can propose some general principles for the couple to follow, allowing them to create a "law" between themselves that becomes a "contract to be fair." Says Coogler, "The basic rule or 'law' of structured mediation is that there should be *no victims.*" Other basic rules are that the family community assets will be fairly distributed according to the needs of all the people involved and the children will not be deprived of access to both parents.

Exactly *how* the money and the time spent with the children will be allocated is the substance of the negotiations. The negotiations can proceed only when the principle of fairness to everyone involved, by everyone involved, is accepted. Naturally, one side's concept of what is fair may change as the negotiations proceed, but "that's the magic of mediation," says John Haynes, a New York psychologist who, along with O. J. Coogler, is one of the country's leading exponents of divorce mediation. "One part of the magic of mediation is to lay out all the options," says Haynes. "I look at every problem in divorce as a skein of wool that has to be carded. We have to look at each problem—children, finances, the family home—one by one. Then I will try to separate out each problem into its component parts. Then I look at all the options I can think of and ask the mother and father to think of options on their own."

Haynes arrived at the concept of mediating rather than liti-

gating divorce and custody from a background as a labor mediator. Some years ago two good friends of his were divorcing
and got into a "horrendous battle." After fighting in court for
nine months, they asked Haynes for help. "In about fifteen
minutes I'd suggested certain ideas to them from my own philosophy that everyone has to win something for there to be a
successful negotiation, and my friends were able to come to an
agreement. We walked back into the court with it and I saw
the judge's jaw drop. Then the husband asked me, 'Why don't
you think about doing this professionally?' And, eventually, I
did."

Experts in divorce and child custody mediation say that
judges, lawyers, and divorcing couples are very narrow in their
thinking about possible solutions to custody and property conflicts. "Perhaps it's the way we were educated," says Haynes,
"but most people come in with this idea that there is really just
one way to do things; that there's just one way to think about
dividing up the children's time, for instance, when there are
perhaps five or six ways, or more, and we begin to explore *all*
the options before making any decisions."

In mediation, options are explored thoroughly, but the divorcing couple's bitter past is *not* a subject for much discussion. With hundreds of mediation sessions behind him, O. J.
Coogler says, "I could spend years trying to untangle things
that people have been into over the last years of their marriage.
I don't do that. The only agenda I've got is helping a family
function as two separate units. What I'm interested in is how,
starting *now,* can these two people sitting in my office start being responsible parents?"

Tony and Nina Charlton (names they have chosen for the
purpose of telling their story) both admit now they were not
very responsible parents during a two-year custody battle over
their little daughter. In fact, the notion of cooperating with
each other as parents seemed totally out of the question. From
the time Carla was eight months old, the Charltons' divorce

file expanded with reports of endless court injunctions, stays, and contempt citations. There was even a police report of alleged assault with a deadly weapon after Carla's maternal grandfather brandished an empty shotgun when his son-in-law came to pick her up for a visit. The thick legal file also contained allegations by Tony of promiscuous behavior on the part of Nina; hospital records of injuries suffered by Tony's girlfriend, who charged that Carla's maternal grandmother yanked out clumps of her hair; newspaper clippings of a drug bust at the house Nina shared with a roommate.

I met Tony and Nina one afternoon in the summer of 1980 at their third session with O. J. Coogler, who was then director of the Conciliation Court in Fort Lauderdale, Florida. They had come to Coogler reluctantly, at the urging of their judge. At the time, they could imagine no way he could help settle their differences, except in a winner-take-all court fight.

Now, entering that third session, Nina, an alluring young woman of twenty-four, smiled and announced, "I'm not happy with our present setup."

Tony, large and powerful, reacted instantly. "I'm sure we'll hear all about Nina's objections to the schedule of my seeing Carla that we worked out last time," he said sarcastically.

The Charltons had been in the same room together for less than a minute.

In the past sessions Coogler had explained the basic rules of mediation:

1. As their mediator he cared about them both, and about their daughter, but he didn't represent either side.
2. Their participation in the mediation process was voluntary, but the mediator would not allow either side to coerce, abuse, or blame the other in an effort to force one spouse to agree to take certain action.
3. Everything that occurred in the mediating sessions was confidential and could not be used in court if the mediation did not succeed.
4. Any agreement the couple came up with must be based upon

adequate information, which meant both sides must agree to disclose fully what they knew about family finances.

5. The mediator could not require the father and mother to cooperate, but he could keep them from negotiating with each other in noncooperative ways. In other words, minimum civility was required during these sessions.

6. The mediator would not endorse any agreement regarding the custody of a child that didn't provide for contact with both parents.

Tony and Nina had been trying to work out what form that contact was to take. Although still antagonistic, they had, for the first time in two years, worked out a temporary coparenting plan, and had stuck to it, more or less, for two weeks. Their main problem seemed to be their working schedules. Nina worked a nine-to-five job, Mondays through Fridays, selling industrial chemicals. Tony worked a twenty-four-hour shift as a fireman every third day. Under the schedule they had designed, Nina ended up, in her words, with "too little quality time with Carla on the weekends, when I don't have to go to work." Often her daughter was with Tony on the weekends, and "half the time he's on his twenty-four-hour shift at the firehouse and the baby is with his girlfriend, Alison," Nina complained.

Tony sat up stiffly and countered, "Well, when she supposedly is with you on the weekends, you're usually at the beach and she's with your mother! But fine, you take Carla on the weekends and I'll take her Mondays through Fridays."

Nina set her mouth in a thin, straight line. "I'm not willing to do that, Tony. I don't want to go a whole week without seeing her."

Coogler asked Nina to go to a blackboard and map out a counterproposal she had in mind. Drawing a makeshift calendar, she chalked in the days she thought she should spend with her daughter.

Tony offered suggestions and adjustments, but there was a

problem: Tony's schedule *rotated* throughout the weeks, which meant that on some days Tony's girlfriend, Alison, would be the only person available to pick up or drop off Carla at Nina's. "I'm sorry, O.J.," said Tony, "there ain't no way Alison is gonna be part of this deal right now. Not after what happened with her and Nina's mother. She doesn't trust Nina *or* her mother, and she doesn't want any big hassles. I can't say I blame her."

Nina took a deep breath and went back to the blackboard. "Listen, Tony, what if I picked Carla up the night before I would ordinarily on the days when you have a conflict with your work?"

Tony paused, studying the chalk marks. "Well," he asked, "how are you gonna compensate me for those twelve hours I miss twice a month by lettin' you have her early?"

Nina had no counterproposal. And the hour-and-a-half session was nearly up.

Coogler's phone rang and he asked the couple to leave for five minutes while he took care of some other business. In the hallway Tony tried to be conciliatory. "I appreciate what you're trying to do, Nina, but we wanna be fair to both of us, remember. I can't forget the past so easily."

Suddenly, it occurred to everyone standing in the hall that the *actual* time with Carla that Tony would lose was time either when Carla was asleep or when Nina was at work and not with her daughter, anyway. Once Tony realized he wasn't being asked to make a bigger sacrifice than Nina, he agreed to the plan.

They returned to the mediator's office, thoroughly pleased. Coogler wasn't surprised. "It's great when parents discover their own options, rather than have the mediator give everything to them. Then they *own* it!"

As he sat down, Tony said, "The court was so blind, always favoring the mother. At least with this mediation I'll break halfway even and I can have a hand in raising my daughter."

Nina nodded. "What bothered me," she said, "was—here

was this judge who's never seen my daughter or Tony or me before and he's going to decide *our* lives!"

I didn't get a progress report on that fragile cooperating arrangement until nine months later. The most interesting assessment came from Tony's girlfriend, Alison. "We've had a few problems," she told me, "but I think Nina is trying. She kept Carla a few days when she wasn't supposed to, and she forgot Tony was supposed to have his daughter on Father's Day and they weren't there when we came to pick her up. And once she didn't show up on time, so we took Carla with us to a family dinner, and that got her mad—but basically, once we changed the schedule, that seemed to help."

Changed the schedule. I wondered how many mediation sessions *that* must have taken. But the mediation process can cope with changing circumstances, and when Tony was promoted to lieutenant in charge of the day-shift rescue squad, he and Nina saw the sense in making an adjustment. They were both working nine to five on weekdays now, so their old rotating schedule ("Which was too much switching around for Carla, anyway," said Alison) was no longer necessary. They agreed to an alternating arrangement in which Carla would spend one week, Sunday to Sunday, with Tony, and the next week with Nina.

"Tony and I are getting along real good now!" Nina told me. "I think working with Mr. Coogler has done miracles for us."

Tony was more subdued. "The new schedule is better for everybody, I think," he said, "especially Carla, and there are fewer hassles between Nina and me now that the transfers come only once a week." But Tony had noticed some problems. "Carla sometimes tries to manipulate us, saying she don't want to go with me or Nina. I always tell her she'll have a good time being with Mommy, but Nina don't do that much to make her want to go with me." Carla was two and a half now, an age when children need "advance notice" about transitions, even from playtime to lunchtime. It is also an age when they are establishing their independence as being separate from their parents (even though, of course, they are dependent on their parents for survival). I suggested that the frequent rapid shifting between two homes may have been too taxing for a two-year-old. Tony agreed that since Carla had started spending a full week at each house she'd improved. "Even with the new schedule, our parents still think we're both nuts," Tony added, laughing, "but mediation has helped us a lot. At least I *see* my daughter now. I'm in a lot better shape than I was this time last year."

Besides reaching accord on a time-sharing formula, Nina and Tony had also agreed that the parent Carla was living with each week would pay her expenses during that time. However, they would split any future education bills or unusual expenses, such as braces; and while Tony would have Carla covered under his firefighter's medical insurance plan, he and Nina would split the cost of any medical expenses not met by his union coverage. The Charltons were also able to work up a plan under which Tony bought Nina's share of the equity they had built up in their $35,000 tract home. And, for the first time, Tony was able to have Carla with him for Christmas Eve and Christmas morning; Nina agreed to pick her up at lunchtime for the annual Christmas feast at Nina's parents' house.

"What the Charltons represent," says their mediator, O. J. Coogler, "is an explosion of the myth that there are people who can't mediate their differences." Many lawyers and judges are fond of saying that only the rich, rational, and highly educated are capable of negotiating a joint custody agreement. "In rare instances," says Coogler, "there are those people who simply cannot use mediation, but we rush to judgment about too many other angry couples who are going through divorce."

Fireman Tony Charlton wishes he and Nina had found mediation sooner. "You can save yourself a lot of heartaches and hassles," he advises, "if you try mediation before you ever go to court."

AM I WILLING TO MEDIATE?

Dr. Sheila Kessler, founder of the Mediation Service at Georgia State University, asks her clients the following questions in order to determine how receptive they are to the idea of mediating, rather than litigating, the conflicts arising out of divorce:

	YES	NO
1. Is the issue (for example, of custody for our children) negotiable?	☐	☐
2. Am I willing to make some compromises?	☐	☐
3. Do I trust my former spouse enough to think he/she will be able to uphold a mutually satisfactory agreement regarding the children? (There is almost always a slight element of doubt.)	☐	☐
4. Am I willing to put aside my anger for a while so that I can deal with the issues (regarding the children) in a rational manner?	☐	☐
5. Can I make a commitment to live up to what I agree to (regarding the children)?	☐	☐
6. Am I capable of listening to the other person's side of the story?	☐	☐
7. Do I see this process (of mediation) in terms of compromise rather than of winning or losing?	☐	☐

SCORING:
If your answers are mostly "Yes" to these questions, Dr. Kessler and others familiar with divorce and custody negotiations say you are a good candidate for mediating, rather than litigating, the issues surrounding the future arrangements for your children after divorce.

For parents willing to try mediation and negotiation as a means of coming up with a shared custody agreement, the first step is to begin thinking about what *you* want to get out of the divorce. That is a difficult assignment for many people because it often seems as if nothing good could ever come out of anything so painful—especially something good for oneself. However, now is the time to start thinking about what results you would like to see materialize. Try to visualize your life five years from now. What do you imagine it to be like?

If you have begun to accept that your marriage is indeed over and that separate parenting is about to begin, what are your *goals* for this new and perhaps frightening state of affairs? What is the reality of your present situation in terms of your finances, employment, and geography; the ages, stages, and health of your children; and the willingness (to date) of the other parent to cooperate with you as far as the care of the children is concerned? These are the circumstances with which you must deal in the near term, and it will be very helpful for you to begin thinking about them as objectively as possible.

This is a time for *assessment,* especially if you think mediation would be a good process through which to address the conflicts facing you and your former spouse. To assess whether or not you are ready to try to mediate your differences, you should be able to answer most of the questions in the accompanying quiz.

AM I READY TO MEDIATE?

	YES	NO
1. Do I know what my current income is and what I can anticipate in the future?	☐	☐
2. Do I know what my former spouse's current income is and what he/she can anticipate in the future?	☐	☐
3. Do I know what the household budget was before I separated?	☐	☐
4. Have I drawn up a reasonable budget for my household if a shared parenting plan is worked out?	☐	☐
5. Have I drawn up a reasonable budget for the parent with the *majority* of child-rearing responsibilities if a shared custody plan is not worked out?	☐	☐

YES NO

6. Have I drawn up a reasonable budget for the parent with the *minority* of child-rearing responsibilities if a shared custody plan is not worked out? ☐ ☐
7. Have I calculated the financial assets from the marriage (the value of the house, cars, investments, furniture, pension plans, etc.)? ☐ ☐
8. Have I thought through how I would like the day-to-day parenting arrangements for my children to be set up for the next couple of months? For the next year or two? Until the children are of age? ☐ ☐

Don't feel overwhelmed if you haven't mapped out all the details mentioned here. These questions are to get you thinking about the future, and you can use them to focus your attention on the kind of "homework" you'll need to do, whether you decide to negotiate, mediate, or litigate the unresolved questions. In Chapter 7 there are some "before" and "after" household-budget sheets to get you started.

Questions to Ask a (Potential) Attorney

At some point you must decide whether you are going to leave it to your attorney to negotiate an agreement in your behalf, whether you will attempt to do the negotiating yourself, or whether, as suggested in this chapter, you will seek out a neutral third party. Whichever way you work out the custody plan, you will probably need an attorney to write it up in legal language and file it with the court. Appendix A will give you some leads on finding mediators and divorce or conciliation counselors in your general area. Representatives of the organizations listed in the same Appendix may be able to suggest attorneys who specialize in family law and are, perhaps, familiar with the shared custody concept, but these groups will not offer personal recommendations. If you know of people who have achieved shared parenting arrangements (even if not an "official" joint custody decree), ask them about their lawyers.

You will be wise to explore thoroughly *on your own* what your options are for coparenting and to seek out an attorney who is receptive to your ideas. This means you will have to *interview* any attorney you are considering hiring. Many consumers (and that is what a divorcing parent is: a *consumer* of legal and/or therapeutic services) find it difficult to question a legal or mental health professional about that person's qualifications to work for them in the manner they have decided. But *you must do this*! Choosing these professionals will be among the most important decisions you will make during this entire process.

You would be wise to interview more than one attorney or counselor. When calling for an appointment, make it clear that the meeting is to explore the *possibility* of working together. Most attorneys or counselors won't charge you (or will ask only a nominal fee) for a "consultation session" in which you are checking each other out. Explain that you do not want to go into the details of your particular situation, but, rather, you wish to use the time to find out some basic information and to see if you both feel comfortable about working together. Any attorney or counselor who doesn't have time for a quick preliminary meeting will probably not have much time for you during your case, so don't worry about anyone who refuses to meet you on this basis. As intimidating as some divorce professionals may be, it is *critical* to set the proper tone from the outset regarding your future relationship. *You,* after all, are the *employer;* you will be paying the bills and living with the results.

Sometimes you will be able to discuss the preliminary issues on the phone, but most likely you will want to do it in person. And, remember, you are paying for expertise, not for friendship or handholding.

In casual conversation you might ask if the attorney has ever been divorced. You are likely to get some interesting answers to that query and even more interesting reactions. Ask if the attorney has children, and if his or her spouse works. You might even ask how involved a parent the attorney feels he or she is in the day-to-day care of any children. The answers aren't as important as the attitudes expressed by the attorney when you ask these kinds of questions. Your tone should be light and pleasant, but by the end of a half hour you will know if this attorney is on your wavelength. Once you've talked to two or three lawyers, asking each one the set of questions in the accompanying questionnaire, you will have a very good idea of what you're looking for in a legal professional. You will also discover whether they can accept, or at least tolerate, the concept of shared custody and win-win negotiations in lieu of the traditional adversarial approach. Most important, your initial meeting will help you find out if a particular attorney has the sensitivity, as well as the legal and mediating skills, to help you work out a sound and sensible plan for your children's future.

Ask all the questions on the accompanying list each time you talk to an attorney, then compare notes before making your selection.

ATTORNEY INTERVIEW
WITH: _____

NOTES:

1. What percentage of his/her work involves divorce and custody matters?   _____

2. Where did he/she take legal training?   _____

3. How many years has he/she practiced family law?   _____

4. Is there a family-law specialty or certification offered by the state bar association? Has this attorney been certified under such a program? For how long?   _____

5. Has he/she ever written any shared parenting agreements? How did they work out for the families? _____

6. What does this attorney think about the concept of former spouses' sharing parenting responsibilities? _____

7. Does this attorney work with or refer clients to mental health professionals when indicated? _____

8. How often does this attorney find that clients need specialized help with their Emotional Divorce? _____

9. Has this attorney ever served in a mediating capacity for spouses who think they might be able to negotiate a custody and/or financial settlement? How often? _____

10. If this attorney will mediate, will he/she agree *in writing* not to represent either side should the negotiations fail? _____

11. What kind of formal training in mediation has this attorney taken? _____

12. Does this attorney refer certain aspects of a divorce to tax specialists or other experts? Under what circumstances? _____

13. What is the hourly fee charged by this attorney? _____

14. What is his/her usual retainer? _____

15. Is this attorney willing to submit to clients an *itemized* bill each month during the time he/she is employed by the client? _____

16. Will this attorney be doing the legal
    work involved in this case, or will a
    "junior partner" have the major re-
    sponsibility for this case?   _____

17. What do divorces similar to yours, as
    you've briefly explained it, cost at
    his/her office? (Approximately, of
    course.)   _____

18. Will this attorney give you the names
    of one or two clients he/she has repre-
    sented or mediated, once the clients
    have been contacted by the attorney
    and have given the attorney permis-
    sion to release their names?   _____

19. Will this attorney agree to keep you
    apprised of all developments in your
    case and make no offers or agreements
    without first consulting you and secur-
    ing your approval?   _____

Interviewing a (Potential) Divorce Counselor or Mediator

Divorce counseling and marriage counseling are *not* the same
thing. The primary focus of a marriage counselor is to try to
help the husband and wife exist in a relationship together. Divorce counseling is aimed at helping the couple "close the book
gently" on the marriage. The skills and training required in divorce counseling are very specialized, and it is important to be
sure the person you've hired to help reorganize your family has
the proper credentials.

Divorce counseling and family mediation are fairly new professions. However, the chances are good that you have connected with a qualified person if the counselor holds an
M.F.C.C. (marriage, family, and child counselor) degree, an
M.A. or Ph.D. in family counseling or clinical psychology, or
an M.S.W. or Ph.D. in social work, *and* is licensed by the state
if there is a licensing program.

As when interviewing lawyers, it is sensible to schedule get-acquainted sessions with *several* counselors, during which *you* ask most of the questions. Again, if the meeting you request is clearly a preliminary one (called in some instances a "consultation" rather than a working session) to see if you both wish to work together, there should be no fee or a nominal one. Even if your spouse is uncertain about committing to the mediation process, you will have the information you need to explain *why* you think mediation is preferable to a legal trial or out-of-court arm twisting.

The mediation organizations listed in Appendix A will guide you to groups and individuals in your general area. However, don't take someone else's word for the competence of a professional whose fees *you* are going to pay. Take the accompanying questions with you and interview two or three counselors so you can compare their training, background, and empathy regarding your desire to negotiate rather than litigate.

COUNSELOR/MEDIATOR INTERVIEW
WITH:＿＿＿＿＿＿＿

NOTES:

1. What percentage of his/her work involves divorce counseling and mediation of custody and financial-settlement issues?   ＿＿＿＿＿＿＿

2. Where did the counselor/mediator take his/her training?   ＿＿＿＿＿＿＿

3. Has this person trained in "family systems" work?   ＿＿＿＿＿＿＿

4. How many years has this person worked in the *divorce* field?   ＿＿＿＿＿＿＿

5. What degrees and/or licenses does this person hold?   ＿＿＿＿＿＿＿

6. Is this person affiliated with a clinic, community mental health association, family services group, or conciliation court in addition to, or exclusive of, a private practice? _____

7. What kind of *specific* training in divorce mediation has this person had? _____

8. How many divorces or custody mediation cases does this person handle in a month? In a year? _____

9. What does this person think the *impact on the child* is when fathers share a significant portion of child-rearing responsibilities? _____

10. Is this person a member of the Family Mediation Association, the Association of Family Conciliation Courts, the Family Service Associations of America, the American Arbitration Association, or church-related professional counseling associations? _____

11. Is it this person's practice to see all members of the immediate family if possible or practical? _____

12. Does this person ever testify in court or through affidavit on behalf of *only one side* in custody matters? _____

13. What does this counselor or mediator think of the concept of former spouses' sharing parenting responsibilities fairly equally? _____

14. Has this counselor been divorced? Does he/she have children? Does he/she have a working spouse? Has he/she remarried? Has he/she participated in the day-to-day care of his/her own children? _____

15. What is the hourly fee for this person's service?   _____

16. Does this person call in or refer certain aspects of a case to a certified public accountant or other expert? Under what circumstances?   _____

17. What is the anticipated number of sessions for the mediation process? At what total (estimated) cost?   _____

As you ask the same questions of more than one mediator, divorce counselor, or lawyer, you will begin to get a feel for the style of each person and have a better notion of what *you* want and what that professional is willing to provide.

Take your list of questions into each interview and keep notes by jotting down the answers next to each query. That way, you can better compare your impressions after you've seen a number of people. Obviously, you won't use these questions to grill them, but you can refer casually to your list as your conversation progresses, and use the questions as a way of guiding you through the interview. Keep the discussion focused on what *you* need to know about this person, with whom you may be working on one of the most important transitions in your life.

You can end each interview by thanking the person for the time spent and saying that you will be talking to several people and will report on how you intend to proceed.

The point of comparison shopping is to find out if you (and, if possible, your spouse) want to work with any of these professionals in a *partnership* to negotiate a plan for being with your children and for settling as many differences in the divorce as possible. However, whether or not you decide to seek counseling or to use mediation as a means of achieving shared custody, if you want a coparenting agreement, the next step on the agenda is to design a cooperative custody parenting plan that is acceptable to both sides. Before you can do that, you have to know precisely what you want that plan to have in it and what you think will work best for your children. So the next question is: What *do* you want?

Chapter 7
Designing a Shared Custody Parenting Plan

So Whadda Ya Want?

Trouble in "paradise." Roy and Betsy Nicholson—plus four.
He who gets the house, gets the kids . . . and other problems.
Asking yourself: "Whadda ya want?" as a first step in design-
ing a shared custody plan. Assessing your needs as a single
parent. The "out-house" parent and the "in-house" parent.
Your Custody Arrangement Fantasy Sheet. Through the eyes
of a child. The "other side": whadda they want? Parent's
Time Survey, or: How much time do I actually spend with
my kids? Designing your Proposed Parenting Plan. The Way
We Were (household budget sheet). The Way We Are (house-
hold budget sheet).

There was trouble in paradise. In an attempt to save their marriage—"for the sake of the children"—a couple I will call Roy
and Betsy Nicholson moved in 1976 from the deep freeze of
the Midwest to Hawaii. But two years later, after twenty-one
years of marriage, they finally concluded that their problems
went well beyond geography. "Our marriage had been in trouble for a long, long time," says Betsy Nicholson. "Being in

such a beautiful place wasn't enough to fix the relationship. I was very happy to be living here in Hawaii, but inside I was miserable."

The Nicholsons had married in their teens, after Betsy became pregnant, and when they separated in 1978, they had four children, ranging in age from seven to twenty-one. Although Betsy and Roy have different views as to what went wrong with their marriage, they agree they can be proud of the way in which they designed their own parenting plan for taking care of the children following their split.

"I think I heard about joint custody in *Time* magazine or someplace," recalls Roy, a salesman. "I sought out a lawyer I had been told was supposed to be an expert in divorce, and when I proposed a situation whereby Betsy and I would both continue to be involved with the kids, the attorney just shook his head and said, 'You'll never be such an involved father as you think you want to be right now.' He actually told me I really didn't want my kids." Roy remembers male friends' saying to him, "You won't be able to boogie, man. *You* can't cope with four children. Let *her* do it and you just see them when you want to." Roy realized that "all these guys giving me advice hardly saw their own kids, and they were *married*."

For Betsy, outsiders were equally discouraging. "I had heard that if a judge was opposed to joint custody, he might slow things up by ordering a case study and questioning everything. It was kind of a scary feeling to me that the divorce and custody issues might be out of our hands when *we* were the ones that agreed that sharing custody was the best thing for our kids." It never occurred to Betsy and Roy that there was no law on the books which prevented them from conducting their private life as they chose, as long as they *both* agreed—as they did—to try to cooperate as parents.

The breakup began bitterly. When Betsy proposed that they divorce and move out of their three-bedroom town house at a Honolulu marina, Roy was extremely upset. "I told her, 'You want to leave so bad, you get your ass outta here and *I'll* stay with the kids in the house. ' " Betsy did leave, and she rented a small wooden cottage at the other end of town. She was convinced that outsiders would think she had abandoned her children, and feared that the children would feel deserted. "I told the kids that moving out was very traumatizing for me, too, but that I was ten minutes away and that I would always be their mother." Soon she found work as a salesperson for a local tourist outfit, her first full-time job in thirteen years.

Roy recalls how miserable they all felt. "I began my year with the kids in the house by myself. I had never cooked or done much housework, and I was scared that my new job wouldn't work out and I wouldn't be able to support this whole circus." Laughing ruefully, he adds, "I guess I felt like a divorced single *mother.*"

Most of what Betsy remembers about that first year is the guilt. "Moving out put a heavy burden on me. *Was* I deserting my kids?" She installed "wall-to-wall beds" in her tiny cottage, but often found herself back at her old town house making a casserole, doing the laundry, "and trying to keep it all together."

Soon Roy and Betsy determined that since there were four children involved, in such a variety of ages and stages, it would be more stabilizing for the youngsters if the children stayed in one place and the adults did the moving back and forth. "We knew what we wanted to do about the kids, and then *later* the tag of 'joint custody' was put on it," says Betsy.

Each week, Betsy tried to spend her two days off with the children, usually at the house on the marina. On those days, Roy would be at work or would stay away for the day. "Sometimes, though," Betsy says, "the little ones would stay overnight at my cottage and I'd drive them to school in the morning." Roy paid the mortgage and all the expenses of the main household, plus $300 a month to Betsy while she struggled to live on her own income for the first time in her life.

Roy's anger at Betsy for leaving him began to abate as she shouldered some of the day-to-day responsibility for the children. "I always knew there were things that the kids could depend on their mother for," says Roy, who often would go out on a date Saturday night when Betsy came over to care for the children. Betsy herself began to feel confident that their shared custody plan could work when she finally "got over the agony of watching Roy fumble through things I'd been doing with ease around the house for years. I had to let myself not feel guilty and realize that it was okay that the laundry was *his* responsibility when he had the kids. He wasn't experienced in taking care of them when they were sick or in making casseroles, but he didn't want to lose the kids, so he became willing to learn."

The Nicholsons shared the view that endless squabbling over money and custody would be self-defeating. "We'd seen the kids of Roy's sister and brother-in-law go through a horrendous divorce," says Betsy. "Roy's sister had the kids; the father saw them on Saturdays—until he remarried a woman with two kids of her own. Then *her* children saw more of their stepfather than his own flesh and blood saw of him, their *real* father. It was so sad." Roy agrees that his sister got bad advice: "It was really bitter, since *he* left her, and she'll probably end up in a mental hospital."

Both Roy and Betsy were determined to avoid having their own problems enlarged by the legal maneuverings of attorneys. "What Roy and I both realized," says Betsy, "is that lawyers, generally, get money when there is trouble. We felt that if we could work things out between us and keep the trouble away from the lawyers, we would be better off, our finances would be better off, and the kids would be better off." Says Roy, "It's in the attorney's best interests to keep conflicts boiling. I don't say they sit down and say, 'Let's stick this guy for another fifteen hundred bucks and start the meter, but the kind of advice they give generates more conflict and keeps the adversary proceedings going." Betsy says, "I think that the amount of money we saved by negotiating with each other instead of fighting now makes it easier for us to do joint custody."

In the beginning, however, when the Nicholsons were trying to design a plan for "doing their joint custody," they had to go through a process that can be called "So Whadda Ya Want?"—the process of asking themselves what they wanted to come out of the divorce in terms of their own, their children's, and their finances' well-being.

Roy and Betsy recognized that they were unique: there were many other divorcing couples in the world—including some with four children—but Roy and Betsy's own situation was different from all other parents' because the Nicholsons were six *individuals*. Other couples with four kids might even want to design a shared custody plan, but Roy and Betsy wanted the Nicholson shared custody plan to be tailor-made to accommodate the specific realities in the lives of Roy, Betsy, twenty-one-year-old Steven, fifteen-year-old Liz, nine-year-old Jimmy, and seven-year-old Jeremy. So they decided that the kids would stay in the family home, and on December 31 ever year, one parent would move in and the other would move out. "For us," Roy says, "it was a workable arrangement." It was workable because each parent had gone through the process of asking the other, "So Whadda Ya Want?"

Roy knew one thing in response to that question: he wanted to keep his kids. "If you lose your wife and your house and your kids, you have no reason to do anything but go out and get a .45." But he did not want to have the *full* responsibility for them during their entire childhood. "I still believe that a man is defined by his work in this world, and my job takes a lot of my time. I wanted to be with the kids, but I wanted Betsy to do her part." Nor did Roy want to become a pauper as a result of the divorce or a shared custody agreement where he was the only financial tent pole.

Betsy also had to ask herself the question "So Whadda Ya Want?" She knew that she, too, loved her children and wanted to continue to be a parent to them. However, she had had more than twenty years as a full-time homemaker and felt she had "burnt out emotionally" in that role. Now she wanted to develop some of her other interests, including pursuing a degree in East Asian studies. She also wanted to become economically self-sufficient, though she needed Roy to subsidize her for a while. "I'd put my energies into house and home and didn't have much to sell in the real world at the time we separated." And, like Roy, Betsy wanted her children to have stability by staying in the same neighborhood and school system. They sensed that their teenagers, especially, might reject moving back and forth between two residences. Moreover, even if they were to sell the family home, the Nicholsons doubted there would be enough money to find two apartments big enough to accommodate two to four children on a regular basis. No, the idea of having the children stay put and the *parents* do the moving made the most sense. The parent who was not living in the house—the "out-house parent"—would have access to the children, and the youngsters could visit that parent at any time. "We knew that with this unusual system the children would lose the comfortable, traditional form most families take," says Betsy, "but at least they still would have a family."

The parents drew up their list of wants and needs and their individual assessments of what they understood to be the needs of their children. They drew up alongside that information a factual account of their mutual finances. And they began to see past the emotional issues and began to focus on *what was actually possible for them* in terms of a negotiated parenting plan of their own design. They also agreed that, if conditions changed, the plan would be subject to renegotiation.

Roy remained in the town house exactly one year. He moved out on December 31, 1979, and Betsy moved in. It wasn't an easy transition for either of them. Says Roy, "I'd hung in there the first difficult year and found out it takes as much work to be a good parent as to be a good salesman. When I moved out and Betsy moved back in, I was supercritical and didn't think she was as attentive to the kids' needs as I felt she should be. We had these horrible knockdown fights over her not spending what I thought was enough time and letting the older ones take care of the little ones. Then she'd say to me, 'Well, *you* weren't around that much when they were little.'" However, the changeover endured because, as Roy notes, "I was at a point where I needed some room and privacy and Betsy needed to be more connected to the kids." He also acknowledges that Betsy was a "good enough" parent. "She wasn't perfect, but good enough; and anyway, back then, I'm not so sure *I* was such a great father."

In the months that followed, each parent learned to respect the other. "It was a step-by-step process," said Betsy on December 31, 1980, when she moved out of the marina town house once again. "Joint custody parents—like all divorced parents, I suppose—have to anticipate a lot of ups and downs. We both found out it can be tough to be an active mom and work outside the home as well as be an active dad and hold down a job." Chuckling, she says, "My kids saw a Macho Man learning to run a vacuum cleaner, and that was great!"

The Nicholsons anticipate that their current plan will be modified when two of their four children become full-time college students. Their expectation is that Roy will stay in the family house with the two younger boys while daughter Liz moves in with Betsy near the school Liz wants to attend, the University of Hawaii. Their oldest son, Steven, plans to be living on his own by then, and Betsy expects to spend two or three days a week with her younger sons.

Eventually, both Roy and Betsy hope to be involved in new permanent romances and relationships. And eventually they want to diminish the connection they have with each other because of joint ownership of the marina house. "If one of us had gone and lived with someone else soon after the separation," says Roy flatly, "then we would have had to come up with a different plan."

Betsy believes that parenting plans must have, as a central tenet, built-in flexibility so they can be redesigned as a family's circumstances change. "The thing that kept me going the first three years when it was so darned difficult was that I kept asking myself, 'How will I feel when things calm down?' I asked myself during those first, bitter days whether a particular way of arranging things concerning the kids or the money would ultimately make me feel upset, ashamed, or proud. We have to realize life *changes.* Be flexible; keep talking to *everyone* in the family, and don't make derogatory remarks about anyone. That doesn't mean not expressing your feelings," says Betsy, "but don't go around blaming others for your feelings." Roy's advice: "Once you have a plan, you're going to need time to let it take hold. Trust your own judgment and don't let others impose their ideas on you."

When Roy's attorney read the custody agreement the couple had worked out, he offered a few suggestions about wording, then said, "This is one of the best plans I've ever seen." The premise only confirmed what businessman Roy Nicholson believed from the outset: "The settlement should be *between the two parties.* That's just good business. When you've got it settled, *then* you should go see a lawyer. I don't think it's any more difficult, now that we've done it, than negotiating a contract between management and labor. Management and labor have completely different interests and yet they are able to come up with agreements all the time. We, at least, had the children in common." Referring to the document that describes the Nicholson's individual parenting plan as "joint legal and physical custody to mother and father," Roy says proudly, "Like us, business and labor simply negotiate."

The need to negotiate custody issues has become the central ethic in the career of Marybeth Webster, a lively and outspoken gadfly in the area of divorce reform. A psychologist by training, Dr. Webster is a cofounder of a private divorce clinic in Honolulu and also coordinates a public education program, "The Divorce Experience," sponsored by the Honolulu Superior Court and subsequently adopted in other cities, including Los Angeles and Minneapolis. As a result of what Dr. Webster calls her own "disastrous divorce" in 1965, which resulted in a three-year custody battle over her four children, she believes that "if people have some facts and background and a little bit of help and some relief from their stress, they become easier to work with as clients—whether they are clients of a lawyer or a divorce counselor."

"The Divorce Experience" comprises three sessions that meet on the first, second, and third Wednesdays of alternate months. The meetings deal with the social and emotional stresses of separation, offer a basic primer in local divorce law, and outline the impact of divorce on children. There are panel discussions, to which Dr. Webster invites lawyers and counselors as well as parents who've gone through divorce and the restructuring of their families and "have lived to tell about it."

As a basis for good child care, what has to happen, says Dr. Webster, is for working fathers as well as mothers—whether married or divorced—to reassess what elements are important in their lives, and to place the care of their offspring, and enjoyment of daily contact with them, higher on their list of priorities than they have in the past. When fathers and mothers both achieve a better balance between the demands of earning a living and the requirements of being "good enough" parents, the crunch in which current children of divorce are caught should begin to ease up. "What we try to do is achieve the greatest sustenance for the children with the least amount of torment for the parents," Dr. Webster says. Children of divorced parents need mothers and fathers who are willing, when it counts, to be reasonably selfless—at least to the degree that each parent is willing to step in for the other when necessary.

A shared custody plan can provide the blueprint for achieving that balance. For starters, it is necessary to discover what, exactly, you—if you are a divorcing parent—want out of a custody arrangement. When she negotiates privately with a divorcing couple, says Dr. Webster, "I say to them, 'Suppose the court would insist on a strict sole custody/reasonable visitation schedule. Imagine *you* are the visiting parent. What would be your ideal visiting routine?" Laughing, she adds, "On paper, anyhow, they each have to be as generous to the 'visitor' as they can." This exercise is the first of Dr. Webster's many attempts to encourage the warring parents she works with to try to empathize with what it might feel like to be an "outside," or, as the Nicholsons joked, "out-house," parent.

Take a moment now to fill out this adaptation of Dr. Webster's "shoe-on-the-other-foot" concept. Remember, in this exercise the judge has awarded your former spouse sole custody of your children; *you* are the noncustodial parent, the parent granted "reasonable visitation." How would you prefer the schedule to go?

VISITING PARENT'S CUSTODY SCHEDULE

1. Time my children would spend with me, the *noncustodial* parent:

    During school year: _____

    _____

    During summer vacations: _____

    _____

    During Christmas/Hanukkah: _____

    _____

    Other vacations (semester break, Easter, Memorial Weekend, etc.): _____

    _____

    Mother's Day: _____
    Father's Day: _____
    Maternal grandparents' birthdays: _____
    Paternal grandparents' birthdays: _____
    Child's birthday: _____
    Noncustodial parent's birthday: _____
    Other holidays (Thanksgiving Day, Halloween, religious holidays, etc.): _____

    _____

    _____

2. Extracurricular activities noncustodial parent would supervise or participate in (scouting, sports, religious observance, school ceremonies, music or dance recitals, and so on): _____

_____

_____

3. Medical decisions noncustodial parent would participate in:

_____

_____

4. Academic decisions noncustodial parent would participate in (choice of schools, colleges, and so on): _____

_____

_____

5. Decisions regarding choice of summer camps, music, dance, or sports lessons noncustodial parent would participate in: _____

_____

_____

6. Areas dealing with problems at school, report cards, parent-teacher conferences, discipline at home, that noncustodial parent would participate in: _____

_____

_____

7. Amount of financial support of child noncustodial parent is willing to assume: _____

_____

After thinking of what it would be like to be the parent relegated to a "supporting role," it is next useful to give yourself permission to consider what you, and *you alone,* would like in a custody arrangement. This does not mean what you think "ought" to be in such an agreement, or what "should" happen according to the perceptions of your family and friends, your former spouse, or your children. It means plumbing the depths of your true feelings, putting down the Deep Wish. In filling out the Custody Arrangement Fantasy Sheet, be as "selfish" as you wish. This may be a document you'd rather not have anyone else on earth see, but that's all right, it's your fantasy.

CUSTODY ARRANGEMENT FANTASY SHEET

1. Custody arrangement:

   Sole to me: _____

   Sole to former spouse: _____

   Joint legal with primary residence to me: _____

   Joint legal with primary residence to former spouse: _____

   Joint legal and physical custody with former spouse: _____

   Other (including split custody, if there is more than one child):

   _____

2. Time-sharing arrangements regarding children:

   Time during school year with me: _____

   _____

   Time during school year with former spouse: _____

   _____

   Time during Christmas/Hanukkah with me: _____

   _____

   Time during Christmas/Hanukkah with former spouse: _____

   _____

   Time during other vacations (semester break; Easter; Memorial Weekend, etc.) with me: _____

   _____

   Time during other vacations with former spouse: _____

   _____

   Mother's Day spent with: _____

   Father's Day spent with: _____

   Maternal grandparents' birthdays spent with: _____

   Paternal grandparents' birthdays spent with: _____

   My birthday spent with: _____

   Former spouse's birthday spent with: _____

   Other holidays (Thanksgiving Day; Halloween; religious holidays, etc.) spent with: _____

   _____

3. Extracurricular activities of children I want to supervise (including chauffeuring to and from), such as scouting, sports, lessons, recitals, day camp in summer, etc.: _____

   _____

   _____

Extracurricular activities of children I'm willing to delegate or share with former spouse: _____

_____

_____

4. School arrangements:

School I would like children to attend: _____

_____

Parent-teacher's conferences to be attended by me: _____ ; by former spouse: _____

Report cards and school communications to go to me: _____ ; to former spouse: _____ ; or to both: _____

Tutoring, if necessary, to be arranged by me: _____ ; by former spouse: _____ ; or jointly: _____

Tutoring, if necessary, to be paid for by me: _____ ; by former spouse: _____ ; or expenses to be shared by both on a ratio of: _____

School tuition, if any, to be paid by me: _____ ; by former spouse: _____ ; or shared by both on a ratio of: _____

School performances, sports contests, or recitals to be attended by me: _____ ; by former spouse: _____ ; or by both: _____

5. Medical care:

Doctor for children I would trust is: _____

Decision on children's doctor to be made by me: _____ ; by former spouse: _____ ; or by both: _____

Dentist for children I would trust: _____

Decision on choice of dentist to be made by me: _____ ; by former spouse: _____ ; or by both: _____

Children to be covered on my medical plan: _____ ; on former spouse's medical plan: _____ ; on our shared medical coverage: _____

Additional medical expenses not covered by insurance to be paid by me: _____ ; by former spouse: _____ ; or shared by both on a ratio of: _____

Extraordinary medical expenses (braces, plastic surgery, etc.) to be paid by me: _____ ; by former spouse: _____ ; or shared by both on a ratio of: _____

Decisions regarding what type of medical care is to be given to the children to be decided by me: _____ ; by former spouse: _____ ; or by both: _____

Physical care of children when ill to be provided by me: _____ ; by former spouse: _____ ; shared on basis of: _____

Medical records regarding children to go to me: _____ ; to former spouse: _____ ; or shared by both: _____

6. Religious education:

   Church or temple children attend to be selected by me: _____ ; by former spouse: _____ ; or by mutual agreement: _____

   Decision *not* to provide religious education for children to be made by me: _____ ; by former spouse: _____ ; or by mutual agreement: _____

7. Schedule of day-to-day arrangements I would prefer:
   (for example: children with me 100 percent; or weekdays with me/Saturday with former spouse; or weekdays with me/weekends with former spouse; or school year with me/summer with former spouse; or children stay in family home/parents move in and out weekly, monthly, yearly; or other formula):

   _____
   _____
   _____
   _____

8. Communication with former spouse regarding children:

   Never: _____
   Through lawyers: _____
   By letter: _____
   By telephone: _____
   In person: _____
   Combination of types of communication, which are: _____
   _____
   Scheduled meetings with third-party mediator: _____
   _____

9. Current family residence:

Family home or apartment and furnishings to be owned/kept by me: _____; by former spouse: _____; or shared equity on a ratio of: _____ until time of sale

Family home or apartment and furnishings used by me: _____; by former spouse: _____; or alternating on a schedule of: _____ until time of sale

Mortgage and/or maintenance to be paid by me: _____; by former spouse: _____; or expenses paid jointly on a ratio of: _____

If you have followed the *spirit* of this exercise, you have filled out the questionnaire with no thought of being fair or self-sacrificing. Obviously, you probably won't get everything you want when it comes time to draw up the actual agreement, but it's important to find out what your true feelings are. Now, having found out, go back to the Fantasy Sheet, but this time imagine you are *your child.* Think deeply about your child. (If you have more than one, you'll have to repeat this exercise for each.) Think about your child's personality, character, temperament, hobbies, likes, loves, fears, and hates. Think about your child's relationship with you, and with the other parent. *Imagine you are your child!* Be your child for the next fifteen minutes and design a custody arrangement you would like best *if you were your child.* Using the Fantasy Sheet as a model, write your answers on a separate sheet of paper, putting at the top of the page: Child's Ideal Custody Arrangement. Complete each section as you think *your child*—not you—would like things to be arranged.

The next and last exercise in this series will probably be the most difficult for you. Again using the Fantasy Sheet as a guide, compose your answers *as if you were your former spouse.* Think as quietly and as unemotionally as possible about that person. Jot down an objective description of your former spouse's personality, character, passions, strengths, flaws, work routine, hobbies, loves, hates, and fears. How involved a parent has he or she been in the past? How would you objectively describe the relationship that this person presently has with your children? *Imagine you are your former spouse* and write down your answers on a piece of paper labeled Former Spouse's Ideal Custody Arrangement. Remember, respond as you think your former mate—not you—would like things to be arranged.

In Dr. Webster's work with divorcing parents, she moves eventually from fantasy and ideal custody arrangements to reality by asking the parents to take a good long look at how their children were cared for during the marriage and in the period following the separation. Sometimes, in the weeks and months following the split, one parent will suddenly be playing a drastically reduced—or enhanced—role. Says Dr. Webster, "I ask both parents to list specifically what a typical week would be like when (or, in the case of some of the absent parents, *if*) the child was with them." She urges each parent to describe realistically what he or she would actually be doing hour by hour, day by day, in the presence of the children or in proximity to them. This includes keeping track of everything from the seven and a half minutes it takes to braid a daughter's pigtails, to the half hour required to chauffeur a son to and from band practice, to the two hours spent watching the *Late, Late Show* on TV when the kids are asleep. Dr. Webster also asks the parents to identify where they are and what they are doing when they are not at home with their children. The purpose is not to generate guilt but, according to Dr. Webster, to find out exactly how much contact and closeness and time sharing of parenting responsibilities is actually taking place. "The parent who hasn't had the experience of having the day-to-day care of the children has more difficulty conducting this time survey," says Dr. Webster, "and many realize, 'Hey, I haven't actually spent much time with my kids.' This doesn't mean they shouldn't in the future; but doing this exercise really makes parents *think* about what skills they don't have yet and what the children need and can get from each parent."

As with the other exercises in this chapter, filling out a Parent's Time Survey is most useful if *both* spouses can complete the information from their individual perspectives. But even if only one parent is willing to participate at this stage, charting a typical week's parenting functions will help you clarify what chores you do well, what aspects of parenting you enjoy most (and least), and how much time you have put, or have been willing to put, into the effort of single parenting. As a guide, I have filled out the accompanying survey for a typical Monday when my son is with me.

PARENT'S TIME SURVEY

Time		Activity	Comments
Day 1 (Monday) MORNING			
	7:00	get up; prepare morning broadcasts at home	feel very rushed
	7:20	Make son's school lunch	split-second timing required
	7:26	edit first script	
	7:40	broadcast "live" first one-minute radio commentary from home studio	
	7:43	write second broadcast	
	8:00	wake son; discuss clothes	feel like lousy housekeeper when no two matching socks are found

Time		Activity	Comments
	8:10	pour out cereal; eat breakfast w/son, quiz him on spelling	little time for conversation
	8:30	car pool arrives to take son to school	
	8:40	broadcast second one-minute commentary "live" from home studio	
	8:43	look over newspaper headlines; feed dog	
	9:00	one-mile walk w/dog	feels good
	9:30	shower and dress for day	
	10:00–noon	write	feel pressure that day isn't long enough for work
AFTERNOON			
	Noon–1:00	lunch	
	1:30–3:00	write	
	3:00–3:20	drive to son's school	always five minutes late
	3:20	deliver car-pool kids	feel like a "good mom"—doing my mom role despite career
	4:00	home again; talk to son re day's events	feels like an obligation some days when work presses; today, nice to talk about book-report assignment

4:15	son starts homework; I return calls	feel fragmented; a professional on phone; helping son with homework in between calls
5:00	start dinner; chat w/son while he feeds dog	fun to work together

EVENING

6:00	watch TV news	
7:00	dinner; talk w/son	third-grade jokes are trying, but nice to be together
8:00	clean up from dinner w/son helping	totally in "mother" mode
8:30	bath for son; I pick up around house; run a laundry	
8:45	read a story together	this is "quality" time
9:00	son goes to bed; I supervise brushing teeth, picking up clothes in his room, etc.	conscious of a mental "countdown"— knowing I'll soon have some time for myself
9:07	watch TV movie, sew cub scout patch	ah, now time for me; put my mind in neutral
10:30	get ready for bed	
10:45	read in bed	irritated that I can't keep my eyes open
11:00	fall asleep	set alarm for 7:00 a.m., and here we go again!

Obviously, each person's survey will be different, and will be quite long when seven days' worth of activities are minutely recorded. For some parents, there is no such thing as a "typical" week. However, merely charting a random week may be very revealing for some people. Dr. Webster says that often, after a mother and father have examined the time they actually spend with their youngsters, and identified the weaknesses and strengths in their roles not only as caretakers but as nurturers of their children, one parent will say to the other something like "I guess I'm pretty weak in this area." The other will reply, "Oh, I'd be willing to teach you that" or "I have a really good cookbook that you could borrow" or "I'm good at helping with algebra homework."

The value of conducting these surveys in the early stages of working out a shared custody agreement is that mothers and fathers can begin to see themselves as separate entities, and "mapping out what actually goes on in their everyday lives with their youngsters often will trigger ideas for collaborating with each other for the benefit of their kids," Dr. Webster points out. In fact, the sheer logistics of life can bring many hostile parents to the realization that the daily routine of such mundane matters as car pools and cub scouts, soccer practice and dentist appointments, school lunches and difficult homework assignments, can be handled far more smoothly for everyone when two parents cooperate with each other.

Now it is time to review all the exercises you have completed in this chapter:

1. "Visiting" Parent's Custody Schedule
2. Custody Arrangement Fantasy Sheet
3. Child's Ideal Custody Arrangement
4. Former Spouse's Ideal Custody Arrangement
5. Parent's Time Survey

With the information they contain before you, you will have a better idea of what kind of *practical* parenting plan can be developed for your particular situation. As you propose and counterpropose various time-sharing formulas based on what you want and what you believe to be your children's needs— while taking into consideration what you know to be the needs and desires of the other parent—your "pilot" plan should begin to take shape. The plan should address all the categories on the Fantasy Sheet. Include all those categories as you now structure your proposed shared custody parenting plan and write it out in specific detail. Label it Proposed Parenting Plan. If possible, ask your former spouse to do the same.

There are many forms this proposed plan could take. Chapter 8 will outline some samples of the creative shared custody arrangements other parents have developed—some under the most difficult of circumstances. Dr. Webster is quick to point out that "if the paper says 'shared custody' and the parents keep fighting, the paper means nothing. On the other hand, if the paper a judge signs says 'sole custody' but the parents are sharing responsibilities for the kids in a meaningful way, then *that* paper has no meaning either." The obvious point, declares the psychologist, is that "what is on that piece of paper is far less important than the attitudes of the people involved." However, it is useful to put proposals in writing in order to deal concretely with the practical issues of the day-in, day-out care of your children.

It is necessary—especially in the beginning, when a parent is not confident the other side will follow through—that it be clear who has agreed to do what, and when. As one joint custody parent with many years of experience of cooperating put it, "The less trust between the parents, the more structure needs to be written into the agreement, at least in the beginning. The more trust that is built up over time, the more flexibility will develop as far as pickups and drop-offs and special occasions are concerned."

In the case of the Nicholsons, Betsy and Roy were able to agree at the time of their initial separation that they would both play an active parenting role and that each would spend time with the children every week. However, they were not able to agree about the financial share each would hold in their three-bedroom Honolulu town house. Roy felt that since *he* had been the parent willing to stay in the marriage, and, once Betsy moved out, he became the parent with more full-time responsibility for all four children, he should have at least a 50 percent share of the value of the house. But when Betsy moved back into the family home and was trying to make plans to go back to college to get an advanced degree, she wanted a 60 percent share because, she said, she had put in many years as a full-time homemaker and mother without pay.

Finally, Roy met with Betsy, hauled out their tax returns and other financial records, and drew a picture of their resources. "I sat down and figured out everything on paper: our assets, our possessions, my income, Betsy's new income, the expenses of running two households, and so on. Then I proposed what I felt *I* could contribute. I said I'd pay the mortgage and maintenance on the town home—regardless of who was living there—as long as Betsy's income was still so small, and that we'd split the equity fifty-fifty when we eventually sold the place when the kids were grown."

Betsy's lawyer, who agreed with her that there was no need to litigate the matter, helped her come up with a counterproposal that represented her needs as she saw them: a deal in which 10 percent of the present value of the house would be paid to Betsy in 1981 for her "rehabilitative" schooling. Betsy's advanced degree would, in the end, help Roy by improving her earning potential, thus making her better able to contribute to the mortgage and other expenses relating to the children at some time in the future. Betsy said that the proceeds could be split fifty-fifty at the time the house was sold. She said that real-estate values in Hawaii most probably would continue to go up, eventually compensating Roy for the 10 percent he'd pay to her in 1981 dollars. Roy discussed the counterproposal with his attorney and decided it was an agreement he could live with. Both Roy and Betsy were pleased with their negotiating efforts and signed the necessary documents.

If financial battles are preventing you and your former spouse from settling on a plan for custody of the children, reverse your order of priorities. First, by completing the exercises outlined earlier in this chapter, begin to work on a reasonable day-to-day plan for caring for the children. Then complete the following household budget forms so that the *entire picture* of your family's resources—both parental and economic—is spread out before you both. Then, and only then, can you begin to see the range of your options. Financial solutions often suggest themselves as parenting responsibilities are hammered out. Remember, there is no "best" solution; there are *many* possible solutions, and it is up to you and your former spouse to start thinking creatively about which custody and financial package (of several you could design) would best fit your family.

The Nicholsons' final divorce papers, which included both a statement detailing their legal and physical joint custody arrangements and an itemized financial settlement, were filed at the Honolulu courthouse in January 1981. The arrangements were acceptable to all parties, including their four children. Both parents described the final agreement as satisfying their needs as individual joint custody parents. As for the children, Betsy told me, "I asked them recently what they thought about the joint custody arrangements and they all said that they don't like divorce, but that sharing is the best thing."

Both Roy and Betsy commented on how pleased they were they could now talk to each other about problems concerning their children. "When it comes to the kids," Betsy said, "we've gotten past a lot of hostility and we're comfortable discussing those things with each other." And a critical step in getting them to that point was their financial agreement, arrived at by compiling the information you can assemble in the accompanying budget worksheets.

The worksheets will be lengthy and tiresome to complete, but you *must know the facts* before you can enter any negotiation as to how to restructure your household from one residence to two. Your joint tax return will have much of the information you will need to fill in these worksheets. Don't hesitate to ask a friend or someone who is knowledgeable enough to help you with the sections with which you may not be familiar—whether you want to learn how to calculate the surrender value of a life insurance policy or how to determine what it costs to feed a family of four for a week. It is important that both mothers and fathers have a clear picture of what it will require to set up separate households.

THE WAY WE WERE*

Assets

FINANCIAL

What We Own Together:

cash in checking accounts	$
cash in savings accounts	$
government bonds: current value	$
cash-surrender value of insurance policy	$
equity in pension plan(s)	$
current value of annuities	$
equity in real estate	$
market value of securities	$
bonds	$
mutual funds	$
investment trusts	$

What We Own Separately:

There may be assets of the type listed above which were acquired *before* the marriage or

---

*Forms adapted from "Divorce Mediation: A Less Painful Path," by Dr. John M. Haynes. Used by permission.

acquired after the marriage as a gift or inheritance to an individual spouse, or assets
that have been jointly agreed upon by both
spouses as being separate. You may need to
consult a professional accountant or other
expert knowledgeable in defining joint and
separate assets. List *possible* separate assets
here. $

TOTAL joint financial assets $

MATERIAL

What We Own Together:

autos (current blue book value)		$
home appliances:		
	washer	$
	dryer	$
	refrigerator	$
	other	$
furnishings:		
	bedroom (1, 2, etc.)	$
	living room	$
	dining room	$
	kitchen equipment	$
	den	$
	outdoor equipment	$
	other	$
TVs		$
radios		$
paintings, other art		$
fine silver, china		$
books		$
records		$
houseplants		$
hobby equipment (including collections)		$
sports equipment (including boats, planes, etc.)		$
pets		$
mementos		$
other		$

What We Own Separately:

You may not agree on items you list as separately owned, but for now, make your claims. $

TOTAL joint material assets $

TOTAL joint financial and material assets $

Liabilities

FINANCIAL

What We Owe Together:

current total bills outstanding	$
amount owed on installment purchases	$
amount owed on personal loans	$
amount due on taxes:	
federal/state income tax	$
property tax	$
other liabilities	$

What We Owe Separately:

Again, these definitions of separate and joint assets and liabilities will probably need an expert's opinion. Often, living in a community-property state will have impact on this question. Seek professional advice if you or your spouse has major debts outstanding. List *possible* separate debts here. $

TOTAL joint financial liabilities $

OUR NET WORTH $

Household Budget

Our Fixed Household Expenses:

rent or mortgage payments per year $
telephone $
gas/electricity $
water $
fuel for house $
garbage pickup $
cable TV $
other $

Our Joint Taxes:

federal income tax $
state income tax $
property tax $

Our Insurance Costs:

life premiums per year $
auto $
health and accident $
hospitalization $
fire and theft $
personal property $
social security $
other $

Our Transportation Costs:

fuel for cars (gas/oil) $
yearly registration $
parking fees $
commuting fare(s) $
auto repair, upkeep $
other $

Our Installment Payments:

auto $
furniture/appliances $

charge accounts $
bank-credit-card balances $
personal loans $
Christmas/Hanukkah Club $
other $

Our Education Costs:

tuition (for children and/or adults) $
room and board $
books $
allowances $
music, dancing, sports lessons $
other $

Our Membership Costs:

union dues $
professional associations $
clubs $
religious groups $

Our Miscellaneous Expenses:

care of aging parents $
forthcoming major house repairs $
forthcoming major auto repairs $
emergency fund $
other $

Our Food Costs:

meals at home $
meals out $
school lunches $

Our Child-Care Expenses:

baby-sitter/housekeeper $
day care outside home $

Our Home-Maintenance Costs:

cleaning services $
yard work $
repair or replacements done this year $

Our Health Costs:
(not covered by insurance)

medical	$
dental	$
drugs/medication	$
counseling	$
other	$

Our Personal Costs:

clothes, children	$
clothes, mother	$
clothes, father	$
grooming aids	$
barber/beauty costs	$
newspapers, magazines	$
stationery, postage	$
alcohol	$
tobacco	$
other	$

Our Entertainment:

theater/movies	$
sports events	$
hobbies	$
vacations	$
home entertainment	$

Our Gifts:

birthdays	$
Christmas/Hanukkah	$
other	$

Our Contributions:

religious	$
charity	$
schools and colleges	$
other	$

TOTAL cost to run our former household $ per year

THE WAY WE ARE
Proposed Single-Household Worksheets

Return to the previous worksheet, The Way We Were. Beginning with the category "Our Fixed Household Expenses," and ending with the category "Our Contributions," estimate on each line what you think it will (or does) cost to run a *separate* household under the following conditions:

1. The cost of running a household *if you had the children full-time.*
2. The cost of running a household *if you had the children on a shared basis*—either throughout the year or for portions of the year.
3. The cost of running a household *if you rarely had the children with you* in your place of residence.

When you have completed this final exercise and added it to the others in this chapter, you will have accumulated a sheaf of papers that can be used as the basis for negotiating a shared custody parenting plan. As with the Nicholson family, once you have outlined a time-sharing formula for coparenting the children, the allocation of *material* resources to put that plan into action will most likely begin to fall into place. With your "before" and "after" budget worksheets as a reference, jot down your proposals for a financial settlement that supports the key elements in your Proposed Coparenting Plan. Ask your former spouse to do the same kind of preplanning. Then take some time to digest all the facts and fantasies.

Meanwhile, let's consider some answers to the key question regarding *children* living in a shared custody arrangement: What hurts and what works?

Chapter 8
Shared Custody Kids
What Hurts and What Works

Sad stories from the front lines. Child-focused custody planning. Scrutinizing the myths about shared custody. Avoiding the "Ain't it awful . . ." syndrome and other mistakes. Seeking the "magic formula" for your shared custody plan: the Perfect Blend. Age-Appropriate Planning for Shared Custody (questionnaire). What we know and don't know about specific shared custody plans that are best for specific ages. Age-Appropriate Plans and Possibilities: infants to two-year-olds; ages three to five; ages six to twelve; adolescents, thirteen to eighteen. Adjusting the time-sharing formula as years go by. Monitor Your Child (quiz): tip-offs, red lights, and danger signs. Suggested Guidelines for Developing Your Own "Magic Formula." The Master Calendar.

"Are you going to tell about the shared custody situations that *don't* work very well?" challenged a friend of mine. She and her husband technically shared legal and physical custody of his ten-year-old son, but the boy's natural mother rarely exercised her right to see the child; when she did, the youngster apparently plopped his sleeping bag down in a different house or apartment every time he visited. The mother had moved sixty miles away from the father soon after the divorce and, wholeheartedly embracing the "Me Decade," had designed for herself what Californians are fond of calling "a very free lifestyle." As a result, my friend and her husband had had the major responsibility for rearing the youngster for the past seven years and also had to deal with the child's questions and occasional sadness about his mother's casual interest in him.

"Believe me," said my friend, "his mother is a joint custody parent in name only!" However, as we talked, my friend was willing to acknowledge that "at least the child has *some* contact with his mother." And the mother, my friend admitted, clearly loved her son, though she seemed unconcerned about the roller-coaster quality of their relationship. Moreover, my friend and the boy's father had provided a warm, stable home for the child. "So I guess he's better off than a lot of children of divorce," my friend conceded. But still, she said, if parents were more aware of "what hurts and what works" in a shared custody arrangement, they would be pushed, if only out of guilt, to build in elements that would give a shared parenting plan the *best* chance of success.

I wholeheartedly agreed with her, recalling the single most devastating comment I had heard during the two years I spent researching this book. It came from a fourteen-year-old boy whose parents had been at war over him since he was seven. The mother demanded sole custody; the father had campaigned vigorously through the courts and every arena he could think of, including the media, for joint custody. When the couple were preparing for yet another round in court, the boy looked both parents squarely in the eye and said, "I don't care *how* this thing turns out. I wish you'd put me in a foster home!"

When I repeated this story to my friend, I added to it the tale of a couple with whom I had appeared on national television. After two and a half years of bitter wrangling, the parents had agreed to try joint custody. During the telecast, the father began putting his arm around the mother and kept inching closer to her as the interview wore on. The mother looked increasingly uncomfortable as she valiantly tried to explain why she was willing to try sharing custody for the sake of her two-year-old son, although she announced pointedly that she was adamant about not wanting the marriage to continue.

The father kept caressing her shoulder and saying how ecstatic he was that they were going to be a joint custody family. Within two months of the telecast the couple were back in court, asking a judge to settle the issue. The mother was now disturbed about the shared custody arrangement, saying her husband wanted it only as a means of staying connected to her. The sharing arrangements had become impossible to carry out, she said, because her former husband used each conversation as a means of begging and bullying her to come back to him.

Clearly, shared custody is not an instant panacea for divorcing families. In the beginning, as with any new enterprise, snags are bound to develop and things rarely go as planned. However, we do know, both from research that has been done on shared custody families and from parents who have *lived* with shared custody, that there are some basic guidelines that can help parents enormously as they attempt to launch cooperative custody plans.

Susan Steinman, in her study of twenty-four joint custody families in the San Francisco Bay Area in the late 1970s, determined that the scheduling of time spent with each parent and the specific living arrangements should focus *primarily* on the needs and capacities of the individual child and *not* on what may be convenient or expedient for the parents. "While joint custody allows a more creative and individually tailored approach to custody arrangements after divorce," she says, "the idea that *any* time-sharing or geographical arrangement made for the child—as long as parents cooperate and the child sees both parents—is okay is *not* supported by the research." What her studies show is that parents may indeed be able to work out a coparenting plan, and may absolutely love the convenience of it and its "off-duty" aspects, while the children fail to flourish under it and, in fact, experience developmental difficulties. Whatever the plan, it must make reasonable sense for the child at his or her particular age and stage.

A good example of an arrangement that may not meet that criterion was the coparenting plan I was told about that accommodated two parents who lived one hundred eighty miles apart. The couple had an arrangement under which their upper-grade-school child spent two weeks with one parent and attended one school, and then two weeks with the other parent and attended a different school. The parents claimed the child had adjusted academically: "It's a statewide curriculum." But as another joint custody kid remarked when asked what he thought of such a plan, "Who takes over your team if you're captain?"

Dr. Steinman did discover, however, in the course of her pioneering study, that some of the myths surrounding shared custody don't hold up to scrutiny. There is no doubt that long geographic distances can create a major obstacle to reaching a shared custody agreement. But short geographic distances are no guarantee of success, either. It helps, Dr. Steinman found, for a child to have a sense of the schedule shared custody is going to follow. The parents of one child in her study lived only a few miles apart, but because the routine wasn't clearly explained and reinforced by each parent, the child worried about his personal safety and was afraid of getting lost and going to the wrong house on the wrong day. Once a schedule has been worked out, it helps to have a Master Calendar in each home and to review it each week with the child if he or she seems uncertain about anything.

Another common fear is that joint custody children will become pawns between parents whose views of life differed seriously enough to cause a divorce. Dr. Steinman found that most of the children she studied were able to accept the differences in the personalities, behavior, and values of their parents and that most of the children were able to adapt to each household with a minimum of conflict and confusion. Where some joint custody children experienced difficulty was when the parents themselves were intolerant of each other's differences and let the children know it.

A parent does not have to endorse behavior in the other house, but each parent, say people who have practiced shared custody for a few years, can learn to adopt a "When in Rome. . ." attitude. A typical answer to a child who says, "But Dad lets me watch TV on school nights," is to reply, "What Dad says goes in his house; however, in *this* house, I've decided no TV on school nights." Period. End of sentence. Will this confuse children? It will not, say psychologists I've talked to, if the children are not made to feel guilty about what goes on at the *other* house. Parents sharing custody have to accept the fact they cannot control the life-style at the other house. What the children often learn from living in two households with different life-styles is tolerance for others and the knowledge that there is, indeed, "more than one way to skin a cat." One distinguished family counselor told me that if a child is not admonished for the way she or he lives at the other house, "a child with a health-nut mother and a junk-food father will probably grow up demanding a balanced diet and an occasional chocolate sundae." As long as they're not told "how bad" the "other" parent is, kids tend to integrate divergent viewpoints, she said, and end up somewhere in the middle.

Another basic guideline is to avoid giving joint custody children even small doses of "Ain't it awful . . .": "Ain't it awful that your mother lives with that man in our big beautiful house and I live in this crummy apartment." "Ain't it awful that your father makes more money than I do and gives us a pittance to live on." "Ain't it awful that your daddy runs around with girls who are practically young enough to be your sister . . . I'm willing to share you with him, but not with *her!*" If something truly *is* awful, it should be taken up with the other parent directly, and *not* in front of the children.

Overall, the youngsters in Dr. Steinman's study were not

torn by the crippling loyalty conflicts often seen in the children of sole custody situations. However, there were loyalty conflicts among some joint custody children when they found themselves in an arrangement designed primarily to be fair to the parents. In those cases, it had become the child's responsibility to divide time and affections in a scrupulously fair manner, which can be a very heavy burden. Dr. Steinman found about one third of the joint custody children in her study exhibiting what she called "hyperloyalty." These youngsters were extremely concerned about being fair to both parents and said they felt compelled to maintain strict equality in feelings for each parent. One little girl remarked, "There should be eight days in a week."

The joint custody children experiencing this hyperloyalty sometimes had tremendous difficulty making decisions in their own behalf because they felt their parents' feelings and desires always came first. Children must be shown that they are not expected to be referees or time-study experts during the process of working out a shared custody plan.

In the course of trying to find out what will work in your particular family, child experts agree, you should *never* ask the question "Who do you want to live with?"—or the subtler version, "Who do you want to spend the most time with?" Florence Bienenfeld, a marriage, family, and child counselor in the Los Angeles Family Court, says that asking a child for input like that means there is no way a child can win. "If a child says, 'With Mom,' he feels guilty hurting Dad, and vice versa."

However, there is a difference between asking a child what custody arrangements would feel the best and making the child *responsible* for choosing those arrangements. Dr. Mel Roman, a professor in the department of psychiatry at the Albert Einstein College of Medicine and director of family studies at Bronx Municipal Hospital Center, has some suggestions. "Of course you want the children to participate in working out a final custody solution in some meaningful way, so you have to find out how the children feel about things, but do it carefully." Dr. Roman suggests that the parents explore various time-sharing possibilities by asking something like "How would you feel [not *"like* it"] if you went to the same school, but spent a week with your mom and a week with your dad . . . or would four days/three days make sense for you because of your music lessons?" Dr. Roman believes parents need to get their children to voice their objections to a *particular* plan, "but I always tell the parents they need to tell the children that the kids aren't making the final decision—the parents are."

What probably impressed me the most as I toured around the country talking to parents sharing custody is the *variety* of time-sharing formulas that people have managed to invent. Some plans sounded absolutely hideous to me, but they seemed to work well for the families who thought of them. However, there are some general recommendations that can be offered for children at various stages of development, and the key seems to be: *Age-Appropriate Planning.*

Obviously, a plan for shared custody that is suitable for a three-year-old may not work very well for a youngster of thirteen. But Age-Appropriate Planning means age *and* stage, since children of the same chronological age can vary widely in adaptability, physical development, and other characteristics.

The plan must be appropriate for the parents as well. A shared custody arrangement involving a mother who stays at home with her five-year-old may not accommodate the working mother of a child of the same age.

To come up with the "magic formula" for your particular family, you must consider the five main factors in the accompanying questionnaire: your children's chronological ages; their stages of emotional development; your own and your former spouse's financial, emotional, and vocational needs; the geographical considerations in your situation; and the degree of cooperation that exists between you and your former spouse.

AGE-APPROPRIATE PLANNING
FOR SHARED CUSTODY

1. What are the *chronological ages* of your children? ——————
   ————————————————————————————
   ————————————————————————————
   ————————————————————————————

2. How would you characterize the *emotional development* of
   your children? (Note any problem areas.)——————————
   ————————————————————————————
   ————————————————————————————
   ————————————————————————————
   ————————————————————————————

3. Briefly, with regard to a proposed shared custody plan, what
   are your *financial, emotional, and vocational needs*—and those
   of your former spouse?
   My needs are: ——————————————————————
   ————————————————————————————
   ————————————————————————————
   ————————————————————————————

   My former spouse's needs are: ——————————————
   ————————————————————————————
   ————————————————————————————

4. What are the basic *geographical considerations* in your situation? ————————————————————————————
   ————————————————————————————

5. How would you characterize the *degree of cooperation* that
   now exists between you and your former spouse in terms of
   dealing with the children? ——————————————————
   ————————————————————————————
   ————————————————————————————

Once you have begun to think about these five main factors,
certain time-sharing formulas will be discarded immediately,

making the final choice much easier. The proper blending of these factors will, in and of themselves, help you plan your shared custody arrangements appropriately and will help you avoid the so-called Ping-Pong Syndrome that fledgling co-custody parents hear so much about. That is the condition, somewhat exaggerated by the critics of shared custody, in which children, saddled with schedules that don't take their needs into consideration, feel literally like a Ping-Pong ball bouncing back and forth between houses.

Dr. Roman, who is the author of the controversial book *The Disposable Parent: The Case for Joint Custody,* told me that he's begun to get exasperated at questions about the Ping-Pong Syndrome. "I haven't seen all the joint custody families there are, but when you hear of reports which blame joint custody for behavior problems, you often see a researcher, or critic, with no appreciation for, or knowledge of, how family systems work. The problems they ascribe to joint custody disregard the fact that a child lives in a *family system.* If a kid is going back and forth on a perfectly sensible joint custody schedule but is being hassled by a grandmother, say, who doesn't like the kid's father—*that* could be the source of the problem, not the moving back and forth."

As you search for your own formula, remember that the accompanying shared custody scenarios are offered only as *plans and possibilities.* There are age-appropriate suggestions culled from interviews with parents all over the country and with the professionals most knowledgeable on the subject of parents sharing custody. As every one of these experts will tell you, there are always families and children (and perhaps yours is one of them) that don't fit into any "typical" category. As you look over these programs, try to keep in mind your answers to the five questions about Age-Appropriate Planning. And remember, these programs are geared to parents living in the same general geographic area. Chapter 9 will take up the issue of long-distance shared custody.

AGE APPROPRIATE PLANS AND POSSIBILITIES

Infants to Two-Year-Olds:

Possibility I

One parent establishes "home base"

Other parent visits on Monday, Wednesday; takes over all day Saturday

Possibility II

One parent establishes "home base"

Other parent visits two days a week; in addition, spends one night and a full day with child

Even the experts researching the impact of shared custody arrangements on children cannot say with certainty what routines of coparenting are "best" for the really little ones. As Dr. Roman notes, "We just don't have enough information. However, the general guidelines are to have as much stability *and* contact with the other parent *and* conflict-free interaction between the parents as possible." A child under two is not too young to be affected when one parent suddenly disappears, and this is especially true with families in which both parents took part in the day-to-day care of a very young child before the divorce.

The parents of an eighteen-month-old boy, who had both participated in his care during marriage, developed a plan whereby he always slept at the mother's house—she was not working outside the home—and the father came over every other day to give the child his bath and dinner. On Saturday the child spent all day and early evening with his father. Then, when the child reached two and a half, he started spending

Friday or Saturday night at his father's, finally working up to three nights a week by the time he was five years old.

Another joint custody family with a boy who was less than a year old began immediately with a plan whereby the father took the child overnight every Saturday and dropped by the family home several times during the week—on a specific schedule, so the mother could plan her free time. This father had witnessed the birth of his baby and had been as involved as the mother in diapering and feeding. The child thrived on the contact with his father, and by the time he was in the third grade, he lived with his father full-time during the school year, since his mother chose to travel for six months a year. When the child was seven, the parents worked out an official joint custody arrangement with primary residence to the father during the school year and with the mother during summertime and several holidays, with visits back and forth.

For very small children there is no way around it: geography is the number one consideration. It is generally agreed that until they are about three, children need stability in their environment as *the* major element in a custody plan. If a child has developed a deep attachment to both parents, then that child probably falls in the minority category of youngsters who would adjust well to being "home-based" with either parent and sleeping over once or twice a week at the other's place. The litmus test for a child under three is: Has the child been cared for by both parents and can the youngster handle shifting environments without major upset? Also, can the parents manage a spirit of cooperation in caring for the child together—separately—after they divorce?

It is important for parents of very young children to educate themselves as to early childhood development patterns, and to learn to monitor the reactions of their children to whatever sharing routine is eventually adopted. In one case in upstate New York, a couple divorced when their child was eight months old. The parents alternated days of care, and the child began to develop sleeping and eating problems. The cause was not the so-called Ping-Pong Syndrome, as was suspected, but rather that the father, who lived in a commune, allowed the child to be taken care of by several people. The lack of consistency and the number of strangers in the baby's life were intolerable—not sharing custody per se. However, until more research on two-home custody and the very young child is available, parents of children under two to three years old would be wise, say many child-development experts, to build in as much consistency as possible when planning a cocustody routine.

Ages Three to Five:

Possibility I

Two spaced overnights a week with one parent

Rest of week at other parent's and at pre-school

Possibility II

One week with one parent

One week with other parent

Phone calls back and forth

Possibility III

Three and a half days with each parent per week

By age three, most children are usually better able not only to tolerate change but to deal with a greater number of people in their lives. This is the time when children generally start nursery school, taking their first steps toward becoming part of a larger society than just Mommy and Daddy and Ralphie, the dog.

At nursery school and prekindergarten classes, children begin to be introduced to the outside world and may be ready to sleep over one or two nights a week without longing for the parent they are not with. Some children might even be able to manage three days without seeing the other parent; a smaller group could tolerate a week with one parent, a week with the other, with phone calls or "drop-bys" in between. The best test for an appropriate routine is to see if the child is cheerful and curious most of the time; if the child is eating well and suffering no major upsets; if the child is able to settle down at night with relative ease, doesn't cry for prolonged periods after leaving one parent or the other, and generally seems at ease.

A three-to-five-year-old may make the transition back and forth with even greater ease if a brother or sister is making the trip as well. In fact, urges Dr. Roman, "I think it's a good idea to keep all the kids in a family going back and forth together for a good while so they support each other." Later on, parents can arrange to spend separate time with the various children. But in the beginning, "siblings are a definite support system," says Dr. Roman, "and the kind of sexist thing some parents do, which is to give custody of the boy to the father and the girl to the mother, can be terrible for them down the road."

Child-development experts such as Dr. Roman believe that parents should be aware of certain other issues that preoccupy preschoolers. "Whether you buy into it or not," says Dr. Roman, "the three-to-five-year-old is moving into an Oedipal phase where it's important to be able to *share* parents. If there is competition with the parent of the same sex, there may be loyalty issues boiling up, or some anxiety about 'driving Daddy away' and winning Mommy as a prize, or vice versa." Sometimes, notes Dr. Roman, children—and especially the three-to-five-year-old set—have a tendency either to idealize or to depreciate a "lost" parent. "If the real parent is around, that problem is usually diminished." If the other parent *isn't* around during the Oedipal phase, there can be long-lasting effects, including the so-called Marilyn Monroe Syndrome of the little girl always searching for a daddy, or the little boy who has won an "Oedipal victory" over his father, securing Mom all to himself—a triumph that has been known to churn up a lot of anger and hostility out of the guilt a little boy may feel.

"We know," says psychologist Roman, "that *two* parents are terribly important to help the child get through all those subtle phases of development." Being exposed to two parents is also important, he stresses, so a child can see different value systems in operation. "It runs the gamut from the superficial to the most profound internalized issues of sexual identification," warns Dr. Roman, "and many times parents won't understand these issues until the child has grown up."

One plan that worked for a three-and-a-half-year-old was the program set up for a child I shall call Joanie Morton. The changes in her life after her parents separated seemed overwhelming: a new nursery school; a new apartment when Mommy moved, leaving Daddy in the old one; going home with her friend Suzy's mom two days a week because Mommy had a new job; and seeing Mommy or Daddy for only a short time before she had to go to bed at night. But the parents were determined to cooperate, with her best interests at heart.

Gene Morton had been willing and able to join in a fifty-fifty partnership for Joanie's after-school care. However, because of all the other changes in Joanie's life, after a trial period during which the child alternated days with each parent, Gene and his former wife decided that, for a while, anyway, Joanie needed a less complicated schedule. She would be based at her mother's and sleep at her dad's on Wednesday and Saturday nights. Joanie chatted with her father on the phone nearly every day, and he picked her up at Suzy's house on Mondays after school, took her for ice cream, and dropped her off at her mom's to sleep. After eighteen months of this routine, the parents shifted into a three-and-a-half-day-each routine, with Joanie's father picking her up after school on Wednesdays and delivering her to her mother's at midmorning on Sundays. Joanie continued to go home at three-thirty with her friend Suzy twice a week, and they played for a few hours until either parent picked her up. Joanie's parents consulted with each other on all major issues, including the decision to have Joanie's adenoids removed. Whenever one parent had an emergency at work, the other filled in to care for Joanie.

Another child in this age range, five-year-old Jessica, was three when her parents separated. Her father, Greg Spencer, had shared all aspects of raising her since he witnessed her birth. As a Lamaze-trained birth coach for his wife, Greg remembers "putting on my sterilized cap and gown while the other fathers were watching cartoons on TV in the fathers' waiting room. I was so elated being part of it, and I've always felt a very strong attachment to Jessica since the beginning."

That attachment strengthened as he shared in changing Jessica's diapers and in helping to care for her when she was sick. Both parents were actors and were home a lot together during the marriage. "The division of labor in the household was fifty-fifty," Greg says. When the couple broke up, Greg saw clearly that the legal establishment viewed with suspicion his desire to continue to be at least a half-time parent of Jessica. *Mothers,* he was told over and over, were the proper custodians of children of "tender years"—especially little girls. "I felt I was fighting *everybody* over this thing," Greg says with some bitterness. No one Greg talked to, except his own parents, felt that what he had to offer little Jessica was important to her upbringing. His only strong suit was that he had had de facto joint physical custody during the couple's year-and-a-half-long separation and that Jessica seemed to be all right during that period. Greg, his attorney, his former wife, her attorney, and a mediator finally agreed to meet, and the couple decided to try joint legal and physical custody for one year, with a review of the situation at the end of that time.

The parents alternate weeks of having Jessica in their home.

"I pick up Jessica on Monday at school and her mother takes her the following Monday after school," he says. That seemed the best arrangement because Greg and his ex-wife don't see eye to eye on several issues, including health foods versus bologna sandwiches. (Greg feels hamburger once in a while isn't so bad; his former wife opts for bran muffins and wheat germ.) Greg has learned to adopt the "When in Rome . . ." solution to many of these differences, and that seems to be working. He is determined to stay in the picture. "Jessica is a part of me," he says simply. "I provide her with a lot of stability. Her needs are so simple and pure: to be loved and taken care of."

Six-to-Twelve-Year-Olds:

Possibility I
Monday, Wednesday with one parent

Tuesday, Thursday with other parent

Parents alternate weekends

Possibility II
Monday, Tuesday with one parent

Wednesday, Thursday with other parent

Parents alternate weekends

Possibility III
Three and a half days/three and a half days

Parents split weekends

Possibility IV
Three days/four days:

Split weekend (Wednesday p.m. to Saturday p.m. with one parent; Saturday p.m. to Wednesday p.m. with other parent) or

WEEK 1
Wednesday p.m. to Sunday p.m. with one
parent

Sunday p.m. to Wednesday p.m. with other
parent

WEEK 2
Wednesday p.m. to Saturday a.m. with one
parent

Saturday a.m. to Wednesday p.m. with other

(Giving each parent a free Saturday and Sunday every other weekend)

Vacation periods with each parent in addition

Possibility V

Two weeks/two weeks, with midweek overnight with other parent

Vacation periods with each parent in addition

Possibility VI

(Ten-to-twelve-year-olds are the more likely
candidates for this schedule.)

One month/one month, with an exchange
weekend or periodic overnights with other
parent

Vacation periods with each parent in addition

For these elementary-school-age children, the outside world
begins to play a much more significant role than for the pre-
school group. As six-to-twelve-year-olds move through the
early grades, they are exposed to democratic issues; they begin
to vote on things at school, and they start asking *why* things

are being done the way they are. They become junior arbitrators and mediators, and they attempt to solve problems "fairly." In fact, elementary-school children have a passion for "fairness." Dr. Roman chuckles when he thinks about all the elementary-school children he has seen in his clinical work. "These kids come home and sit around and talk about whether the teacher was fair . . . they want to know the *reasons* things were decided one way or another."

Divorced parents who enact a well-thought-out shared custody plan will probably be perceived as being "fair" by children between the ages of six and twelve, Dr. Roman believes. But, he warns, "it's not just a matter of 'You're going to live here and you're going to live there—how do you like it?' and the kids say 'lousy' or 'great.' Parents need to sit down and explain what is *meant* by sharing custody and cooperative parenting. Talk with the kids about what shared parenting implies: that both parents love the child and will share in deciding what's best for him or her; that you think it's the best arrangement for everyone that the child has both of you and that both of you will participate in the raising of the child."

For the six-to-twelve-year-old, a fifty-fifty arrangement (or as close to it as makes sense for a family willing to stay in the same general area) may be a viable option. This doesn't mean that the parents must divide the time spent with the child to the exact *minute,* or be rich enough to provide duplicate living quarters. In fact, one working-class family in New York with elementary-school-age youngsters decided to reorganize things like this: the mother, a secretary, remained in the family apartment in the Bronx, and the father, a subway conductor, moved nearby to a much smaller place—which was all they could afford. The two children came over to their father's several times a week, unrolled their sleeping bags on the living-room floor, and sat at the kitchen table to do their homework. The apartments were ten blocks apart, so the children continued to go to the same school and were doing well with the arrangement.

They didn't have fancy surroundings, but they had something else: two parents.

Dr. Susan Steinman, in reviewing the findings of her study of twenty-four joint custody families in California, says, "My study does suggest that geographical proximity and continuity of school and friendships are very important for a dual-home arrangement." Dr. Roman agrees: "I really think it helps these kids whose families are changing so radically to feel that they're important enough for the parents to stay reasonably close and that the parents are taking their needs and desires into account." When children are given this consideration, they don't feel so powerless in the aftermath of divorce. "Kids learn to *think* about decisions and they see the process by which decisions are made," notes Dr. Roman. In fact, the psychologist has noticed that children he has seen in shared custody arrangements tend to be much more open and articulate about their feelings than youngsters in sole custody situations. "Those [sole custody] kids often feel they don't have any power and they better be quiet and make the best of it or they might lose the parent they're with."

That wasn't the problem of a ten-year-old with the pseudonym Gillian Walters. Her parents worked out a system in which she stayed with each on alternating days. Michael Walters was a free-lance writer in New York, and Gillian's mother worked for a major TV network there. Gillian was pleased that she saw both of her parents following their divorce, but soon it seemed she could never keep track of her favorite pair of shoes and missed her battery-operated pencil sharpener when she forgot to throw it in her backpack. Tentatively she asked first one parent and then the other if she could stay a week in one place and a week in the other. Both parents had seen how hard it had been for Gillian to keep the paraphernalia of her life organized, and realized that for this particular child a change in schedule made sense.

Both parents said they were open to revising their schedule, at least on a trial basis, and soon they shifted to a one-week-on,

one-week-off routine. Gillian divided her vacation times between her parents and they worked out an individual holiday
schedule with relative ease.

In contrast, my own son, when he turned seven, suddenly
began to forget his schoolbooks, his cub scout shirt, and his
soccer shoes with unbelievable regularity. Wherever *he* was,
his prized possessions were *not*. For the last four years he had
been spending Tuesdays and Thursdays at his father's and we
split the weekends. True, there was a good deal of going back
and forth, but our residences are only a mile and half apart.
Alarmed by his apparent confusion, his dad and I asked if the
alternating schedule was too hard for him, and we proposed
trying another arrangement—perhaps one week with Mom,
one week with Dad, the same schedule chosen by ten-year-old
Gillian in New York. "Oh, no!" Jamie said. "Then I would
miss both of you too much." Our son was apparently going
through a quite normal phase—for him—of "the forgets." We
kept the weekday schedule the same, but alternated weekends
and worked on teaching Jamie how to make a mental checklist
before he left for or from school each day. As a result, he now
has a remarkable memory for trivia.

These two examples point up an important lesson to keep in
mind when trying to determine what hurts and what works:
parents should be careful about making *assumptions* when
snags in a particular plan develop. A first step is to check
things out; get the *facts* before diagnosing a problem. Explore
various *possible* reasons for what you or your child is experiencing. Make sure you've talked to everyone involved.

As you contemplate plans for six-to-twelve-year-olds, you
can see there are many variations. John and Ginger Albert of
Madison, Wisconsin, were aware of this fact in 1976 when they
began divorce proceedings. At the time of their separation
their son, David, was six and Sarah, their daughter, was three.
"Our experience seemed to tell us that three to four days was
about the period of time the kids, especially Sarah, could last
without being with the other parent," reflects John, an attor-

ney who "does not do divorce law!" The couple had started out with a system of "grope and feel," remembers John. "We decided that wasn't working, so we structured it." What they came up with was this: every week from Wednesday evening to Saturday afternoon David and Sarah live with their father in the original family home. Late Saturday afternoon John drops his children off at their mother's apartment three miles away, where they stay until John picks them up at school on Wednesday. The children move twice a week, but they don't carry suitcases, "only a *lot* of heavy coats and boots in the winter." They attend the same school all the time.

Everyone who meets the Albert family always asks, "But isn't it confusing for the children?" John Albert sighs patiently, he says, and answers the question as honestly as he can. "At first Sarah, who was only three when we split, cried when one of us put the kids in the car to go to the other house, but she stopped in two blocks." Before long, both children adjusted well to the routine, and John has since decided that their arrangement may be confusing for everybody else, but it's not confusing to the kids. He tells the story of Sarah at age seven getting a phone call from the mother of a new friend inquiring about her staying overnight. "The woman said to her, 'Let me talk to your mom,' and Sarah replied, 'I don't have a mom here . . . talk to my dad.' She handed me the phone, I made the arrangements, and then I asked her, 'Did you say that just because it was easier to do it that way than to explain the whole thing?' She said, 'Yeah.' " John smiles wryly, "The *kids* aren't confused."

Young David, too, seems clear about what form his life has taken. The "house rules" are pretty much the same in both places, he says. "No wrestling in Mom's house; no wrestling at Dad's . . . but sometimes bedtimes are a little different: nine o'clock at Dad's and eight-thirty at Mom's." When asked what he would say to children who want to know if shared custody is a good idea, David replied, "I'd say it would be good because we're happy with it. Why shouldn't they be?"

David's father says that one issue parents sharing custody of children six to twelve years old may encounter is the question: "If you and Mom get along so well doing joint custody, why didn't you stay married?" John says he and Ginger have talked about their divorce at different times with the two children. "We had to come up with a real explanation here," he says. "We told them, 'We tried living together and we just couldn't get along. We had arguments and we weren't happy. We thought that would make you unhappy, too. Now we're both happier and it's easier to be parents together and to be nicer to you.' "

When the Alberts were in the process of getting divorced, Wisconsin had not yet passed its statute allowing for official joint legal and physical custody of children. In fact, they were told by a judicial officer that what they wanted to do with their own children was "illegal." Eventually their decree simply spelled out how the children would live, without awarding legal custody to either parent. "*Whatever* the court said," John notes firmly, "we knew what we were going to do."

As the years have passed, John and Ginger have been able to be more flexible in their schedule. When John wants to get away for a week of skiing, for instance, Ginger, who has a new man in her life, is willing to have the children stay with her full-time. John does the same for her. "With our particular schedule, we have weeknights when we can each work or do something on our own, and weekend nights when we can each go out, plus nice blocks of time when each of us spends time with the kids." Smiling, John adds, "Three days/four days is a magic division for all of us."

In New York City, the formula that worked for a Manhattan family was two weeks with the father and two weeks with the mother. The father was an airline pilot who could cluster his flying time into the first two weeks of the month. When he was flying the New York–London–New York route, his former wife had their two elementary-school-age children with her. When he completed his last flight of the month, the mother turned the children over to him for the next two weeks. In this case, too, the parents lived reasonably close to each other, so that the children could attend the same school.

Adolescents, Thirteen to Eighteen:

Possibility I

Home base with one parent

Flexible but constant time with other parent for dinners, trips, activities, and overnights during each month

Possibility II

Children stay in family home

Parents move in and out of home base each week, month, half year, or year; "out-of-house" parent spends flexible but consistent time with children for dinner, trips, activities during each month

Possibility III

Parents maintain separate family homes

Children attend same school but live in home-base houses in alternate years

"Out-of-house" parent spends flexible but consistent time with children for dinners, trips, activities, and overnights during each month, as schedules permit

Possibility IV

School year with one parent/summer with other parent

If parents live in same area, "out-of-house" parent spends consistent time with children for dinners, trips, activities, and overnights during each month, as schedules permit; if

geography a factor, midwinter holidays
spent with summer parent; all decisions
made jointly by parents throughout the
year

There are many possible arrangements that parents of teenagers can devise. However, divorced parents of teenagers
should be aware that around the onset of puberty a definite
shift seems to take place. This is a time when their youngsters
take tentative steps toward becoming more independent. As
they begin the process of depending on their parents less and
on themselves more, these budding young adults often want to
spend a lot of time with their friends. Yet the adolescent needs
to know his parents are still available and will tolerate him as a
"kid" occasionally, as well as "almost a grown-up."

Some children who have been raised as joint custody kids for
a few years may be perfectly happy to continue with whatever
pattern developed before they became teenagers; others will
suddenly discover at around thirteen or fourteen that the old
system, which seemed just perfect when they were in grade
school, doesn't work very well for them anymore. Instead of
going bowling or taking in a museum or spending the weekend
with one or the other parent, on a prescribed schedule, teenagers may want to go to a school basketball game with friends,
attend an all-day music clinic, or spend a Saturday tinkering
with a neighbor's car. Youngsters who were already teenagers
when their parents divorced may simply reject the notion of
going back and forth between two houses.

While children thirteen and older may need to be granted
more freedom in whatever plan is devised, parents should not
assume that because they are older they don't need supervision
or won't have serious problems adjusting to the parents' breakup. In the past, parents, family members, and even experts on
divorce tended to be more concerned about the impact of the
family split on younger children than on their older brothers

and sisters. However, from the Wallerstein and Kelly research discussed in Chapter 5, it is clear that the same amount of care is needed for children in their teenage years. One man approaching forty told me that when his parents announced shortly after his seventeenth birthday that they were getting a divorce, great care and sympathy were offered to his younger brother and sister. No one seemed to notice how depressed the older son became when the first holidays rolled around and the family didn't sing carols or spend Christmas Day together. The kids had lunch with their dad and dinner with their mother and nothing was said about the fact that they weren't all together for the first time in his life. To this day, he says, he dreads the Christmas season. Dr. Mel Roman warns, "The one thing parents need to be cautioned about is *generalizing* about adolescents. You simply have to tailor *your* decisions about what teenagers need to specific aspects of your own family's situation and the stage of development your particular teenager appears to be in."

Many child-development specialists believe parents can grant a certain amount of power to their older youngsters when determining shared custody arrangements. Dr. Roman, who does not think a twelve-year-old, unless very mature, is ready to decide the specifics of custody plans, says, "I do think, however, that a thirteen- or fourteen-year-old girl or boy should have a great weight in deciding the living arrangements." He brings up, as an example, a family he worked with. At the time of the parents' divorce, the three teenaged children were consulted for ideas on how the living arrangements should be set up, but were told that the parents would make the final decisions. "Eventually they worked out a very nice living situation," Dr. Roman told me. "The mother moved into a two-room one-bedroom apartment, and the father stayed in the family home, where each kid had a room. Frankly, I couldn't imagine those three teenagers with their mom in her little apartment. Sheer space and their needs as adolescents dictated that they make a home base with their father." The family agreed to joint legal and physical custody, with all major decisions to be made by both mother and father.

The youngsters agreed that they wanted to be based at the family home, but worked out a routine for seeing their mother often—at dinners out together once or twice a week, on trips to the movies, on weekend jaunts, and on sleepovers at her apartment occasionally, one by one. "I don't think that family is going to have any big problems," says Dr. Roman. "Those teenagers ended up with their rooms, their same school, and everything that was critical to their lives as increasingly independent people." They had access to both their parents and an established routine for spending time with the "out-of-house" parent, so they wouldn't drift away by default. "The mother couldn't afford a bigger place," notes Dr. Roman, "so reality helped this family decide what to do." Reality *and,* he adds, taking the needs and wants of the teenagers into consideration. "They needed their two parents, but they also needed some degree of controlled independence."

Ailene Hubert, a divorce counselor in Fort Lauderdale, Florida, agrees with Dr. Roman's assessment of what parents should consider when devising a custody plan involving teens. Her perspective comes not only from her professional work but also from personal experience as the divorced mother of five children, ages eleven to twenty-two. "When I went back to school to get my master's and started working full-time," she recalls, "we sat down and talked realistically about what their wants were. Their dad was financially able to handle it, so the two boys, who by then had their driver's licenses and could get around to see both of us, decided to live with their dad for a year while I got launched at school." (The three other children lived with their mother.) Hubert admits that it was a hard decision for her because she knew that in her community, and among her set, "people literally thought I must have had a nervous breakdown to have 'let' the boys' father have primary physical custody."

When counseling other parents who are trying to come up with their own "magic formula," she urges them to remember that whatever they decide at the time of the divorce isn't irrevocable. Parents who keep track of their children's changing needs often have to adjust the arrangement several times over the years. "I say to them, 'We may as well establish in the beginning that we want to design a custody plan that has flexibility and recognize the fact that this plan may be modified as the years go by.' " What is important, she says, is the *principle* of parents consulting each other about what is going to be best for their children at particular stages in their development and then mutually carrying out a plan of action based on the parents' current assessment. Many parents get "hung up on the notion that joint legal and physical custody means everything's fifty-fifty." For Hubert, and for so many others, joint legal and physical custody means the parents *remain* parents, with equal rights and responsibilities regarding their children, but that the time-sharing formula will be adjusted over the years to suit realities and the needs of "a particular child at various stages of his or her development." Says Hubert, "Parents, and especially parents of teenagers, are so excited when they learn that a shared custody plan isn't carved in stone, and that where the child will live on what days will redefine itself according to what is happening in the lives of various family members in the years following the divorce."

Most researchers of custody sharing submit that we simply don't yet have a full body of knowledge on the best forms of two-home arrangements. What we *do* know, however, is that children who are doing well under such arrangements have parents who cooperate with and respect each other as they raise their children. These parents support the relationship of the child with both father and mother and arrange things so the child is able to spend time with each. That often means making a commitment to stay close geographically. Parents sharing custody have told me over and over that agreeing to stay within the same area was the factor that did the most to promote the success of their efforts. "If you don't make that commitment to stay close," cautions John Albert, "you'd better examine your motives as to how sincere you are about co-parenting." As we have seen, children who thrive as joint custody kids are those not living in arrangements designed primarily for the convenience of the parents, but rather in a daily routine that takes into account youngsters' moving through childhood with traits and genes and habits and quirks that are uniquely their own.

There are plans that work—and plans that hurt. Certain tip-offs may indicate that a custody arrangement, whether shared or sole, isn't working well for a child. Sometimes, however, these symptoms indicate that the problem lies in the *way* in which a custody plan is being carried out by the parents, and not in the time-sharing formula itself.

MONITOR YOUR CHILD

Has your child shown:

	YES	NO
1. Problems with sleeping (restlessness, fear of the dark, fear of falling asleep, bad dreams and night terrors, a desire to sleep with a parent)?	☐	☐
2. Problems with eating (refusing food, overeating, stomachaches, constipation)?	☐	☐
3. Problems at school (grades dropping, fights with other children, misbehaving in class, unwillingness to participate in activities, few friends or none)?	☐	☐
4. Medical problems (sudden headaches, nervous stomach, asthma, lethargy, accident-proneness)?	☐	☐
5. Withdrawal from close friends or overdependence on large peer groups?	☐	☐

It is important to remember that there may be problems that existed *before* the divorce; also that, even in a shared custody arrangement that has been working perfectly, major changes— a move, a change of schools, the remarriage of one or both parents, the absence of a parent for prolonged periods—can trigger reactions in children. Before revising your cocustody plan, examine *all* the major elements in your own and your children's lives.

In the beginning stages of putting a shared custody plan into practice, you may notice that your children show unusual behavior before or after spending time with one or the other parent. A child may seem upset or withdrawn after being with one and shifting to the other. In many cases this is *normal behavior* and does not necessarily mean that a parent is not doing a good job of taking care of the children during his or her time "on duty." It usually means the children are in the difficult process of adjusting to a major change in their lives—the divorce—and need all the help and understanding they can get. If you think about it, it's easy to see how children can grow angry and frightened over the breakup of their family. Dr. Roman believes that it is important for parents to tolerate that anger for a while even if it makes them feel guilty. "Remember, though," he cautions, "during this angry phase it is not a good time to ask what the child thinks about a particular custody arrangement."

During these initial phases of putting together the plan, it is particularly important that both parents, working together, offer the youngsters the comfort and support they are desperate for. However, if the problems listed under "Monitor Your Child" persist, then, as parents, you may need to reexamine the nuts and bolts of the plan itself and make adjustments and "mid-course corrections."

Even if all immediate family members are alert and concerned about making a new shared custody formula work, trouble can come from other sources: grandparents, aunts, uncles, and well-meaning friends and acquaintances. Nothing can torpedo a cocustody arrangement faster than, say, a grandma who suggests to a child that his mother doesn't love him because she "gave him up" to his father, with whom he spends substantial time. Dr. Roman urges parents to help other family members and friends understand right from the start why they've chosen to try sharing custody. "Sit down with your mother-in-law and tell her *why* it's important to both of you and the kids to share parenting. This often will head off efforts to sabotage." Dr. Roman also recommends, if it's at all possible, that the grandparents and other important family members be involved in the plan. Let them see it is *in their interest,* if they want continued contact with the children, to support the idea of shared custody. "Set time aside for them to be with the children if they want to stay involved," he says. If outsiders prove uncooperative, you, as parents, must acknowledge that is happening and work together not to let others harm your efforts.

The true experts on the question of which particular shared custody plan will work best for you are you, your former spouse, and your youngsters. As long as you and your former spouse are tuned into the developmental and individual needs of your children, you two will be the best ones qualified to decide what, if any, corrections are needed. Not too long after my son's father and I made the decision to alternate weekends with Jamie instead of splitting his time each weekend, I was driving Jamie and a group of first-graders home in the car pool. One of the children mentioned that a classmate was moving to Arizona " 'cause his mommy and daddy are gettin' a divorce and his mommy is mad at his daddy." From the back seat I heard my son chirp, "Gee, that's too bad. My mommy and daddy got one of those *good* divorces where I got to keep both of 'em!" It may be easier than you think to tell what hurts and what works.

SUGGESTED GUIDELINES FOR DEVELOPING YOUR OWN "MAGIC FORMULA"

Some plans are obviously easier to put into practice than others—especially if the major obstacle is geography, as we will see in Chapter 9. But first, here is a recap of suggested guidelines for tailoring a joint custody plan to meet your family's needs. In thinking about your own pilot plan:

	YES	NO
1. Have you focused the shared custody parenting plan *primarily* on the needs and capacities of your children, taking into account, of course, your own basic requirements in order to come up with the right mix?	☐	☐
2. Have you reviewed what you and your former spouse have done as parents in the past that worked?	☐	☐
3. Have you thought things through on the basis of units of time (work schedules, school periods, vacation time, holidays, etc.)? Where possible, can you share the responsibility for your children's care around these natural transitions, as well as sharing other responsibilities of child rearing, such as dental and medical appointments, scouting, music and dance lessons, etc.? (Let "reality" assist you in figuring out a sensible day-to-day arrangement.)	☐	☐
4. Have you let your children know that the ultimate decision on the living arrangements will be made by both parents, but that you would like each child to respond to various proposals you are considering? (*Never* ask a child, "Who do you want to live with?" or "Who do you want to spend the most time with?")	☐	☐

5. Have you asked yourself *why* you would like custody arranged in a certain way? Have you checked to see if you are using shared custody as a means of staying connected to your former

YES   NO

spouse as a marriage partner—either to rekindle the relationship or to punish the other parent for the hurts of the marriage?   ☐   ☐

6. Have you resisted the temptation to tell your troubles to your children during the often difficult first months or year or so following your separation? Have you avoided confiding in them in a way that burdens them or makes them feel responsible for your welfare? (Talk to a counselor if your own emotional well-being is shaky; get expert advice if your financial security seems threatened. Remember, a kid is a *kid.*)   ☐   ☐

7. Have you been supportive of your children in their relationship with the other parent, even if you acknowledge to yourself (or privately to friends) that it is sometimes difficult for you to sustain many good feelings about your former spouse?   ☐   ☐

8. Have you been businesslike in dealing with the other parent? Have you stayed focused on the issues that relate to the children and resisted going over "old territory" regarding the way things were in the past?   ☐   ☐

9. Have you been sensitive to signs of "hyper-loyalty"? (Are your children overly concerned with being equally "fair" to both parents? A successful joint custody parenting plan is one that is good for and fair to everyone, not just competing parents.)   ☐   ☐

10. Have you accepted the differences in the other household—unless there is objective evidence that those differences are truly endangering your children physically or emotionally? (Be sure of your facts before you make a "diagnosis" as to what you think is wrong with your cocustody plan. You don't have to endorse what goes on in the other house; simply be firm about the rules in your house. Remember *you cannot control your child in the other house.*)   ☐   ☐

	YES	NO

11. Have you gotten into the habit of communicating with the other parent regarding important events in your children's lives or in your own that may affect your children? (Share the "high points" or successes that the other parent may not have seen—as well as the problems.)   ☐   ☐

12. Have you developed a Master Calendar, once you have decided on your schedule?   ☐   ☐

The Master Calendar

Make duplicate Master Calendars—one for each household—and go over the routine so your children have a clear sense of where they are going to be and when. Two samples of possible plans—for early-elementary-school-age children whose parents live close enough so the children can attend the same school—have been translated into the accompanying Master Calendars. When you actually plot out the day-to-day schedules, you can see clearly where the blocks of time fall and begin to have a sense of what it would be like to live with a particular plan. You can also spot the potential trouble areas a month in advance and make any needed adjustments. After studying these samples, plot out your own proposed plan in calendar form.

SAMPLE MASTER CALENDARS

Key:

M = Mom

D = Dad

( ) = time blocks

Sample I: six-to-twelve-year-olds

Sun.	Mon.	Tues.	Wed.	Thurs.	Fri.	Sat.	(Example:
	M	M)	(D	D	D	D	Mon., Tues. =
D)	M	M	D	D	(M	M	Mom; Wed.,
M	M	M)	(D	D	D	D	Thurs. =
D)	M	M	D	D	(M	M	Dad (parents alternate weekends)

Sample II: six-to-twelve-year-olds

Sun.	Mon.	Tues.	Wed.	Thurs.	Fri.	Sat.	(Example:
			D) (M	M	M	M)	3½ days/3½
(D	D	D	D) (M	M	M	M)	days; parents split
(D	D	D	D) (M	M	M	M)	weekends)
(D	D	D	D) (M	M	M	M)	

Chapter 9
Shared Custody and Geography

Can Your Child Commute?

The big "what if." The price you pay for getting divorced when children are involved: somebody loses something. When shared custody becomes "a tale of two cities." The New York–Los Angeles connection: bicoastal kids. Caroline and love at six thousand miles. The benefits of shared custody, even as a "temporary" solution. Communication Contract for Long-Distance Shared Custody. Two-Town Plans and Possibilities for Long-Distance Shared Custody: preschool children; school-age children. Calculating Your Time/Distance Formula.

My future husband and I looked at each other wordlessly across the kitchen table, with tears in our eyes. The "what if" we had always pushed to the back of our mind had come to pass. "What if you have to move? How can shared custody work then?" "What if the man you someday marry gets a fabulous job in another city? Do you expect him to put his career on hold while you wait for your son to grow up?"

My son, Jamie, was four when the "what if" call came from

New York. For two years Jamie had been living in two West Los Angeles homes a mile and a half apart, and one thing had become clear to everyone involved: he adored his dad, and his father was devoted to him. And now a national business magazine wanted to change all that by offering the little boy's future stepfather a prestigious by-lined weekly column out of New York and a lot of seductive perks to go with it. I was furious. I was terrified. I felt that just when I had finally gotten my life back on the rails, some rotten managing editor three thousand miles away was going to ruin everything. I was torn between my commitment to a life with an extraordinary new man and my commitment to a child I had given birth to with another man. The situation was even more difficult: not only had I seen the benefits of cooperative parenting for our child; I had also experienced the benefits to me *personally* in terms of being able to build my own career as a writer and broadcaster in a city it had taken me ten years to learn. And sharing parenthood after my divorce had left me *time* to really get to know this new man.

I remember the precise moment the decision about whether or not to go to New York settled into me with comforting clarity. I didn't feel like a martyr and I didn't feel noble. I simply knew that I couldn't move. Jamie wasn't even out of nursery school. How would he maintain contact with his father from three thousand miles away? He couldn't even dial a phone. Perhaps when he was older, I thought, geographic proximity wouldn't be so crucial. But his father and I had agreed in good faith that for the foreseeable future we would stay in the same area if at all possible. It was still possible for me to stay; I was still single. I told Tony that night in the kitchen that I wouldn't be able to go with him.

It was hard to say (and mean it) that I felt that my fiancé had to make his decision about taking or refusing the job offer *solely* in his own interest. But I did say it: if he felt that he wouldn't be happy if he didn't make this career move or if he should resent staying in California out of obligation to me, then we would be in trouble as a couple, and that wouldn't be good for any of us, including Jamie. I didn't want him to go to New York, but I didn't want to have to pay the price if he stayed in California with part of him longing for the challenge and rewards that New York had to offer. Could he really afford to pass up this promotion by the magazine he'd worked so hard for for three years? "Please, please. Do what is best for you!" I pleaded, holding my breath.

Tony's decision to remain in California with Jamie and me was the first "feminist" choice I'd ever personally seen a man make, and it convinced me, if I needed convincing, that we both had our priorities in the same order. As it turned out, the magazine soon began passing him over for choice article assignments—as a form of punishment, I suppose, for turning down their plum job. Eventually Tony knew he had to find another employer—which he did, fortunately. However, the lesson in all of this for us was that *there is a price you have to pay for getting divorced when there are children involved.* The bigger surprise is that you never know how many or which people will have to pay that price. In our case, Tony was the one who had to make the greater sacrifice. If he had taken the magazine's offer, *I* could have been the person to lose out—or Jamie's father and Jamie himself could have come up short if I had changed my mind and followed Tony to the East Coast.

But not all parents can make, or are willing to make, the choice to stay geographically close. What happens when sharing custody becomes "a tale of two cities"?

Thousands of families have had to face the hard reality that the parents cannot remain in the same area until their children are grown. These families are struggling to come up with formulas that will diminish the negative impact that long distances can have on divorced parents and their children. By opting for shared custody in those circumstances, many have worked out creative and often ingenious ways of maintaining close contact despite the miles between them. These parents acknowledge that no matter where they live, they are still the mother and father of their children. Together, they will continue to make major decisions on schooling, health care, summer activities, and other important matters; hence, they are still joint *legal* custodians of their children. And though the amount of time the children spend with each parent may not be split fifty-fifty, the parents continue to participate in the actual care of their children; hence, they are both still joint *physical* custodians of their youngsters. Some shared custody agreements include a clause which says that the parent electing to move from the area will relinquish primary or cocustodial care to the other parent so that the children can remain in the same school and familiar surroundings.

Some plans clearly demand less adaptation on the part of the children than the others. Take the case of a man I shall call Bill England and his nine-year-old-daughter, Dorothy. Bill considers himself a lucky man—and a very active father, although for more than half the year his child lives three thousand miles away from him.

Every May 15, or thereabouts, since 1977, Bill has rushed out to JFK International Airport to welcome his blond daughter for her annual four-month stay at his apartment in Manhattan. Dorothy spends the school term with her mother in California and she spends the summer and every Christmas and Easter with her father in New York. When Dorothy is living with her mother, she talks on the phone with Bill once a week, and father and daughter exchange at least a postcard every week. "Our contact when we're apart is something she looks forward to during the school term," says Bill. "She knows that I'm alive." He's proud of the fact that after several years of trial and error, he and his former wife share "those great moments when the other parent isn't around. The day she passed her intermediate swimming test in New York I said, 'Call up Mom and tell her, too.' "

Dorothy's basic routine with Bill during the summer is to attend day camp during the hours he is working as the director of a nonprofit foundation. Much of the summer, however, he reserves for his vacation, when he and Dorothy take trips. "We plan our vacation time together, since it's her vacation too. We consult each other all winter. I send her brochures and we write back and forth."

It took Bill and his former wife a few years and a near tragedy to figure out how to manage long-distance coparenting. "My ex-wife and I, two Americans, met abroad and had a mad, three-month whirlwind romance and married. The problem was, we simply turned into different people from the ones we'd married."

After the Englands split up in 1973 in Washington, D.C., Bill took a job in New York, and Dorothy, who was then three years old, used to toddle onto the New York–Washington air shuttle by herself every weekend. "Basically, she was a 'visitor' in my life, and the flying back and forth once a week wasn't a natural father–daughter thing. I said to her mother, 'Hey, this ain't going to work.' Fortunately, her mother agreed with me and we began to talk about what schedule would work better for Dorothy."

The couple decided that Dorothy would live with her mother during the school term and be taken out of school in the middle of May until she was at an age when final exams in June were important. "Our first major crisis occurred when the doctors misdiagnosed Dorothy as having leukemia. Suddenly I was flying to Washington every weekend and, despite all the hassles we'd had over our divorce, I realized that I had to give my full support to my ex-wife and be there when certain tests were being done." After several months Dorothy recovered and the family faced its second major crisis: the Big Move. His former wife, whose parents in California had offered her the kind of support system she felt she needed after all she'd been through with Dorothy's illness, decided to live in Southern California. Fortunately, the shared custody plan they had been using between Washington and New York could be adapted to New York–California. "It's not as convenient as Washington–New York, that's for sure," Bill admits, noting that he must forgo a lot of luxuries to be able to afford to bring Dorothy back East for Christmas and Easter, but "a big plus is that my ex has always been great about telling Dorothy what an exciting time she'll have coming back to be with me."

Bill acknowledges that it takes a good chunk of his income to stay connected to his daughter over the three thousand miles that separate them—but he gets good value for every dollar. "It all started in that delivery room at the hospital the day Dorothy was born. I remember looking at the baby coming out and thinking, 'Here's our kid!' My connection started right then and the benefit has been that that connection has made me very, very happy. I feel like a very wealthy man. I have a friend. I have totally unqualified love—which is very difficult to get these days—and I have a happy child." Thinking back over the decade of long-distance shared custody, he adds, "I feel that my existence is meaningful."

For another family sharing parenthood since their divorce, the distance between the two households stretched from six miles to six thousand. In 1979 Julie Cornelia (not her real name) lived with her second husband in a small Southwestern town. Her former husband, whom I will refer to as Charles, lived fifteen minutes away with his new wife, her daughter by a previous marriage, and the couple's new baby.

Julie and Charles's daughter, Caroline, then eleven, split her time between them fairly evenly. Then, in December 1979, Charles and his new family moved to Japan, where he had been assigned for two years by his company. Caroline went with them; Julie had agreed to the move after a time of agonizing indecision.

"I didn't know how I was going to handle the experience of Caroline's being so far away," Julie told me. "My present husband, Ray, and I talked it over when Caroline's father told us about the move, and we decided it was such a wonderful opportunity—one we couldn't give her right then—so we all agreed that Caroline should at least try it if she wanted to go."

The evolution of such cooperation was slow, touched by a heartbreaking past history. In 1973 Julie and Charles's younger child, a three-year-old girl, had run into the street and been killed by a speeding auto. Charles and Julie's marriage came apart one year after that and she moved out with Caroline. Caroline had severe trouble dealing with the double loss: first of her little sister and then of her father.

Both parents found new partners fairly quickly after their separation. With counseling, Charles and Julie went through an excruciating process of trying to determine what was truly in Caroline's best interests. And they were able to conclude eventually that the girl should go to Japan.

During Caroline's eighteen-month stint overseas, she and Julie talked once a month by phone and wrote regular letters. "Caroline's stepmother gets a great deal of credit for making their stay abroad bearable for me," says Julie. "Charles was gone on the job quite a bit, and she made sure that Caroline wrote me and sent birthday cards to her cousins." The difficulty of long-distance shared custody should never be minimized, warns Julie. "Charles would send me copies of Caroline's report cards from her school in Japan, but I always longed to know *more*. I had mixed feelings the whole time, especially when our birthdays and Christmas rolled around." Julie believes, however, that the experience seems to have been a good one for Caroline. "It was much stricter over there in her school and she had a lot more homework. She developed good study habits and got all A's and B's. She traveled all over the country and thought the entire adventure was just great."

This was a tremendous relief for both parents because, immediately following their separation, "Caroline used to cry about little things all the time," but "now she gets along with others really well," says Julie. "Now she's very verbal, has a lot of friends, and is full of fun and humor."

In the summer of 1980, the two families pooled their resources to bring Caroline back to California for a three-month visit, and in 1981 Caroline returned to the United States for good. Her father and his new family stayed on in Japan for several more months.

By this time, Caroline had turned thirteen, and her parents decided to let her have a major voice in the choice of where her headquarters would be during the following school term. At the end of the summer her father returned to the United States and bought a house about two hours' drive from where Julie lives. Caroline chose to spend the school year with her mom and see her father every other weekend. Now, on alternating Fridays the two parents drive to a point between their homes and Caroline skips from her mother's car to her father's to spend the weekend with her dad, her stepmother, her half sister, and her stepsister. "I usually leave it to Caroline to set things up," Julie comments. "She's free to see Charles whenever she can persuade the two of us to make that drive other than the scheduled weekends, and, of course, she can talk on the phone all the time."

Caroline's father supported his daughter's decision to make her mom's house home base for a while. "When Charles returned from Japan," recalls Julie, "it was his turn to be in transition and he couldn't offer what we could in terms of school and so on." Julie believes that Caroline is now old enough to know where she's most comfortable. "Right now that's with Ray and me, and she's made a commitment, as I insisted, to stay through each school year she chooses to spend with us."

Julie Cornelia believes that children *can* commute "if you've got communication between the parents. It cannot be worked out without support from the *new* spouses also, if they're in the picture. Each parent must support the other to an acceptable degree and *never* talk each other down," she advises. "A lot has to do with the age of a child—can he or she talk or write to keep up the connection with the parent who is far away? It is crucial," she emphasizes, "that during the separation the child call and write, and that the 'away' parent do the same. Having to deal with long distances is not the easiest way of doing joint custody, believe me, but let's face it—what are the alternatives?"

For many families, the question Julie Cornelia posed is the crucial one: What *are* the alternatives, other than permanently amputating one parent from the lives of his or her children? Whether the distance is seventy miles or seven thousand, children who seem best able to commute with reasonable ease do so between two supportive, cooperative parents. *Especially* when there are significant distances involved, shared custody arrangements need as their cornerstone a commitment by both parents to work out a plan that is *appropriate for the child*— even if it places some inconvenience or hardship on one or both of the parents.

However, what is appropriate for the child often turns out to be appropriate for the parents as well. As Julie points out, "Letting go and giving Caroline my blessing to go to Japan was a terribly hard decision for me, but because of everything that had happened to us—the death of our younger daughter, our divorce and remarriages—I knew Caroline needed that time with her father. At the time the Japan trip came up, Ray and I were starting a new upholstery business, which was a six-days-a-week, twelve-to-fourteen-hours-a-day commitment. I missed Caroline horribly, but, to be honest, it worked out well for us not to have the major responsibility for her during that period. Now that Caroline is with us, we have the time and concentration to give her." Julie is sensitive to the fact that Charles misses having his daughter with him full-time and that Caroline misses daily contact with her father and her half sister and stepsister. "Eventually, Caroline may wish to be based in a bigger family again," acknowledges Julie.

Regardless of where they have lived over the last few years, Julie and Charles have continued to look on each other as *equals,* with neither parent having superior rights—merely shifting obligations. Together they have made all major decisions regarding Caroline's welfare; they've accepted the idea that the physical arrangement of their shared custody agreement can be reworked to fit new circumstances, and that regardless of the addition of stepparents, no one takes the place of Caroline's natural mother and father. In this family, Caroline's stepparents are *parents,* but everyone involved is clear about the fact that Charles remains the father and Julie remains the mother.

The issue of geography is undoubtedly the toughest hurdle in working out any feasible custody plan, sole or shared. The situation is made even more difficult when one parent moves out of the neighborhood right after the family breakup, thereby adding to a child's sense of loss. From clinical observation of families sharing custody, we know that children who have been lucky enough to have lived in a two-household situation for a couple of years before their parents remarry and/or move away seem better able to cope with the physical loss of one parent than they would have if that loss had come at the time the marriage was falling apart. In addition, the child's relationship with both parents appears to be stronger if the youngster has had time to redefine the bond with them following their separation. Children seem better able to withstand the strain of physical separation if parent and child have forged a new connection and developed new ways of being with each other in the period immediately following divorce.

The critics of shared custody argue that coparenting after divorce is often only a temporary solution because so often people remarry, move, or radically change their life-style. However, children with a couple of years of successful shared custody under their belt have learned enough by that experience to know that parents continue to be parents, even if marriages fail and grown-ups cannot always keep their commitment to stay geographically close. This good experience of even *temporary* physically shared parenting often will have fortified children to the point where they don't feel that a later move by one parent is a form of abandonment. And if significant sharing lasts only for a while, parents have often built up the trust they need to be able to adapt to the geographical changes in their lives, so that they have fewer difficulties working out new shared custody arrangements.

But as Julie Cornelia has said so poignantly, "Long distance isn't the easiest way to share custody," and parents who cannot or will not remain close are asking their children to help pay the dues their parents owe for getting divorced. It may be a long time before parents who divorce acknowledge that they don't automatically have the freedom to move wherever they want—at least not ethically—and to take the children with them. However, if geography is the hurdle your family is attempting to overcome, the accompanying guidelines may be of some help in trying to work out an arrangement that keeps parents and children connected despite the distances between them.

COMMUNICATION CONTRACT FOR LONG-DISTANCE SHARED CUSTODY

Communication, even more than distance, will affect the success or failure of long-distance shared custody. To estimate the likelihood of your creating a successful long-distance shared custody arrangement, see how many of these statements you—and your former spouse—can agree to:

	YES	NO
1. I agree to work out a preplanned schedule of telephone and mail contact and agree to assure the other parent I will make every effort to adhere to it.	☐	☐
2. I agree that the parent with whom the children are living should encourage the youngsters to keep in touch on a regular basis with the "away" parent.	☐	☐

YES NO

3. I agree to keep the other parent informed of major developments involving the health, school progress, and general ups and downs of our mutual offspring, and I agree to consult with my former spouse on all major decisions. ☐ ☐

4. I agree not to demean the other parent in blatant or subtle ways while the children are with me, or to put pressure on our youngsters to prefer my household over the other. ☐ ☐

5. I agree to try to get together with the other parent on issues such as bedtimes, how much TV watching is allowed, junk foods, and allowances in an attempt to present as united a front as possible in the two households. ☐ ☐

6. I agree that, if space permits, both parents should try to have an area reserved primarily for the children. The children and I will try to go shopping together to pick out items that will define that area or room so the youngsters really feel they have a place in my home. ☐ ☐

7. I agree to plan the children's departures and arrivals with the other parent so they go smoothly. (Some families plot out the distances on a map and calculate how long it takes to get from one place to the other.) ☐ ☐

8. I agree to reassure the children that I will be there to pick them up after their journey to my house. (Some parents make a "dress rehearsal" trip to the airport, train station, or bus depot before a new long-distance shared custody plan is put into operation.) ☐ ☐

9. I agree to welcome pictures of the other parent or mementos of times spent at the other house into my own house. I will allow mail and telephone conversations to be private if my children wish them to be so. ☐ ☐

10. I agree that if the other parent has a new spouse or "live-in," the new person in my children's life will not mean "the end" of the other parent. I

will tell my children that, regardless of the geography or other adults involved in our arrangement, my children will *always* have a mother and a father, even though the new adult on the scene will be a "parent" to my children as well.   ☐   ☐

TWO-TOWN PLANS AND POSSIBILITIES FOR LONG-DISTANCE SHARED CUSTODY

As with any other shared custody plan, there are no "perfect" formulas or "right" ways of arranging things when developing a long-distance shared custody plan. Nor are the following shared custody plans the *only* arrangements that might work for your family. The Plans and Possibilities below are merely suggestions distilled from interviews with parents who have had to cope with geographic challenges, and with counselors who have worked with families sharing custody who faced these kinds of problems.

Preschool Children Under Three Years Old

Most experts on child development agree that continually shifting very young children from home to home, especially over long distances, is not recommended. It is primarily the *parents* who should do the commuting in order to spend time with children under three. Sadly, few parents can afford to accompany a small child back and forth over substantial distances, or even to pay for roundtrips for themselves. Divorcing parents of very young children who remove youngsters from the possibility of spending time with the other parent—if that parent wants to stay involved—are robbing their children of their birthright. The one hope for the cooperative parent is to try, perhaps through counseling with a neutral third party, to educate the other parent about the developmental needs of young children to know and spend time with both parents, and to emphasize the possible later negative repercussions on children who are deprived of one parent. The objective is to persuade the parent who wants to move to acknowledge his or her obligation to stay at least a few years until the child is five or six, so that the child can forge and maintain the important bond with both parents. If such arguments are rejected by the relocating parent, the absent parent will simply have to face the difficult task of building a relationship with his or her offspring when the child is older. There are no easy answers for this group—period.

Children Three to Six Years Old

There are no easy answers for this group, either, although older sisters and brothers are very helpful in easing transitions for these young children. If three-to-six-year-olds are able to shift long distances, it will probably be within the context of a home-base parent and a second-home parent, with the amount of time spent away from home base gradually lengthening as the child matures.

School-Age Children

LONG AND MIDDLE DISTANCES:

Possibility I

School term/vacations

School term based with one parent; vacations based with other parent; holidays and overnights apportioned depending on distances and finances involved

Possibility II

School term/vacations, plus visits

School term based with one parent; vacation time based with other parent; once- or twice-monthly weekends spent with other parent, depending on distances and finances involved

Possibility III

Alternating school term/vacations

Yearly or every two years based with one or other parent with proviso that older children (around twelve and up) will have major weight in deciding residence for school terms

DISTANCES OVER TWENTY MILES, UNDER EIGHTY MILES:

Possibility I

Week/weekends

School week with one parent; weekends, vacations, and most holidays with other parent

Possibility II

Week/weekends, plus "nesting"

School week with one parent; weekends, vacations, and most holidays with other parent; several times a year, distant parent moves in for a long weekend and home-base parent moves out

Possibility III

Split time

School remains the same; two weeks/two weeks with each parent (or month/month, etc.) if distances are drivable and children adjust well to travel time

Calculating Your Time/Distance Formula

The plans and possibilities suggested for longer distances may also be suitable for parents living twenty to eighty miles apart if commuting appears to put too much of a strain on the children. As youngsters get older their focus tends to turn away from the homefront, somewhat, toward school activities and friendships. Long-distance planning will have to take that factor into consideration, as well as the importance of maintaining contact between the children and the out-of-town parent. Foremost, with all ages, parents should do everything possible to make their children's commute as painless as possible.

With that in mind, calculate your own Time/Distance Formula if geography is a major factor in your life.

SHARED CUSTODY TIME/DISTANCE FORMULA

1. *Distance*
      Father lives in: _____
      Mother lives in: _____
      Miles between: _____

2. *Time*
      Travel time by car: _____
              bus: _____
           train: _____
              air: _____

3. *Children's Ages and Other Factors*
      Children's ages: _____

      _____

      _____

      _____

      Schools available
        in father's area: _____
        in mother's area: _____
      Parents' occupations and time demands
        father: _____
        mother: _____
      Financial factors (parents' income, transportation costs, etc.): _____

_____

_____

_____

_____

4. *Time Proposals*
      Residence with father: _____
      Residence with mother: _____

5. *Transportation Agreement*
      Expenses paid by father: _____
      Expenses paid by mother: _____

6. *Adjustment and Renegotiation Agreement*
      If situations change or problems develop: _____

_____

_____

      then we agree to
        negotiate: _____
        mediate: _____

Chapter 10
The Shared Custody Agreement

Get It in Writing

Tears and empathy on D (Document) Day. Professor Jay Folberg on the language of shared custody. Legal documents and love: the two are compatible. Cut the legalese! The new interdisciplinary approach to writing shared parenting agreements. Why put it in writing? Issues to be covered in your shared custody document. Your day in court: what might the judge ask? Preparing your answers. What to do if the judge turns thumbs down. Working with your attorney in drafting your agreement. Spoon-feeding clauses to lawyers. Adapting to local legal forms. A sample shared custody and child support agreement and order.

Law professor Jay Folberg passed the custody agreement to the tearful couple facing him across his desk. He suddenly realized he had only one handkerchief ready. "I didn't know what to do," he says, thinking back to the truck driver and his wife who were with him that day to finalize the documents regarding custody of their children. The three sat in Folberg's glass "treehouse" office overlooking the majestic evergreens of

Tryon Creek State Park, on the campus of Lewis and Clark Law School in Portland, Oregon. "This was one of the most emotional signings I'd witnessed and there was great sadness," Folberg says. "I think that agreement marked the official end of their marriage and it made their divorce real. It was the end of an important life phase for them and they were both in tears."

Folberg smiles as he decribes how he always keeps one big clean handkerchief available for such occasions. "I didn't want to be chauvinistic about it and only offer it to *her!*"

The man and wife tried to compose themselves as, sharing Folberg's handkerchief, they picked up their pens to sign the documents. The most unusual feature of the agreement was its language. It began: "We believe each of us to be fit parents and recognize the unique contribution each of us has to offer our children.... We wish to continue to cooperate as parents and disrupt the children's life pattern as little as possible. Our primary concern has been, and shall be, the best interests of the children within the reality of our dissolved [marriage] relationship."

The documents went on to describe the day-to-day specifics of the children's schedule, including holidays, vacations, and the youngsters' birthdays. The words of the agreement held no undertone of victor or vanquished; the children were not described as possessions of the parents, but rather as valued mutual assets to be nurtured and cherished. Unlike the more traditional agreement stipulating custody, the document did not "award" custody to one parent over the other. Neither parent was relegated to the role of "visitor." Nor did the children find themselves with a "primary" and a "secondary" residence—the euphemism for living with one parent and meeting the other at the corner drugstore for a weekly soda and an occasional overnight.

Says Professor Folberg of the joint custody agreements he has authored since 1976, "I try to use words that are appropriate to what is actually going on in the lives of the divorcing family. I want the words to be ones that kids or their parents can read years from now and feel there wasn't any lack of love on the part of the parents toward their children."

Professor Folberg has served as chairman of the Oregon State Bar Association's Family Law Section and as chairman of the American Bar Association's Mediation and Arbitration Committee—Family Law Section. His first experience drafting joint custody prose came when he and his former wife agreed in 1976 to share the responsibilities of raising their three children. "Facing that blank sheet of paper was probably the best thing that could have happened," he says. "We outlined the type of arrangements we wanted and cut through the legalese to write it out." The agreements Folberg uses today are based primarily on what he and his former wife drew up for themselves, adding, of course, sections that reflect the needs of a particular family. "Originally I started with a statement that both parents were fit. Now I add that not only are they fit, but that the parents agree to *foster* love and affection between their children and the other parent," says Folberg. "Meyer Elkin [former director of the Los Angeles Conciliation Court] had been talking for years about how we have long sets of words that we use in these things when shorter ones will do just fine."

Professor Folberg says that a variety of events and experiences influenced his thinking about how custody agreements should be written. "I started out in this business as a litigator. I litigated all kinds of cases: business, primarily, and even some custody cases. I was trained as a legal advocate and I was a good trial lawyer." He was so good, in fact, that he won a few custody cases that later upset him. In one, he represented a woman who had walked away from her marriage and her family, leaving the father in charge of their child for several years. "It was not unlike the movie *Kramer vs. Kramer,* and I was trying to regain the child for the mother. In fact," recalls Folberg, "I really came to empathize with the mother's position, thinking she just *had* to win that case." But when the father got on the stand during the trial, it was equally clear that he, too, had much to offer the child. "They *both* had something special to give to their child," Folberg remembers sadly.

Folberg became the director of the Association of Family Conciliation Courts, an interdisciplinary group of lawyers, judges, and therapists "all trying to figure out how we could use the understanding and training of mental health counselors in the legal system to make family law help people, instead of hurt families. The given policy in family law is supposed to be 'what is in the best interests of the child,' and so the issue became for me: how do we achieve a custody solution that is truly in the best interests of the child? It certainly had been shown to me that it wasn't through the adversarial approach."

In a series of law review articles, Professor Folberg urged a reexamination of the ways in which various disciplines interact on the issue of child custody. He suggested that lawyers, judges, and mental health professionals look at the "bigger picture." And he determined that a practical way to influence how children are to be cared for is for the parents and their lawyer to compose a coparenting plan in legal, but understandable, language. "If parents are attuned to the child's need and their own needs, they can figure out—just as married people do—what is to be done."

Professor Folberg believes it is important to have an agreement in writing and to process it through the courts, so that both the mother and the father know what the ground rules are. "It avoids a lot of little arguments," he says, then offers a comparison to the U.S. Constitution: "You don't go into court to litigate every time there's a minor crisis; however, if there's a revolution brewing, you've got the main document to fall back on." A written agreement also provides the framework for discussing, and coming to an understanding on, important points. "It's like any other contract," he points out. "You don't really need a contract for most things you do, but the contract *form* helps you work through the 'what ifs.' What if you remarry? What if you move? What if you die? All those things you hope and assume you won't actually go through, but the exercise of writing a joint custody agreement makes you think about those issues in case you do."

When Folberg works with a couple, he normally helps with the financial aspects of the divorce as well as the issues of custody. "You can separate custody from financial issues to a degree," he notes, "but it's a superficial separation, to my way of thinking. We start off with the easiest things first, so if the couple is arguing over the kids, I'll start by working with them to resolve the money issues first." He points out, however, that "it is important to avoid the trade-offs of money for kids."

Among the many issues that may, in part, affect the way in which the parents approach how the children are to be cared for are such questions as: Who will take the children as tax exemptions? How is their future education to be paid for? Which parent will provide medical and life insurance? How are wills to be drawn? What expenses will be included in setting child support payments? How will support payments be categorized for tax purposes? "Near the end of our sessions together I'll go over all the things we *have* discussed to make sure my notes are right before I draft the agreement. Then I'll say, 'I don't have notes on the following points: educational expense, pension plan payments (or whatever). We need to cover them one way or another in the agreement.' "

One of Professor Folberg's cases involved a physician and his wife, who ended up with a twelve-page agreement. It detailed everything from the two-week/two-week schedule of joint physical custody, to a joint checking account requiring the signature of both parents to disburse funds for the children's support, to a clause detailing the continuing joint ownership of their considerable art collection, which would be traded back and forth over the years until it was given in trust to the children. "Even with agreements as comprehensive as that one," warns Folberg, "the judge in some jurisdictions may—and probably *will*—question the divorcing couple." Parents, he cautions, should be prepared and should expect to be quizzed. "Even in states where joint custody statutes are on the books, in most cases it is still discretionary; it's up to the judge to approve your shared custody agreement." Folberg advises that the best way to deal with possibly hostile questioning from the bench is to show the judge you have really thought through all the ramifications of what you have put in writing. "Show him or her that the agreement is not merely a compromise to avoid further fighting, even if initially that may be what it was. Let the judge see that you realize there may be difficult points but that the agreement itself is proof that you have some ability to cooperate." What the judge is probably worried about, cautions Folberg, "is that your case might be like some case which the judge was eventually forced to rehear."

If the judge refuses to approve a couple's shared custody agreement, Professor Folberg says, there are three basic alternatives: (1) appeal your case; (2) maneuver your case to a more sympathetic judge *before* the final part of the case is heard; or (3) simply go ahead and *live* joint custody according to the written plan to which you've both agreed. However, none of these alternatives is ideal, as Folberg sees it. "It's costly and time-consuming to appeal. Attorneys have to really know their way around the court system to find out how to avoid Judge X by scheduling your case on Wednesday afternoons when His Honor is playing golf. And merely living joint custody without a court-ordered plan leaves one parent at the mercy of the officially designated 'custodial parent'—which could be difficult if circumstances change." However, Folberg believes that if parents present a united front and show they've thought about the types of questions the judge is likely to bring up, and if they've prepared good answers, courts are often disinclined to meddle.

Before meeting with an attorney to draft the legal language of a shared custody agreement, says Professor Folberg, "you need to already have made it clear to the attorney early on that you, as the client, want control of your own case. Be specific about what details you want included in the legal document."

Professional ethics require that clients be allowed to make their own decisions once they are informed by their attorneys of the implications and possible repercussions of various choices. However, Folberg warns, many attorneys may not have had much experience in writing shared custody agreements, and some may simply find the notion unworkable. "Women, particularly, sometimes have a difficult time," he says, "with attorneys who are uncomfortable with females who insist that the decision about how the custody agreement should be written is theirs to make." And men as well as women, he adds, sometimes have a hard time holding firm against authoritarian lawyers.

Professor Folberg urges parents to make certain from the start that their attorney is willing—and able—to implement, through a sound, written agreement, the shared custody principles they want in the document. And once the agreement is drawn up, he says, parents should scrutinize it line by line to be sure it *precisely* reflects their wishes.

A sample joint custody and property settlement agreement will be found in Appendix C. A clause-by-clause breakdown dealing *only* with the custody section of such an agreement follows here. The provisions in each division of this sample agreement are a blend of those developed by Professor Folberg and by James Cook, a legislative advocate who is the author of California's joint custody law. The language in the following sample agreement is meant only as a guide for you and whoever helps you draw up your own document. Each family, of course, has individual needs that must be expressed in legal language. In addition, changing tax laws and rulings must be considered, as they may impact the most favorable financial arrangement.

The precise legal forms required by the state and court in which your custody document is to be filed also vary, and your document should be written to meet legal and local stylistic standards. For general help, though, you may wish to show this chapter—and the sample agreement in Appendix C—to the person helping you draft your agreement. Discuss each point as you work to make your own shared custody agreement reflect the needs of your family.

Jay Folberg
Attorney at Law
Portland, OR 97208
Attorney for Petitioner

IN THE CIRCUIT COURT OF THE STATE OF OREGON
FOR THE COUNTY OF WASHINGTON
DEPARTMENT OF DOMESTIC RELATIONS

In the Matter of the Dissolution of
the Marriage of

JOHN DOE	)	
Petitioner,	)	
and	)	CASE NO. _____
	)	
JANE DOE	)	STIPULATED CUSTODY
Respondent	)	AND SUPPORT AGREE-
		MENT AND ORDER

We, John Doe, here referred to as the Father, and Jane Doe, here referred to as the Mother, are husband and wife. We have one child of our marriage, a boy, here referred to as John Jr., who is nine years old.

Irreconcilable differences have arisen between us causing the irremediable breakdown of our marriage and we have agreed to file a petition for dissolution. We have lived apart approximately two years.

(BASIC STATEMENT OF INTENT)
We have continued to share physical and legal responsibilities for John Jr. and have cooperated in providing for his

needs. He appears to have adjusted well to the existing situation. We each have a significant nurturing relationship with our child that is important to all of us.

(FITNESS OF BOTH PARENTS)

We believe each of us to be fit parents and recognize the unique contribution each of us has to offer our child. We wish to continue to share responsibility for the care of John Jr., and each fully participate in all major decisions affecting his residence, health, education, and welfare while disrupting his life pattern as little as possible.

(AGREEMENT TO SHARE CUSTODY)

IT IS HEREBY STIPULATED BY AND BETWEEN PETITIONER AND RESPONDENT that:

1. Mother and Father will share and participate in the joint physical and legal custody of John Jr. The parents shall share custody of John Jr. as set forth below:

(INDIVIDUAL SHARED CUSTODY SCHEDULE)

2. John Jr. shall reside with his Mother Monday and Tuesday of each week, and with his Father Wednesday and Thursday of each week. Parents shall alternate weekends from Friday after school through Monday morning before school.

3. Holidays shall be spent with the parent that John Jr. is scheduled to be with, with the following exceptions:

Mother's Day—with Mother

Father's Day—with Father

Maternal grandparents' birthdays—with Mother

Paternal grandparents' birthdays—with Father

Week preceding Christmas through Christmas Eve—with Mother

Christmas Day from noon through following week—with Father

(Parents alternate this schedule each year.)

Thanksgiving Eve through 2 p.m. Thanksgiving Day—with Mother

Thanksgiving Day from 2 p.m. through Thanksgiving Night—with Father

John Jr.'s birthday—with Mother, alternating years

Summer school recess— six weeks with Mother; six weeks with Father unless regular schedule prevails by mutual consent (Each March, parents will confer to review plans for John Jr.'s summer activities.)

One-day "tax holiday"—Each parent alternates years if necessary to establish Head-of-Household Status

(DEFINING CUSTODIAL RESPONSIBILITIES)

4. The parent with whom John Jr. is staying shall be responsible for daily care and shall make necessary decisions regarding emergency medical or dental care. All major decisions regarding John Jr.'s education, religious training, cultural and artistic training, nonemergency health treatment, and general welfare shall be made by both parents together. Each parent agrees to confer on a regular basis concerning the child's needs, growth, and care, and will share and make accessible all school records and report cards. Each will permit and encourage communication by the other with teachers and school administrators regarding John Jr.'s educational progress.

(COOPERATION DEFINED)

5. It is expressly understood that the above-enumerated times that each parent shall be with John Jr. and responsible for his care are subject to modifications by mutual agreement. Flexibility in child-care responsibilities and involvement are to be encouraged and the terms of this Agreement are to be liberally interpreted to allow John Jr. the maximum benefit to be derived from the love, concern, and care of both Mother and Father. Each parent agrees to promote in John Jr. respect and affection for the other parent.

(CHANGES IN CIRCUMSTANCES)

6. Should any change of circumstance occur, materially affecting the care of John Jr. or either parent's access to him, the residential care and arrangements for him shall be considered

by the parents in light of then existing circumstances. Should either Mother or Father change residences, so that he or she no longer lives in the same school district, or if either changes job patterns, every effort shall be made to facilitate the continued exercise of joint custody, so that John Jr. continues to enjoy the benefit of both parents in as close to equal time proportions as practicable, taking into consideration, among other factors, the needs and developmental stage of John Jr.

7. In considering future living arrangements for John Jr., Mother and Father shall have regard for his preference and the environment and care which each parent can provide.

(FINANCIAL SUPPORT OF CHILD)

8. Each parent shall deposit by the third day of each month an amount of money for support of John Jr. in a joint checking account requiring both their signatures and restricted to payment and reimbursement of expenses incurred on behalf of John Jr. The parents will share child-support costs proportional to their gross income over $10,000 for the previous calendar year. These expenses will include food, child care, education, lessons, summer camp and activities, clothing, grooming, allowances, medical care, health insurance, travel, major gifts, and agreed-upon amounts of other expenses incurred for John Jr.'s benefit until he becomes eighteen years of age. The parents will discuss near the end of each month the expenses for that month to determine the necessary total contribution required. Such monthly total shall not, in any event, be less than $200 per month.

9. Each parent agrees to contribute to a tax-deferred annuity or trust account for the benefit of John Jr. a total of $100 each month on the same formula and condition set forth in Paragraph 8. The income and principal of this annuity or trust account is to be applied to pay to John Jr., or for his benefit, necessary amounts for his support, maintenance, books, and tuition while he is under twenty-one years of age and a student regularly attending as a full-time student a school, community college, college, or university, or regularly attending a course of

vocational or technical training designed to prepare him for gainful employment. If the annuity or trust account is not used for John Jr.'s advanced education as above provided, or is not exhausted by his twenty-first birthday, then the account may be used for his benefit or paid to him as his Mother and Father may agree, or divided between the parents proportionate to each of their contributions to it.

(MEDICAL INSURANCE PROVISIONS)

10. Father agrees to declare John Jr. a dependent for medical insurance purposes and will include him under his employer's medical insurance program for so long as such insurance is available as an employee benefit. Additional medical expenses will be assumed by both parents on an identical ratio reflecting the child-support formulas as set forth in Paragraph 8.

11. Both parents agree that all medical, surgical, and dental records of John Jr. will be available and accessible to both of them.

12. Each parent will permit and encourage communication by the other parent with doctors, clinics, and other health providers regarding John Jr.'s health and welfare.

13. Each parent agrees to provide advance notification to the other parent about proposed and forthcoming medical care and each will inform the other of any medical emergencies.

(TAX PROVISIONS)

14. The parent contributing more than 50 percent of John Jr.'s child support for that calendar year shall be entitled for that year to the dependency exemption for John Jr. on federal and state income tax returns. In the event that the parents each contribute one half of the support for John Jr. in any year, the parents shall alternate claiming John Jr. as a dependent, beginning with the Mother.

(LIFE INSURANCE PROVISIONS)

15. Father shall keep current insurance on his life in an amount of not less than $100,000 and Mother shall keep current insurance on her life in an amount of not less than $50,000, with John Jr. as beneficiary until he reaches the age of twenty-

one, for the purposes of securing his support and expenses to that age as set forth in Paragraph 8.

(REMARRIAGE)

16. This agreement is intended generally not to be affected by the remarriage of either parent.

(REVIEW OF SHARED CUSTODY ARRANGEMENTS)

17. Mother and Father will annually confer and review the shared custody plan as to its adequacy, feasibility, and appropriateness in consideration of John Jr.'s age and developmental progress. This review shall take place at a mutually convenient time between spring school break and summer vacation.

(FUTURE DISPUTES—MEDIATION)

18. Both parents will attempt to work together to avoid any further disputes. Should any disputes arise which they cannot resolve, both parents wish to avoid the expense and acrimony of formal court proceedings. Therefore, any controversy arising out of, or relating to, this Agreement or breach of this Agreement shall first be submitted to the process of mediation through the services of their mediator or anyone else on whom they mutually agree. Both parents agree to follow the process of mediation to its conclusion prior to either party's seeking further relief or modification from a court.

(CONSEQUENCES ARISING FROM DEATH OF ONE OR BOTH PARENTS)

19. Mother and Father agree that should either parent die before John Jr. becomes twenty-one years of age, the surviving parent shall assume custody and provide for his needs until John Jr. is twenty-one years of age. Should both parents die before that time without remarrying, both parents agree that John Jr.'s maternal aunt, Mary Smith, shall assume custody, acting as guardian for John Jr. according to the spirit of this stipulated Custody Agreement and the provisions in the Will of the last surviving parent. If one or both parents have remarried at the time of the death of both parents and John Jr. has developed a significant relationship with either or both stepparents, future living arrangements shall take into account, among other considerations, John Jr.'s preferences and the environment and

care which his stepparent or stepparents may provide.

(BINDING EFFECT OF SHARED CUSTODY AGREEMENT)

20. We accept the foregoing as a full, final, and complete settlement of all of our custody and child-support rights arising from or growing out of our marital relationship. In consideration of the terms expressed, we release and relieve each other from any payments or obligations now or in the future regarding such custody and child-support rights, other than those specifically set forth in this stipulated Agreement, and we acknowledge and accept this Agreement as full settlement of all obligations and demands that either or both of us might or could have in any form against the other's estate on account of any matter whatsoever regarding custody and child-support rights arising from or growing out of our marital relationship.

21. We understand and agree that this stipulated Agreement will be submitted to the court for its approval and may be incorporated with full force and effect in any decree that may be entered in any proceeding for the dissolution of our marriage.

IN WITNESS WHEREOF, the parties have solemnly agreed and signed their names.

IN WITNESS WHEREOF, the parties have solemnly agreed and signed their names.

_____	_____
JOHN DOE	JANE DOE
Petitioner	Respondent

APPROVED AS TO FORM AND CONTENT

_____

Jay Folberg
Attorney for Petitioner

_____

Attorney for Respondent

Dated:_____

Mary Brown
Attorney at Law
Los Angeles, CA 90002
Attorney for the Respondent

SUPERIOR COURT OF THE STATE OF CALIFORNIA
COUNTY OF LOS ANGELES

In re the Marriage of

Petitioner: JANE DOE	
and	Case No. _____
Respondent: JOHN DOE	STIPULATED AGREEMENT FOR MODIFICATION RE CHILD CUSTODY AND ORDER

IT IS HEREBY STIPULATED by and between Petitioner and Respondent that the Court may order that the Final Judgment of Dissolution of Marriage entered on May 22, 1978, and all subsequent orders, be modified as to the custody of the minor child, JOHN DOE, JR., born February 20, 1972, from Petitioner's Sole Custody with Respondent's Reasonable Visitation, to an order for Joint Custody with physical custody shared by the parents in such a way as to assure the child frequent and continuing contact with both parents.
Dated: _____

_____   _____
JANE DOE [signature in   JOHN DOE [signature in
script]   script]

ORDER

IT IS HEREBY ORDERED, ADJUDGED, AND DECREED that:
the Stipulated Custody and Support Agreement set forth above be incorporated with full force and effect in the Final

Judgment of Dissolution of Marriage entered this date in the matter of Marriage of Doe, Case No._____.

Dated: _____

_____
JUDGE OF THE CIRCUIT
COURT

Part Three
Living with Shared Custody

Chapter 11
Shared Custody
Day-to-Day

Running a Two-Household Family

What's it like to be a "shared custody kid"? Setting up the three-ring circus. Involving the children in the process of establishing two homes. The Nuts-and-Bolt Department: clothing, toys, books, records, and lots of et cetera. Making the telephone work for both families. The ins and outs of pickups and drop-offs. Coping with school and homework in a two-household family. Coordinating extracurricular activities and holiday plans. How to throw a shared custody birthday party. Adult dating and shared custody. Fine-tuning the daily schedule in two homes. What to do when things get confusing. Kid conferences.

"Shared custody," said my nine-year-old, squinting thoughtfully, "is sleeping in the bottom bunk at Mom's house and the top bunk at Dad's." Warming to his subject, he began ticking off items on his fingers. "It's brushing with Crest toothpaste at your mom's and Aim at your dad's. It's white bread sandwiches in my lunch bag from Dad's place and whole wheat from Mom's." Jamie was laughing now. "I have spelling homework on Tuesdays at Dad's and math homework at your house on Wednesdays. I brought my clay elephant and the cobra snake I made in art class home to Dad and the sea otter and duck to you." Jamie looked up at me with a big grin. "The dog and cat stay at your house and the pet rats and turtle stay at Dad's, and my report cards go to both of you."

He had forgotten to mention that four parents cheer from the sidelines at his Saturday soccer games but only two plan his birthday parties.

"If someone asked you, 'But where do you *live?*' what would you say to them?" I asked, a little alarmed at how different his life sounded from that of the typical nine-year-old. My son shot back a slightly quizzical look. "I tell them I live at my mom's and my dad's," he explained patiently. "I live with *both* of you." Even so, I responded, it might sound pretty confusing to other people. "It's *complicated,*" agreed Jamie, "but it's not confusing to *me.*"

I was relieved to see that Jamie had apparently worked things out to his own satisfaction. None of the experts can yet say if living in two homes is good or bad for children. Their preconceived notions about sharing custody are clear, however, when they call it a "social experiment." For conclusions, social scientists will have to wait until Jamie and thousands of other joint custody kids grow up. All any divorced parent has to go on now is how his or her child seems to be getting along. Jamie, I could see, knew that he still had a family, which happened to live in two different residences. After a period of developing a routine, he knew that he was supposed to ride home to his mother's house in the car pool on Mondays, Wednesdays and Fridays, and to catch the school bus home to his dad's on Tuesdays and Thursdays. This child who slept in the top *and* bottom bunk understood his life and its own peculiar rhythms. His good humor, his good grades, and his good friends told me that he felt little conflict and lots of love.

How does a family finally arrive at this arrangement? How does it set up such a three-ring circus? How does it make the circus run reasonably smoothly, so that the communication circuits between the two homes rarely blow out?

As I traveled around the United States recently, I asked those questions of many families sharing custody. What I learned from them was what I had experienced myself: you achieve organization by trial and error. As the other joint custody parents and I compared our triumphs and tragedies in running a two-household family, we kept coming back to a central theme: if only we'd known *then* what we know *now*, things would have been so much easier in the early days.

Setting Up a Shared Custody Household

"The first thing to remember," one joint custody mother told me, "is that there is no escaping it: the shared custody routine will be stressful in the beginning. Anything new takes getting used to, so when things blow up, put your energy into detecting *what* went wrong, not *who* went wrong."

In a two-household family, one of the major problems will be accountability. Children seem to know instinctively that it is more difficult for parents to keep track of things when they no longer live under the same roof. A first step might be for both parents to say to the children (together, or at separate times, if that feels more comfortable), "Look, it's going to be hard for Dad and me (or Mom and me) to keep track of everything, so we're going to need your help. You could probably get away with a lot in this kind of situation, but we don't think that would be good for you, so we need your cooperation to make shared custody work well for everybody." Involving the youngsters in the process of setting up the two-home system and securing the children's commitment to cooperate in that effort will help give the operation a good start.

Another important general guideline is that children are anxious, especially in the beginning, to know the specifics of the shared custody routine. As mentioned in earlier chapters, it is much easier for children as well as their parents to imagine what shared custody will be like if the youngsters can see it in black and white. A first step would be to make two Master Calendars, one for each house, with "Dad's" or "Mom's" written in each square, so the child has a clear idea of the schedule and any changes that have to be made as you go along. Go over each week's routine Sunday evening so the children can understand what is on their agenda, and encourage them to refer to the calendar themselves if they can't remember certain details. If grandparents, other relatives, or friends are also involved in the logistics of transporting children or have child-care responsibilities, a photocopy of each month's calendar should be given to them.

Once the basic daily routine has been worked out, the next step is to decide where—physically—the children will sleep in each home. In some cases this may simply involve a fold-out bed or even sleeping-bag space, but a room or area should be designated in both homes. Children need to know what is their "turf" and will settle into the regimen much more easily if they have a place of their own in each house. One joint custody father with severely restricted living space declared a convertible couch, a kitchen table and chair, and a bulletin board the exclusive province of his eleven-year-old. The child knew where he was to sleep and where he could do his homework undisturbed. Before long, his favorite rock 'n' roll posters went up on the bulletin board and a red plastic laundry basket became a storage bin for his schoolbooks and dictionary when he wasn't actually sitting at the kitchen table working.

Regardless of how lavish or how modest the two homes are, the commuting child needs to develop a sense that he or she belongs in *both* places. In addition to helping parents plan how a room or area will *look,* children who are old enough can be given an appropriate amount of responsibility for the care of their allotted space in each household. One California joint custody family paid the same amount of allowance in both households, with "payday" alternating in each home every week. For this "pay" the child's assigned chores were pretty much the same in both households: at one residence the eight-year-old had to make his bed every day he was there, pick up his clothes and toys, and feed the dog. At the other house his room duties were identical, and since there were no animals to take care of, he was responsible for sweeping the patio and taking out the garbage.

Nuts and Bolts Department

Clothing, Toys, Books, and Records

A joint custody stepmother once told me, laughing, of a local television news producer who wanted to do a feature on a family sharing custody. The producer asked if the TV crew could photograph her husband's children in both homes so the viewers could see what the routine was like. "The first thing this young producer—who was not married, by the way—suggested was that the crew film the children walking out of our house with their little suitcases in hand. Isn't that a riot?" she giggled. Well, it is and it isn't. Sadly, the perception of outsiders is that joint custody waifs have no real home, but are merely visitors at both places, hauling their few precious possessions around in a tattered satchel. For a family in the process of setting up two households, the first thing to do is to decide:

1. What items you need duplicates of
2. What items you divide between the two homes
3. What items go back and forth between the two homes

Items You Need to Duplicate

Old hands at sharing custody will tell you that you will need, at a minimum, duplicates of: toothbrushes; hairbrushes; certain toiletries; nightclothes; dictionaries, rulers, some school supplies; medicine for any chronic condition; socks.

Socks, I must mention here, can be the source of tremendous aggravation, even in intact households. The "Sock Fairy" seems to take great joy in stealing *one* of each style and color. In a joint custody household, missing socks can literally drive parents around the bend. One joint custody parent warns, "It's easy to get in fights with the other parent over stupid things like lost socks. One time I bought ten pairs of the damn things, and within two weeks only two pairs ended up at my house. It was so easy to blame the other parent." Her suggestion: each parent buys a lot of the *cheapest* socks available—all alike—at a discount store and then simply accepts the inevitability that most of them will be lost. "Just blame the Sock Fairy and have a good laugh," she counsels.

Items to Divide

A child's wardrobe can be apportioned in measure with how much time is spent in each residence. If a child owns six pairs of underwear and spends three days with Dad and four with Mom, you can divide them three-and-three and make Mom responsible for recycling one pair each week, or, divide them four-to-Mom and two-to-Dad and make Dad responsible for washing a pair in time for reuse. School clothes, play clothes, and shoes can be divvied up this way. For toys, books, and records, however, many parents let the children decide which objects stay where. In my son's case, I gave him a train set on Christmas, but it ended up being housed at his father's, where there is a playroom and a big table where the rig could stay assembled. His father once gave him a miniature plastic paratrooper with a real parachute attached, which worked much more dramatically from the top of the staircase at my house. Both his father and I had to realize that the toys belonged to our child, not to us, and that they should be headquartered where it made the most sense to the owner. After an initial gulp or two, we adults got past any feelings of being "betrayed."

Other things, like favorite dolls, drift back and forth. The child, however, needs to know he or she is responsible for the "drifters' " whereabouts. Unless there is a very convincing case to be made, parents will avoid a lot of arguing if they institute a "no doubling back," "no special trip" rule for forgotten toys and other paraphernalia. Naturally, the concept of responsibility must be introduced gradually and must be geared to the age level and capabilities of a child. But many parents report that after an initial period of adjustment, their commuting children appear to have gained maturity through the experience of learning to keep tabs on their own possessions.

Items That Go Back and Forth

In addition to cherished toys, transported between houses from time to time, there are other items that should be thought of as joint custody possessions.

Sporting equipment usually falls into this category, since soccer balls, Little League uniforms, and riding boots are simply too expensive for most families to duplicate. Musical instruments, bicycles, and house keys also can become sources of irritation unless members of both households learn to do a "mental countdown" on transition day. Some parents have found it helpful to jot down on the appropriate square of the Master Calendar such notations as "send flute" or "library books due." Says one parent with four years' experience sharing custody: "There is no total answer to the problem of keeping track of the minutiae. It's one of those occupational hazards of being a joint custody family ... but the pluses of our system add up to more for us and our kids than the minuses of misplaced notebooks and lost belts."

Part of the answer in making the logistics run smoothly is for both parents to anticipate what will be needed for children's lessons, activities, and events. For women, there is often the danger, as one mother explains it, "of becoming a rescuer. I always seem to be racing to the other house to fetch Charlie's only sports jacket from his father's or doubling back to pick up his saxophone before the band concert." One family, to cope with this problem, made a game out of having their eight-year-old, who had just learned to print clearly, write out her checklist. Before she went out the door, the parent in charge would read from her list and cry out, drill-sergeant style, "Bookbag?" and the little girl would answer "Check!"; "Brownie uniform?" . . . "Check! It's *in* my bookbag!"—and so on.

The Telephone

To make the most of the telephone as an instrument to improve communication in a two-household family, a couple of basic ground rules may help. As in a business, when two parents sharing custody call each other on the phone, the conversation should, in general, be restricted to the project at hand: making arrangements, adjusting the schedule, asking for information regarding the children, or disclosing information. If there has been some foul-up (which often happens in the first year or two of a new shared custody arrangement), a good way to start that conversation might be "Hi . . . let me tell you what's happening on my end . . ." rather than blasting the other parent with "Hey, you jerk, do you know what *you* just did?" Parents can find out when the most convenient times to call each other are and try to stick to that plan—except, of course, in an emergency.

Once the two households have been established, parents sharing custody told me over and over again, the best way to save each home tremendous aggravation is to give the telephone numbers of *both* parents to everyone important in the children's life: friends, relatives, scout leaders, coaches, school administrators, teachers, the music teacher, the Sunday school teacher. Also, be sure most of these people have the number for the children's pediatrician jotted down somewhere.

To get past the embarrassment some parents initially feel

about publicly acknowledging their divorce and their shared custody arrangement, a mother or father might use a simple statement: "I'd like to give you two telephone numbers where you can get hold of Johnny, his dad/mom, and me. If you don't get us at one number, feel free to try at the other." If you're beginning to feel comfortable about sharing custody, you might add, "Johnny's dad/mom and I have a pretty cordial shared custody arrangement, so feel free to call either one of us if you need to get in touch."

If a child's friends call while the child is at your former spouse's home, you can handle it obliquely ("Let me give you another number where I think you can reach him at the moment") or directly ("Johnny's at his dad's today . . . let me give you the number over there, but if you miss him, I'll tell him to call you right away").

Joint custody kids have told me that sometimes they have trouble remembering telephone numbers. One mother complained that her six-year-old daughter, who spent alternate weeks with the father, rarely called her just to say hi. "Her excuse was that she couldn't remember my number and didn't always like to ask her dad. I made her her own little private phone book, which she keeps in the front pouch of her bookbag. I put my number right on the first page and then added the telephone numbers of her grandmother, her piano teacher, and all her best friends. I even put her father's number in it so she wouldn't feel I was putting pressure on her just to call *me*." This mother also made it a practice to give out both home numbers "whenever I registered her for *anything!*"

Perhaps the best use of the phone parents sharing custody can make is to call each other when there is *good* news. "Just thought you'd like to know that our son got the top reading grade in his class—here, I'll let *him* tell you," a voice on the phone once said to me. It was my son's father, and that call marked a major turning point in our relationship as coparents. I realized that my former husband was now willing to share the good as well as the bad, the successes as well as the hassles, and it made me feel as if *I'd* gotten the highest grade in the class.

Another effective way of building trust between parents is to show some appreciation for the contributions the other parent is making toward raising a happy, healthy child. Also, sharing information about events the other parent is unable to attend can be an important gesture of goodwill. One mother called her former husband to describe how their sixteen-year-old daughter looked on prom night, when her first real date came to pick her up. "It could just as easily have been *me* who missed out seeing Heather float out the front door on her night-of-nights, and, as her parents, I felt we *both* deserved at least hearing about it," she said.

Pickups and Drop-offs

One of the greatest areas of conflict in any custody arrangement—sole or shared—is the process of picking up or dropping off children at the other parent's house. There is no magic formula to avoid friction, but some good basic ground rules are:

1. Be clear about time, day, and place.
2. Keep your end of the bargain.
3. Be fair about making schedule adjustments.

If animosity from the divorce still exists, making it difficult for two parents sharing custody to meet face-to-face, they can make arrangements over the phone and choose neutral territory for the drop-off and pickup spots: the child's school, his or her play group, a friend's house or a relative's. This is far preferable to the type of exchange one mother described to me: "My former husband still gets upset when he picks the children up at what he still considers to be 'his' home, even though we finally worked out our financial settlement. So he just pulls up to the curb and *honks!* If he has something to say to me, he does it through the kids. It drives me absolutely crazy. I can see the kids feel bad that he'll only come in the house if I'm not here."

At the other extreme, another mother complained that her former husband "never knocks. He walks right in to pick up the kids as if this were still his house. My second husband can't stand it!"

One family told me they rendezvous in the park or some other place that provokes no memories and where they can be pleasant and businesslike as the children shift. "But don't do what my husband does," urged one stepmother. "We pick up his daughter in the parking lot of a fast-food chain. The poor little thing gets out of one car and into the other and the parents never say a word."

Another family established a rule requiring the parent who is to have the child to *pick up* the child. This routine helps keep signals from getting crossed. Also, explained the joint custody father, "if my ex-wife doesn't arrive by the appointed hour to pick up our daughter and I have made plans, it's now understood by both of us that my daughter and I will go on our way and a later exchange will be arranged at *my* convenience."

Another source of potential conflict is the question of which parent is responsible for providing the meal that precedes the exchange. When drop-off or pickup times are discussed, parents should be clear about meals as well. One mother who cherishes not having to cook Sunday dinner anymore always tags her conversation with "So, the plan is, *you'll* have supper with the kids before you bring them back at eight?"

For parents who live long distances from each other, the most important consideration is that the children feel as secure as possible getting on and off buses, trains, or planes. One joint custody family told me they always print triplicates of itinerary, so that the youngster and both parents have exact travel times and phone numbers to call on both ends. A couple of dimes are taped to the information sheet that goes into the child's pocket before takeoff. And once the child arrives at her destination, the parent meeting her calls the other to confirm the child's safe arrival.

Even when commuting between two homes in the same neighborhood, some children need a period of time to adjust to each change of surroundings. As the shared custody routine becomes more familiar, most children will need less time to make the transition, but parents who notice that a child seems moody or sad should not jump to the conclusion that the other parent has done something negative. Allow the youngster the right to feel the emotions he or she is experiencing, even if that includes feeling sad about the absence of the other parent for a time. If children are supported at both ends of their commute by parents who accept their feelings and assure them they'll be seeing the other parent in the future, the anxiety created by the transitions will diminish and eventually disappear for most children.

In my own case, about a month after my son's father and I had established a true joint custody arrangement, I noticed that my normally cheerful four-year-old seemed depressed on Sunday evenings when he was brought back to my house. Like so many divorced parents, I went through a range of emotions: Jamie must love his father more than he loved me, since he was so blue when he arrived at my place; he probably had more fun with his father, who took him to the pony rides every week; his father was, no doubt, telling him I wasn't a good mother because I had a full-time career and kept him in nursery school till five o'clock every day; his father was, I suspected, telling Jamie how sad he felt living in an apartment instead of in our old house.

As I put Jamie to bed one Sunday evening, my suspicions seemed to be confirmed when he cried and asked why his daddy couldn't live with us. When I explained that Daddy and I would never live together again, he began to sob as if someone had died. When he finally calmed down and fell into an exhausted sleep, I remember walking downstairs, convinced that joint custody wasn't going to work after all.

Then one day on the way home from nursery school, I tried to find out what, *exactly,* was making Jamie so sad on Sunday nights. It is difficult interviewing a four-year-old, especially when you're afraid what the answers might be. What I discovered—finally—was bothering him had nothing to do with any "treachery" on the part of my former husband. Jamie, after considerable probing on my part, revealed that he felt sad when he came home on Sundays because "*we* all live in our house . . . me, you, Tony, Beowolf [our dog], and Pen-pen [our cat], and Daddy has no friends or animals at *his* apartment. He's all alone when I leave," he sniffled. "He doesn't have any fun if I'm not there."

As soon as I could get to a phone, I called Jamie's father. We both realized that my former husband was the only person who could convince Jamie that the child wasn't responsible for his father's happiness—or unhappiness. The next time Jamie went to his dad's, his father explained to him that, although he missed Jamie very much when he left the apartment to come back to my house, big people *like* being alone sometimes so they can do such enjoyable things as read, watch television programs that little kids wouldn't be interested in, or have friends over for dinner and go to movies and parties that Jamie wouldn't enjoy. He carefully reinforced the idea that Jamie didn't have to worry about him when he wasn't there; that life had good things in it apart from the wonderful time he spent with his son.

The change in Jamie was magical. The next time he marched upstairs after an early Sunday supper with his father he told me proudly, "Daddy's having a friend over tonight so he can beat him in backgammon!"

If transition days are causing you problems, do some objective investigating to see if you can discover *what* is causing the difficulty, rather than *who* might be causing it.

School and Homework

The absent parent in a sole custody arrangement often has little to do with the daily routine of his or her child's school activities, but parents sharing custody usually both want to be
informed of, and participate in, day-to-day activities. However,
one mother says, correctly, "A lot of things can fall through
the cracks if you're not careful. My son sprained his right arm
skateboarding, and I didn't find out about it till I went to the
weekly band concert and he wasn't there playing his tuba. I
wasn't so worried about band; I was worried about how he was
going to do his homework. Finals were in two weeks, but his
father just assumed one of the kids would tell me about the accident."

One way to prevent problems is to have a note put in the
child's file at school, advising that both parents share in the
care of the youngster and would like any notices or information pertaining to their child to be sent to *both*. Tell teachers
the same thing at the beginning of each school term. One family told me they schedule a conference with each child's teacher early in the fall and spring. If one parent can't attend, the
other takes along a tape recorder and tapes the meeting, ex-
plaining the situation to the teacher and asking for cooperation. "I told Kathy's teacher we were a joint custody family
and that both parents wanted to help with homework," said
the mother. "I couched what I said in terms of our wanting to
make *her* job easier. I'm sure she thought our living situation
was a little strange, but she seemed impressed that we both
wanted to participate." The mother gave the teacher both telephone numbers and told her to call either parent "or *both* if
there were any problems cropping up."

Many joint custody parents I talked to said they asked the
teacher for a typical week's schedule so both parents could anticipate when homework assignments were due. "My son was

getting his spelling assignment on Monday when he was with me," another mother told me, "and had to study for the test on Thursday night when he was with his father. It wasn't until we saw the C-minus on his report card that we realized he was getting away with murder." This family's answer was to tape a homework schedule to the refrigerator door at both houses, so parents *and* child knew what the teacher expected.

Long-term assignments pose other potential problems. The mother whose son got the C-minus in spelling now asks her child every week what book reports or science projects have been assigned. Then she puts a note to her former husband in her son's bookbag. It says something like "Hi . . . here's another Early Warning Signal: Jake has a book report due a week from this Thursday, during the time he's with you. I'll see that he starts reading his assignment this week at my house and send along the book. Will you follow through on your end? Thanks." These two parents are also underscoring to their son the need for *him* to keep tabs on his schoolwork, so that eventually he will learn to be totally responsible for completing what's expected of him at school. "In one term, once he knew his father and I were both concerned and involved, his study habits improved and his grades came up dramatically," she told me.

Extracurricular Activities

Parents sharing custody who want to participate in their children's extracurricular activities have three basic issues to deal with: logistics, available time, and the degree of comfort they feel when they're around each other.

Some old hands at sharing custody have no problem when both households applaud in the audience of a ballet recital or cheer from the sidelines at a Little League game. When the father or mother is called upon to explain the various relationships to other parents, an easy way to handle introductions is to be prepared with something like "Have you met my son's father, John Jones, and his wife, Jane? And I'd like you to meet *my* husband, Jack Smith."

Some parents, especially in the beginning of a shared custody arrangement, simply may not be ready to meet each other at the annual YMCA picnic or the school carnival. In these cases, it is probably a good idea to agree beforehand which parent will attend a specific function. If you can't agree or both feel strongly about attending, sometimes you can schedule your appearances for different times. It is important to remember that neither parent has an inalienable right to attend a particular event. One father was upset because his former wife had become a "team mother" for her son's soccer club. He told her she should quit because he believed *fathers* automatically were the ones to go to the sports activities of their sons. His former wife replied that she would be at every game—period—unless, of course, he was willing to bring cookies and orange juice every week, attend all practices at three-thirty after school, and call the parents of the other team members regarding important announcements. The father wasn't willing to commit to being a team parent and angrily stayed away from the Saturday games. As his son's soccer team began its march toward a championship, he couldn't stand not being there to see the games and began sneaking onto the field. By the end of the season, both parents were rooting for their youngster from opposite ends of the field, giving each other the thumbs-up sign whenever their son, the goalie, made a save.

Participation in extracurricular activities can also take root from one's natural inclinations. My son and I share a love of horseback riding, while his father, who was raised in the Bronx, wouldn't be caught dead on one of those beasts. The riding class I enrolled my son in met once a week, but at eight-thirty on Saturday mornings. Through his father's distinct lack of enthusiasm for this early-morning activity, it was clear to me that if I felt Jamie's riding lessons were important, I would have to be the one to drive him to the stable, even on the weekends he was at his dad's.

A year or so later, his class was switched to a later time, and his father and I began alternating responsibility for the driving. Still later, Jamie had reached a level of competence where we could take class together, and I took over the entire responsibility for chauffeuring to and from the activity. If his dad had consistently refused to participate in any aspect of the riding, I still would have been willing to assume all the driving, since I was the parent who was eager for my son to learn this skill and it wasn't a top priority for the other parent.

Holidays

The scheduling of plans for summer vacations and holidays often can cause problems. The secret of avoiding them, say many of the joint custody parents I talked to, is to get into the habit of thinking ahead. If you would like your child to go on the school's ski trip during the February semester break, or want to take the youngster back to visit Grandma in Michigan next summer, raise the subject early enough to discuss it thoroughly. And have specific dates in mind. Once you agree, write it on your calendar, even if it is scheduled months in advance. One mother told me, "My former husband actually called me in *January* to get my commitment about his taking the kids to Death Valley over the holidays the following December. It made my second husband, who hates to plan ahead, crazy, but at least I know when he's taking them, so eventually we'll make our plans with that in mind."

One of the best suggestions to combat the "holiday blues" that I heard came from a family who decided it wasn't necessary to celebrate a special occasion on the same day everyone else did. Scheduling became virtually impossible in their case because the wife's second husband shared *his* children with his former spouse. "We had double trouble," the wife complained.

"More often than not, we couldn't arrange to get all the kids home with us on the right day, so we actually celebrated Hanukkah, for instance, *one week* before everyone else did. We lit our last of the eight candles on the day the rest of the world was lighting the first, but it was the spirit of the thing that counted, we thought, and the kids accepted it easily. In fact," this parent told me proudly, "I think that the children put more true meaning into their holidays now than they did before."

Children's Birthdays

A child's birthday is the kind of holiday that can trigger major problems if a reasonable compromise isn't worked out. "The first year after we separated," one mother told me, "Robert and I tried to pretend Shawn's birthday was just like it had been the year before. We planned his party together, but it turned out to be a disaster. Robert announced the day before twelve kids were due to arrive at my house for a swimming party that he wouldn't come if David, a new man in my life, was going to be there. Shawn cried because he wanted both David and his dad at the party. I was ready to tear my hair out. Birthdays are supposed to be happy occasions," she complained bitterly.

If feelings between former spouses are still raw (and even if they're not), parents may want to take turns throwing the actual birthday party, or each be responsible for a separate part of it. One year my son's father had five youngsters over for pizza and cartoons; I picked them up later and they had a slumber party at my house. Another child I know had dinner with her mom on the actual day of her birthday, and her father took her and her closest friend to a movie and for ice cream on the following Saturday.

The critical factor is: How comfortable are the two former spouses in each other's company—and in the company of any "supporting players" who may be involved? If the answer is

"Not very," do yourself a favor and head off trouble by thinking over—*ahead of time*—what your options are. You probably have more than you realize.

Adult Dating

Not all schedules that must be planned concern the children.
What about the social lives of the adults? How can they best be
integrated into the routine?

"During the first year after the divorce," a joint custody
mother from New York told me, "my son, Jim, used to give
my dates the third degree when they'd come to the house to
pick me up. And there was hell to pay if a man was still there
for breakfast." Even with casual dates the situation became
horribly embarrassing "and a lot of the men—nice ones, too—
never came back. Jim became a pint-sized tyrant."

This mother decided to schedule most of her adult social life
on days when Jim was at his father's. "When he was with me, I
was with *him*. Until the cocustody routine became more a matter of course, I tried to focus my attention on Jim during the
times he was with me." Eventually, she reports, her son grew
to accept the reality of his parents' divorce and let his mother's
adult male friends "off the hot seat."

Compared with sole custody parents, joint custodians have
greater freedom to establish adult relationships without the
constant demands of children. They also have more privacy to
nurture those relationships, since the big question of "Should
he or she sleep over?" can be handled with tact and with the
option of utilizing those days when the children aren't home.

Fine-tuning the Daily Schedule

As parents go through the initial process of trying to put their
shared custody schedule into practice, there is simply no way
to anticipate the problems. However, parents should assume
that it probably will be necessary to adjust the schedule, at

least slightly, and try not to feel threatened if the other parent proposes some alterations.

The need for fine-tuning will be especially apparent for working parents. Time conflicts you never dreamed of may pop up once you start living as a two-household family. A spirit of cooperation and understanding (within limits) is necessary. There can actually be some rewards when one parent fills in for another, who, for instance, is suddenly sent out of town by the boss. The parent who has been a good scout can "bank" some time so that when something comes up later there is a baby-sitting "credit" on file. A father in the Midwest told me that is how he gets a week every year just to go off fishing by himself.

One woman told me that when a conflict arises and she can't be with the children, she first offers to trade time with her former husband before making any child-care arrangements. If her husband can't, or is unwilling to, change his schedule, then their agreement is that the parent wanting to make the change must be the one to make other arrangements.

Since children spend only part of their time with you when you're sharing custody, you have to make a strong effort to be with them when they are living at your home. If, when a child is with his father, his dad works late every night, and when he's at his mom's, his mother is taking classes at night school and dating a lot, that child has, in effect, lost both parents as a result of the divorce. "When my daughter is with me," one mother told me, "I schedule all my other activities around her comings and goings as much as I can." Instead of accepting an invitation to dinner at midweek, for example, "I'll make the extra effort and invite my date for drinks at my house at eight-thirty, and put my daughter to bed before I go out. I give her time to be with me after school and get used to the baby-sitter before I leave." Often, this woman told me, she offers to make a romantic supper at nine o'clock "and just stay home. I ask him to bring wine and dessert."

However, there are times when working parents can't be

home with their children as much as they might like. One tactic is to schedule their music lessons, sports activities, or scout functions at these times. Another is to enroll them in an after-school play group or a class at the "Y," or to arrange to have them play after school with a neighborhood friend and offer to reciprocate in some way on the weekends, rather than leave them with the baby-sitter frequently, or at home alone.

Occasionally those alternatives aren't available. One father I know couldn't afford to hire after-school help, had no near neighbors, and couldn't find a suitable after-school program that provided the children, aged nine and eleven, with transportation. The father explained to his youngsters that he had enough confidence in them to allow them to let themselves into the house after school, lock the doors, and spend the next two hours doing homework and playing quietly. The children were instructed, when strangers called, to say their mom or dad was taking a shower and would return the call, and they were told *never* to open the door to someone whose voice they didn't recognize. The children had their father's telephone number at work written next to the phone, as well as the numbers of a close family friend, the police, and the fire department. "I would feel better if I didn't have to do it this way," the father said, "but my kids have actually acquired a greater sense of responsibility for themselves and they help each other when they do their homework."

When Things Get Too Confusing

No matter how well-meaning coparents may be, there are times, as any long-term joint custody parent will testify, when everything seems to tangle up in a perfectly dreadful mess. When this happens, one mother told me, "I give my kids an opportunity to tell me what *they* think went wrong and I give them my view. They tell me about their confusion and I tell them about mine. I let them and their father know that I don't think that what we're trying to do is so easy, either, and I say,

'Let's see what we can do to make things better.' Sometimes I can't think of a solution, and, lo and behold, the kids themselves come up with an answer."

When problems start piling up, she suggests, "Freeze frame. Sometimes I just yell, '*Stop!*' I slow everything down for a while and get the facts about what seems to be going wrong. We try to scale things down immediately and we don't plan anything additional in our lives. Sometimes we subtract a few activities from our routine or simplify the schedule for a while until the whirlwind subsides."

Periodic Conferences

Even when a shared custody situation is working smoothly, many coparents try to plan periodic conferences to review various areas of their own lives and their children's. These get-togethers—whether in person or on the telephone—don't have to be rigidly scheduled, but, from time to time, one parent or the other might initiate an appointment to compare notes. These meetings should be businesslike and stay focused on a fairly precise agenda. One parent might say, for instance, "When you have some time, I'd like us to talk about what we could do about getting Melissa to wear her retainer at night. The dentist told me her teeth aren't improving as rapidly as they should. While we're at it, are you ready yet to discuss summer plans? I heard about a terrific day camp and I'd like you to see the literature." These periodic reviews and planning sessions can be a way of troubleshooting situations that, if left alone, can cause problems later on.

Learning to talk to a former spouse in nonjudgmental, neutral, information-sharing ways is rather like learning a foreign language. This is particularly true if the parents had great difficulty communicating during their marriage. But the language of shared custody *can* be learned, and you, too, can join the ranks of parents who are learning the art of Win-Win Negotiating.

Chapter 12
The Shared Custody Game

Win-Win Negotiating

Sally and Gerry across the bargaining table. How family discussions can go haywire. Mock negotiations and picking an issue. Tricks of the trade from labor negotiators and diplomats. Blocks to good communication between former spouses—and how to leap over them. Negotiating skills made easy. Prepare to meet thy former spouse.

Ten divorced parents watched attentively as a man and woman faced each other in the middle of the room. The woman's lips had tightened into a straight line; the man's hands clenched the arms of his chair. Her face was flushed; his voice had grown louder and more hard-edged. Only minutes earlier, the two had been chatting amiably during a coffee break in their shared custody workshop. Now they seemed on the verge of a tense argument.

The pair were only pretending to negotiate, but the problem was real—and so were their emotions. Sally Matson (not her real name), a music teacher, had come to the workshop with this dilemma: her former husband was a professional singer, and she wanted him to spend time helping their daughter practice the piano, a responsibility he was reluctant to take on. At the workshop, she was trying to deal with this reluctance, as a man named Gerry played the role of her husband. Gerry responded as Sally had instructed him to: he flatly refused to go along with Sally's request, complaining that she was always trying to control him and dictate how he should spend time with Janie, the daughter, when the child was with him.

As their debate heated, Gerry and Sally seemed to have forgotten the other workshop members. Gerry, as the "father," was actually getting angry. "I don't send her back to *you* and say, 'Okay, before I see Janie again, I want her to do this and this and this!' " he snapped. "I don't see why you should always be telling me how *I'm* supposed to spend my time with her!"

Sally, who clearly had had the same argument with her real ex-husband many times, rolled her eyes and sighed. "You have a piano at your house, and I can't *afford* one at mine," she said. "It would be easy for Janie to spend time practicing at your place, but you don't seem to care very much about her or her music, do you?"

As Gerry opened his mouth to answer, a voice from the side of the room shouted, "*Stop! Freeze frame!*" Simone Katz-Savlov, a family therapist and my partner in a workshop called Custody Options for Divorcing Parents, walked to the center of the room. Looking at Gerry and Sally, she smiled. "You can go back to your corners. You were wonderful!" The rest of the class relaxed.

The assignment had been for each member of the class to tell about a *minor* issue of contention with his or her former spouse. One man and one woman in the group actually had been married to each other; the others, including Sally and Gerry, were attending the shared custody class without their previous mates. Simone, their leader, had asked them to pick the smallest, least significant issue they could think of. One class member chose "picking Joey up on time." Another selected "not letting the children watch TV all Saturday morning." Simone had cautioned the class that parents sharing custody must start with a simple issue in order to prepare and practice as negotiators. "If you start with the big issues before you're ready, you'll lose."

Now Simone asked the group, "Okay ... what did you all pick up about how this couple went wrong in their negotiation? How could they have handled the issue of Sally's daughter practicing the piano at her father's differently? What did you think of the *language* they used?"

As the group began to analyze the argument between Sally and Gerry, Simone and I pointed out that divorced couples with children are called upon to resolve issues every day, using the same bargaining techniques as labor relations experts and foreign diplomats. The common blocks to good communication between divorced spouses are similar to those in labor and diplomatic negotiations: unwillingness to listen to what the other side has to say; false information; inaccurate assumptions; attacks on one another; and introduction of side issues to diffuse the focus as to what the negotiation is actually about. "Former spouses have to learn to get *past* these blocks," Simone told the class. "If they don't, it will be just as difficult to put a successful cocustody relationship into practice as it is to achieve an acceptable disarmament agreement or hammer out a labor-management pact in the auto industry."

We advised the workshop participants that as parents sharing custody they would have to learn a new language and a new way of listening if they were ever to negotiate successfully with their former spouses. "You'll have to know very clearly what you want and be able to express it," I cautioned them from seven years' experience as a joint custody parent, "and you're going to have to be able to figure out what, *exactly,* the other side wants. You'll have to act like reporters—get the *facts,* because assumptions are the enemy in any negotiation."

Simone emphasized that the workshop members might *think* they knew what their former spouses wanted, but because there might be some unhappy history between them, that "old baggage" might distort their perception of what they thought the other person wanted. "Before coming to any conclusions about what the other parent wants, you have to check it out," said Simone.

Nodding at Sally, who had taken her seat in the group again, Simone noted that Sally had never told her ex-husband whether she wanted him to spend ten minutes or three hours a weekend supervising their daughter's piano practicing. "What did you have in mind?" Simone asked.

Sally looked startled. "Well, I was only thinking in terms of ten or fifteen minutes of actual supervision."

Gerry, her workshop partner, blinked in surprise. "Gee, I figured you expected me to take at least an hour with her at the piano on Saturdays, and since you told me she is with her daddy only two weekends a month, that pissed me off."

Simone nodded. "No wonder your negotiations didn't get very far. The transmission of information got garbled right from the start because Sally didn't make her desires known clearly enough and Gerry didn't check out his assumptions as to what Sally did, in fact, want from him."

The first rule of negotiating with another parent, we explained, is to be clear about what you want and to be sure the other side understands what you're asking for. You must constantly check out what you *think* you're hearing. The next step is to learn to use words that avoid "pushing people's buttons." "Who knows better than an ex-spouse where those buttons are?" Simone joked. We began to itemize the kinds of words and phrases that are guaranteed to cause friction.

Overgeneralizing Statements

Example: "You're *always* telling me how I should spend my time with Janie!"

Most likely Sally, as our example, has not "always"—*every single time* she has ever talked to her husband—told him how he should spend every minute of his time with their daughter. Overgeneralizations exaggerate and irritate. Gerry could have told her frankly that he didn't like feeling she was scheduling his limited time with Janie. He could have confined his disagreement to *this* particular request at *this* particular time regarding *this* particular activity. "Gerry could have made his complaint specific, restricting it to the manageable proportions of the piano-practicing issue," said Simone. "By using the word 'always,' he escalated the issue far beyond the piano, to what was probably a basic problem in the marriage: Who is manipulating whom? Sally wasn't prepared to defend herself on that one, and so she retaliated with a put-down of her own."

Put-down Statements and Questions

Example: "You don't seem to care very much about her or her music, do you?"

This is the kind of question that is not asked to gain information, but rather to communicate indirectly how dissatisfied Sally is with her former husband's performance as a parent. There is no way a person can answer a question that is, in reality, a blaming statement. Instead, Sally could have stayed focused on the need for Janie to practice the piano. She could have said something like "This problem of Janie's practicing really concerns me. She loves music, but she seems to be the kind of kid who needs more structure. I was thinking that fifteen minutes of practicing when she's with you, since you have a piano, might go a long way in terms of her learning that kind of self-discipline." Sally would have expressed her concerns without demeaning her daughter's father and his role as parent, and would have given him the room to respond to her request—not to her blaming attitude.

Closed-ended Statements

Examples: "I don't want to talk about it anymore!" or "This is a perfectly pointless discussion!"

These kinds of statements cut off communication in order to avoid unpleasant feelings *without* providing a time to continue the discussion when tempers have cooled. When parents are tempted to close off a discussion that seems to be getting nowhere, they could substitute a simple statement as to why they'd like to call a "time-out": "I think I'm getting as frustrated as you must be about the fact we're having such trouble resolving this. Let's stop for now, but how about tackling this again next week, when we've both had some more time to think about it?" *Buy time* until both sides are ready to address the problem on another day. Keep doors open when you negotiate with the other parent because undoubtedly there will come another day when you *have* to sit down with this person to discuss other important issues regarding your mutual children.

Long Statements and Lectures

Most parents react negatively to the feeling they are being harangued as if *they* were the children. "Finger-wagging" lectures do nothing to bring about understanding of the other person's position, but instead bring to mind the overbearing parents we as adults thought we had escaped. The person receiving the lecture becomes totally frustrated in any attempt to resolve the issue at hand and usually gives up, grows angry, and shuts down negotiations. Say what you have to say as succinctly as possible and then give the other side a chance to respond. If you really try to *hear* what the other person is trying to tell you, you may discover information that you weren't aware of before, and this could speed a resolution to your problem.

Judging Statements

Examples: "You don't care about anybody but yourself!" or "You're just being selfish!"

When you pronounce judgment, it means you are placing responsibility—and often blame—on someone or something other than yourself. "You" statements (judging statements) merely shift your feelings about a problem onto the other parent without disclosing anything about how you feel except your dissatisfaction with the former spouse's behavior—a reaction not calculated to motivate any change in that behavior. "You" statements merely say, in effect, that the *other* person is bad. If your pronouncements aren't completely accurate, the other person stands unjustly accused and, understandably, becomes angry. Angry people have trouble negotiating solutions they can live with. A good negotiator takes responsibility for how he or she feels about a particular issue rather than resorting to blaming the other person for how he or she feels. Thus, on the issue of her daughter's musical education, Sally might have said, "I'm worried that Janie isn't getting the guidance she needs in practicing the piano, and yet I don't want to be the only parent keeping tabs on her practicing."

"Should" Statements

Example: "You should be more aware of how badly Janie plays the piano if you really care about your daughter."

"Should" statements imply that one parent knows what's right or wrong about an issue—which can be highly irritating if you are the other parent. "Shoulds" often stir up feelings left over from childhood, when your parents said you *should* eat your carrots and *should* be more considerate of your elders and *should* send thank-you notes. No one enjoys being told what he or she "should" be doing. Often, the person lectured is motivated only to do the exact opposite of what is being urged. Again, take responsibility for what you'd like to see happen. Sally might have said, "I'd like to find some way both of us could set some standards about how much time Janie practices the piano. I was thinking around fifteen minutes on the weekend might make sense." ("I" statements communicate clearly.)

Contaminating Statements

Negotiations between two former spouses over an issue concerning the children can often get sidetracked when unrelated problems are dragged into the discussion. If one parent wants to talk about vacation schedules and the other says he or she can't afford a vacation on the paltry sum provided for child support, the discussion will go nowhere. One way to avoid bringing "everything but the kitchen sink" into these sessions is to be ready with something like "Child support is not the issue we're talking about right now; we're trying to set up vacation schedules. Let's plan to talk about child support at another time—how about the beginning of next month?" If someone is trying to contaminate, you have to bring him or her back to the issue at hand and offer some relief by agreeing to tackle the unrelated issue at another time.

Counterattack Statements

Example: SPOUSE 1: "I'm anxious to try to set up some guidelines as to how much TV we let the kids watch."

SPOUSE 2: "*You* should talk ... how about setting up some guidelines for picking your kids up on time *just once!*"

Often when one parent brings up a specific issue to discuss, the other parent will feel defensive and launch a counterattack.

Like the person who contaminates with other issues, the parent who has been hit with a counterattack has a difficult time trying to stay focused on the original issue and usually shifts to defend himself or herself from the counteroffensive. One way to respond to a counterattack is to acknowledge that the other parent sounds angry about the second issue and agree that you'll talk about it at another time *if* the counterattacker will concentrate on the original subject. It requires supreme self-discipline not to respond to such provocation, but it helps to remember that your main goal is to resolve the issue *you* brought up first.

Past-History Statements

One of the easiest ways to "push the buttons" on a former spouse is to bring up disagreements from the past in an attempt to prove how impossible you think the person is being in the present. When parents are having trouble resolving an issue, one will often say in exasperation, "We've gone over this a million times before and you *never* admit you're late. Remember the time you were four hours overdue last summer and you never called me to let me know? I missed picking my mother up at the airport and we never did find her garment bag!"

If lateness is an issue, make it an issue *in the present.* When a former spouse is constantly unreliable about time, you can use "disclosure" to get across how it affects you: "I have a hard time coordinating my life when you bring the kids home after the time we agreed upon. It is especially tough those times you don't call. Can we agree we will both stick to the time schedule we've worked out and that we'll call each other when there's an unavoidable problem?" State how you feel about a problem and tell the other person clearly what you would like to have happen in order to fix things.

Use of the Behavior of Others to Excuse One's Own Actions

Example: SPOUSE 1: "Well, every other kid in his class gets to play with guns. Why are *you* such a stick-in-the mud?"

SPOUSE 2: "Only macho warmongers like you and your hunting cronies let their kids near guns. Decent parents like Ruth and Bill wouldn't dream of it."

Many people try to justify their own decisions or opinions by pointing to "the Joneses." If parents are debating whether or not to allow their children to play with guns, for instance, communication stops when they introduce the behavior of outsiders in order to strengthen their positions. Quoting other people's actions is often an attempt to demean the position of one parent and gives that person very little room to maneuver—effectively putting an end to any meaningful discussion of the issue.

Direct and Indirect Criticism (Nagging)

Criticism of the other parent's style of caring for children can quickly destroy whatever fragile trust has been built up between two divorced parents. Typical of this style would be "I don't know why you always buy Johnny so many of those cheap toys that are advertised on TV. Don't you know they break as soon as he gets 'em? He's never going to learn the value of a dollar. Don't you want him to be responsible when he grows up?" Etc., etc., etc. While it may be very true that Johnny has been indulged with TV toys by your former spouse, and that you are concerned about the child's lack of respect for his playthings, try not to nag. Just say clearly that you're concerned about how Johnny seems not to appreciate his toys and describe how he is constantly whining for more because he sees them advertised on TV without understanding they tend to be cheaply made. Rather than merely blaming the other parent, a good negotiator would propose some sort of reasonable limit on the number of toys that each of them would buy for their child.

Accusations

Example: "You always bring this up just to start a fight. You don't care about our child; you're just using this to get back at me!"

     The accusation is like the counterattack, but with the "personal touch" whereby one parent accuses the other of deliberate sabotage and conveys the obvious conclusion that the other parent is bad, bad, bad. The accusation is often used to fend off debating something unpleasant while getting in one's own licks for good measure. Instead of accusing the other party of bad faith (even if you have good cause to suspect it), stick to the issue at hand and keep focused on *it* rather than on the other spouse's shortcomings.

The Amateur Shrink

Example: "You're just saying that because you think *your* parents neglected you when, in fact, you were really treated like a spoiled brat!"

     Some put-downs of one parent by the other are bone-crushers; others can be fairly subtle. Either way, the Amateur Shrink tries to gain the upper hand by appearing to know more about you than you do about yourself. If your ex-spouse, for instance, claims to be disturbed because the children spend so much time with the baby-sitter, forget trying to psychoanalyze his or her *motives* for making such a statement; rather, attempt to see if what he or she is telling you has validity *on its own merits,* in terms of the welfare of the child.

Tit-for-Tat Threats

Example:　"If you *ever* don't call me to say you'll be late bringing the kids home, I'll move so far away you'll *never* see them again!"

Some parents are masters at tit-for-tat threats. They don't discuss a conflict, they merely up the ante. Good negotiators can show something has made them angry, but tit-for-tat escalation leads straight to the courthouse and is to be avoided. As any negotiator knows, bringing out the heavy artillery at inappropriate times leads to full-scale warfare. Instead, state precisely what made you angry and then ask for specific remedial action.

Playing the Victim

Example:　"You're always trying to control me and make me feel guilty about not doing things your way."

Some parents fall into the role of victim, rarely asking directly for what they want. They complain that their former spouses aren't fair or treat them badly. They have a long list of all the terrible things the other parent does to them. To get out of the habit of being victimized, you must stand up for what action you think is best and not worry about wanting your ex's approval. State clearly what you are and are not willing to do about a particular situation: "I don't like being told what I should be doing with my daughter during my weekends with her, but I am willing to spend fifteen to twenty minutes with her, supervising her piano practicing."

Sneak Attacks

Example:　"You have a piano but I can't afford one. It would be so easy for you to practice with Janie."

Many parents are experts at the sneak attack, in which they *imply* the former spouse has failed miserably in his or her responsibility as a good parent. Sneak attacks practiced in front of the children can be especially harmful to the negotiating climate and to the youngsters themselves. One little boy once told his counselor, "Whenever my mom says something bad about my dad, it feels like an arrow that she shot at him that goes right through me."

Discounting the Other Parent

Example: "Look, you jerk, I don't agree with anything you've said. We're not married anymore, so shut up and buzz off!"

Perhaps the most damaging conflicts come when one parent closes down all communication by telling the other that, in effect, he or she doesn't exist anymore. A statement like "I never want to discuss anything with you ever again, you idiot!" leaves the other parent with absolutely nowhere to go. Someone who tries to eradicate the other parent may win the argument but lose all chance of giving the children a cooperative, nurturing atmosphere in which to grow up.

Tricks of the Trade

By offering these specific examples of good and bad communication between parents, Simone Katz-Savlov and I hoped the class could see how easily the circuits between ex-spouses could get jammed. The hostile "dumping" phrases that come from two adults who presumably once loved each other stem from residual anger, frustration, grief, and loss. Some couples never get past this phase, but continue their emotional involvement as former lovers, almost the way addicts stay hooked on heroin. Therapist and author Isolini Ricci calls these people "hostility junkies." Their need to stay connected in destructive ways overshadows their need to get on with their lives as individuals and parents. They find some payoff in staying hooked as a victim, or attacker, or nag, or blamer, and continue to be "married" to the ashes of their old destructive relationship.

To reduce the tension both in their children's lives and in their own, couples must bargain with each other as two adults trying to resolve problems in behalf of their mutual children. Most commonly, communication circuits jam because parents forget to follow the rules of negotiation or because there has been some basic misunderstanding. These problems are relatively easy to remedy if each parent strives to give information and ask for it in an accurate and neutral fashion. For example, a good negotiator who sees his or her child walk into the house with another cheap TV toy after both parents agreed to cut back on presents should ask in a nonjudgmental voice *how* the child got the toy before coming to the conclusion the other parent has welshed on the bargain. After all, the youngster could have traded his dump truck and seventeen baseball cards for the toy of a kid down the block.

Sometimes parents who are in the process of setting up a shared custody arrangement and detaching themselves emotionally from each other still get hooked into rerunning old arguments. This is known as "hooking" because former spouses know just where to catch each other in the most vulnerable places. When one parent is feeling angry or sad, he or she can lash out with a verbal punch—a kind of emotional left hook—bound to find its mark. "You always play the martyr" is a classic way to hook a former spouse who has actually been making an effort to stop playing the victim.

At one of our workshops, a man said that it felt to him as if he were "taking a course at Berlitz. If my wife suddenly heard me talking in this strange jargon, she'd think I was pretty weird. She'd say I was just trying to manipulate her." It was true: communication techniques could be used to control the other spouse.

"You can't just parrot what we've told you here tonight,"

said Simone. "You've got to make the key phrases and concepts your own by putting them into your own words. It *is* rather like translating to English from a foreign tongue, but once you become fluent in your *own* style of negotiating, you'll be able to communicate better."

We asked the class to take out notebooks and label a page "Negotiating Skills for Conflict Resolution—A Summary." Then we asked them to write down the following headings:

Stay focused. Once you identify the issue that needs to be discussed, keep to that issue until it's resolved, and avoid bringing up other subjects. Be precise about what you are thinking, wanting, or feeling.

Ask for information in a neutral fashion. Monitor yourself and the other parent before coming to any conclusions about the facts. Don't guess the facts; *get* the facts. Act like a newspaper reporter and ask questions *as if you had no idea what the answers might be.* Don't make assumptions or try to read the mind of the other parent. If you want to elicit an opinion, start with the question: "What is your feeling about so-and-so?"

Disclose information accurately. If you are asked a question, don't embellish or exaggerate. Avoid out-and-out distortion. Avoid words like "always" and "never." Use sentences that start with "I feel, I like, I don't like, I think, I don't think" rather than "you seem, you feel, you like, you don't like, you think, you don't think," and so forth. Let the other parent speak for himself or herself. Don't put words in other people's mouths.

Listen actively. Really listening to what the other person says is a well-known communication technique and is especially helpful during discussions between former spouses. Rather than allowing the other parent to get half a sentence out and then interrupting with a "yes, but," let the *entire* sentence get out and *listen* for clues to the meaning *behind* the words. When discussing whether a child is ready to go to summer camp, one parent might say, "Don't you think a month is a long time for an eight-year-old to be away from home?" An active listener might pick up on the possibility that a month sounds like a long time for the *parent* to be separated from the eight-year-old. Constantly evaluate what you are hearing. You can do this by restating what you think the other person said. Continuing our example, you could ask, "Does four weeks of camp seem like a long time for you and Jamie to be away from each other?"

Be alert to nonverbal communication. Look for cues and clues as to what may be behind the words by listening to the *voice tones* of the other parent. Check to see whether your former spouse's hands are clenched or relaxed. Watch facial expressions and note the speed of breathing. Being able to read a former spouse's body language is a necessary skill in good negotiating. It is also a skill that can tell you when to keep talking, when to stop, and when to put things on "hold" for a while.

Time the negotiations. Be sure you know what has been going on in the recent past before you decide to negotiate a major issue like changing the coparenting schedule or talking about summer plans. Try to be aware if your former mate has just been fired, lost a lover, contracted a disease, or been through a death in the family. Negotiations between former spouses succeed best when both sides are feeling reasonably fit. At a minimum, try to hold your negotiations when you are feeling good about yourself and when there is enough time to permit a full discussion of what you want to talk about.

Summarize and validate. In the early minutes of a negotiation, try to find something the other parent is saying that you can agree with. Even if you think the other parent is making some fairly outrageous statements, you can always respond with something like "I can understand how you might think that, but for my part, I think that ..." When it appears you and your ex-spouse have come to a tentative agreement, it helps to summarize where you both are on an issue. You can say, as an example, "I guess we both want to spend about the same amount of time with the kids this summer. Perhaps I could take them in June and you have them in July if your boss okays your time off. Does that sound about right to you?" And before you finalize a negotiation, be sure you both understand—and agree out loud—to the deal.

Parents who share custody and who have long-term experience in dealing with their former spouses have learned to speak the language of negotiation as a way of getting through the shared chores of everyday child-rearing. A major key to their success seems to be *understanding the motivation of the other parent.* Once you have some awareness of what your former spouse really wants, it will be easier for you to negotiate for what *you* want and what you think is in the best interests of your child.

In working with parents who share custody of their children, Simone Katz-Savlov and I jokingly began to develop a cast of characters we call the Seven Species of Spouses. Although no person fits a particular category precisely, the negotiating methods used by various individuals can be classified into general groupings. The next chapter may help you determine which negotiating profile comes closest to describing you and your former mate, and, once you see how those styles affect your negotiations, show you how to put that information to work to improve your relationship as parents sharing custody.

Chapter 13
Seven Species of Spouses
Pick a Profile

Know who is sitting across that bargaining table: Despotic Dads/Moms. Make-Nice Mamas/Papas. Phantom Fathers/ Mothers. Earth Mothers/Fathers. Passive Papas/Mamas. Saboteur Spouses. Straight-Shooter Spouses. Changing your negotiating style. Using visualization to become a better negotiator. Basic principles to keep in mind.

Despotic Dads/Moms

These types tend to want to be controllers, and act as if they must always have their own way. They have a difficult time tolerating people—and especially ex-spouses—who think and act differently from themselves. They have an exaggerated respect for authority and insist on laying down the law, even in other people's houses. They won't hesitate to use intimidation to get what they want. Threats are the mainstay of their aggressive arsenal.

Negotiating with this type of former spouse requires great control on your end. You will have to acknowledge when the Despotic Dad or Mom has a good idea and does something well with regard to the children. In fact, give credit whenever possible to this person in order to build his or her respect for you as a coparent. As you probably learned in your marriage to a Despot, this type's strong suit is intimidation. You can't fake being prepared when dealing with the Despotic Dad or Mom, and, frankly, this type does not make a very congenial coparent.

Make-Nice Mamas/Papas

These ex-spouses will never give you a straight answer. They can't stand conflict, so, rather than give you some bad news, they gloss things over, leading you to believe they will deliver the goods, when often they won't. They're the type that, when you ask, "Can you pick up the children by nine-fifteen, please? I have to get to a class by ten o'clock," will say, "Oh, sure, probably," and slide into your driveway forty-five minutes late. Make-Nice Mamas and Papas will do anything to avoid having an out-and-out fight and will try to appease you with tales of all the terrible things that befell them on the way to trying to get to your house on time. They are experts at making you feel guilty for putting so many impossible demands on them and at making you responsible for their problems, since life has a way of victimizing people who fit this profile. Since they always have a good excuse (and you buy it), you might end up carrying most of the burden with regard to the children's needs.

One possible way of negotiating with them is to be sure you both understand very clearly what the issues are and the mechanics of how things are to be managed. Make-Nice types need approval desperately, so give it to them whenever you can. Written lists and breezy notes detailing very specifically who-does-what may be helpful with Make-Nice Mamas and Papas, so there simply won't be room for excuses like "I didn't *realize* you expected to have Johnny with you on Father's Day/Mother's Day."

This species of spouse does not respond well to harangues and long lectures about how irresponsibly they've behaved.

Your best bet is to focus *solely* on the needs of your mutual children and not on what is fair and reasonable behavior on the part of the adults.

Phantom Fathers/Mothers

If your ex-spouse fits this profile, you're in trouble. This type avoids nearly *all* responsibility, including caring in a practical way for the children. Parents who are rarely involved with their children and refuse to take on active parenting roles see only their adult needs and wants and are unable or unwilling to perceive that what their children want and need may be different. Some Phantoms, however, are absent parents because their ex-spouses have made life so miserable for them that they can't bear being involved, even if it means giving up the children. Some fear that the ongoing parental conflict puts their children in an equally painful position, and so, in a form of misguided sacrifice, they fade into the distance.

It is important to analyze which kind of Phantom you're dealing with, and that will require some degree of self-examination on your part. The self-centered Phantom is the hardest type for a willing coparent to handle. These types have to be shown that it is in *their* interest to pay attention to their children; that they are needed as role models, as providers for their youngsters, as *alternatives* to what *you* can offer the children. They need to see that if they don't cooperate they may be burdened with problem children later on. Sometimes, persuading a Phantom to stay involved as a parent requires taking a very tough stance—and you still may not win. One wife formerly married to a Phantom was awarded extra support from a judge who recognized that she was overburdened. The judge announced in court that the mother needed some time away from home and children and job and ordered the Phantom Father to pay more child support so she could hire a baby-sitter on each day the father didn't show up to take the kids.

Earth Mothers/Fathers

This is another variety of despotic, controlling spouse, only he or she appears to be the nicest person in the world—baking cookies, driving the car pool, or taking the entire scout troop on a fishing trip. The trouble is, these folks are often very manipulative and they use their "devotion" to the children to try to gain the upper hand with both the youngsters and the other parent. Their absolute "goodness" somehow emphasizes your "badness"—or, at least, your glaring shortcomings as a parent in comparison to their total absorption in your mutual children. Watch out if your former spouse fits this negotiating profile. Earth Mamas and Papas can be crafty. They give the appearance of being empathetic to your position and the needs of their children, but often they have their *own* needs and desires uppermost in mind.

Perhaps the most effective way to deal with a manipulative former spouse is simply to refuse to be manipulated. Let him or her run ragged being the Perfect Parent. Don't try to prove to these types how good you are; they'll always be better. When it *is* your turn to do something, be sure to do it—or you'll never hear the end of it—and do it on time. Don't expect to get much applause from this type of former mate—after all, he or she is perfect, right? Be sure you've let an Earth Father or Mother know that you've considered his or her needs and the needs of the children and then firmly state your own. Whenever you can, praise them as parents, and while you're at it, give yourself a pat on the back; you won't get it from many Earth Mothers or Fathers.

Passive Papas/Mamas

These are a combination of Make-Nice types and defeated Phantoms who tend to be victimized by their former spouses.

They could also be called Doormat Daddies or Doormat Moms, because they get rolled over constantly by their more aggressive ex-spouses. Their hearts are in the right place, but they are often consumed by self-pity. Behind their "poor me" exterior, Passive Papas and Mamas can be very angry about what is going on in their lives but they show their hostility only in *indirect* ways—like "forgetting" to send the support check, or not signing important documents on time.

As parents, they often imply what an uncaring person *you* are toward them and the children, but they rarely state what's bothering them.

As a former mate of a Passive Papa or Mama, you must avoid feeling responsible for all of that person's problems. You must keep some psychological distance and try not to expect much mutual respect or support. In making plans with a parent who fits this profile, a direct, practical approach is best. Transact your business quickly by laying out the options first and checking back briefly for a response. This type of negotiator does not disclose things easily and is not a "schmoozer." In fact, Passives will rarely express their emotions, so you're unlikely to get clues from their facial expressions or body language. However, Passives can be *scared* into action. If negotiations are stalled, shift gears suddenly with a totally new proposal and the Passive Papa or Mama may suddenly respond to your original offer.

Saboteur Spouses

These can be worse than Despots because they always seem to have a "hidden agenda": revenge against anyone they feel has hurt them. Saboteurs usually have very low self-esteem and will go to almost any sneaky lengths to pay back real or imagined slights. As with the Phantom spouse who refuses to take responsibility for a child's need to experience two parents, the Saboteur may be bent on depriving the children of one parent—and that parent is you. A Saboteur can't see that the need to hurt a previous mate is separate from the children's needs to have a loving relationship with the parent the Saboteur is trying to exclude.

The best antidote for Saboteurs is to support any effort they make toward building their sense of self-esteem. It's not possible, nor is it a former spouse's responsibility, to create a feeling of self-worth in the other parent, but you could be encouraging if he or she is going back to school, starting a new job, or exploring a new relationship. Once the ordinary Saboteur feels better about himself or herself, the urge to make the former spouse unhappy usually diminishes.

It is wise to *keep quiet* about your own successes and be prudent about revealing new relationships with anyone who fits the profile of a Saboteur. This is especially true immediately following separation and perhaps for a year or so after the divorce. If the Saboteur is trying to wreck your relationship with your children, sit down with your youngsters privately. Tell them you love them and want to be with them and that you know the other parent is feeling sad about the divorce. Tell them you hope the other parent will feel better soon, but that *you* will always be their parent, regardless of your former spouse's attitude about you.

When you deal directly with the Saboteur, be ready for the attack and try to stay focused on whatever it is you're negotiating regarding the children. Check out your own sense of self-esteem before sitting down at the bargaining table and pick a time when you are feeling really good about yourself.

Straight-Shooter Spouses

These are dreams because they can tolerate *your* coming out of the divorce all right for the sake of the children you had together. In fact, even if *you* do well in a negotiation, they have enough self-esteem so that they don't feel *they* have lost. The Straight-Shooter Spouse has severed all the links with you that existed in the marriage *except* the parental link, so that together you can do what has to be done to provide physically and emotionally for your youngsters.

Straight-Shooters tell you what's on their mind and try not to offer unwanted advice or to render judgments on your behavior. They will be clear with you as to how much to expect, as to how far they will go on a particular issue. Straight-Shooters are not afraid to confront issues openly. They feel good enough about themselves to allow you to maintain your dignity during a disagreement. They can share your child with you because they don't feel deprived. They are aware of their personal needs and attend to them, and they understand that your needs—or the children's—may be different. They make excellent coparents.

Negotiating in "Real Life"

When one man I know (I'll call him Stanley Roberts) first began to share custody, he would have categorized himself as a cross between an Earth Father in his dealings with his children and a Passive Papa in his relationship with his former wife. He acknowledges now that his pattern was to store up resentment until there was an explosion. "It was always the same old issue with us and the same old anger: my former wife thought I was using her to get what I wanted; I thought I was always getting dumped with the unpleasant parts of child raising."

At the same time Stanley was attempting to adjust to a shared custody schedule, he was also working hard at his job. "Things were pretty chaotic then and it was extremely hard to keep all the balls in the air," he says. But at the same time he was learning to juggle school, children, a former spouse, and coparenting, he began to receive some counseling in how to look at the divorcing family as a *system*. "I was learning to examine how each person has a part in what's going on." No longer did he have the luxury of blaming his former wife for the problems the family was experiencing. Stanley had to take a look at what part his behavior played in the family dynamic.

"I was an overachiever and my ex-wife was an underachiever," he says, laughing. "I was steeped in the work ethic from my father, who worked in the professions; books were *everything* as I was growing up. My ex, on the other hand, wanted life to be fun. She hadn't been encouraged to go to college by her father, who was a steelworker, and she stressed having a good time, which always made me feel like an ogre." When the couple married, he had graduated Phi Beta Kappa from college. His wife was a clerk. After ten years of marriage and three children, the couple filed for divorce "and kind of fell into a sharing arrangement with the kids."

During the first months of shared custody, as their routine became established, "my house became the Study Hall, and hers the Funhouse," Stanley says. "I wanted the kids to work; she wanted them to play. Within a few months, my oldest daughter's grades began to slip badly. She hadn't been able to integrate my philosophy (which was probably too conscientious) with her mother's philosophy (which was probably too loose). Instead of being somewhere in the middle and getting B-minuses, she was getting C's and D's. She wouldn't do any homework at her mother's house and then would try to complete long-term projects at the last minute when she was with me." Stanley was particularly distressed that the shared custody arrangement had become a convenient excuse for his daughter not to do her schoolwork. "We were all furious with one another. My ex-wife's attitude was that it was our daughter's responsibility and she didn't want to be the taskmaster. She also didn't like what she felt was my manipulation of her to feel guilty about our daughter's not doing her work. My attitude was that our daughter needed guidance and what kind of lousy mother she was being not to back me up. Meanwhile, our daughter was overwhelmed by the increasingly difficult work at school and was sinking fast." Stanley discovered that no amount of pleading or demanding did any good. "Both my ex and my daughter simply resisted, and there was no use arguing over who was right and who was wrong."

Stanley began to learn about a technique that therapist Simone Katz-Savlov calls *visualizing*. Simone explains it as follows: "Ideally, it would always be great to get divorcing parents into a room together to talk about what plan would be best for the kids, but in many cases that is really not feasible. So, instead, I work with the parents separately, having them visualize what it would feel like to be the other parent so they could get off dead center. I have them go through a day in the life of their ex-spouse *mentally* as I describe out loud to them the experiences that other men and women had told me about—things like feeling lonely in a small furnished apartment, or returning home to an empty house once shared with a mate. I talk them through such experiences as finding out two months later that your child won some award or suffered a broken arm."

Stanley tried visualization exercises, and, he says, "It became a very nonblaming way to look at problems, and I could see the way my ex-wife and I had been 'negotiating' issues between us: we communicated negatively, pushed each other's buttons, and blamed each other for our predicament."

He tried to visualize what it felt like to be his ex-wife. "I realized that as a Make-Nice type she was always having to appease me but was operating on the premise that I was always trying to get something out of her, to control her, to take advantage of her by getting her to do things my way." It was clear to him that she had been smarting from his implied messages that she was not a very caring parent since she didn't value education as highly as he did. "Basically, we were involved in a power struggle. After she remarried, I could see she was under even greater pressure *not* to listen to me. She couldn't give herself permission to listen to *my* need for our daughter to do well in school."

By trying to visualize what it felt like to be his former wife, Stanley came to realize that she loved the children very much and wanted good things for them. "She actually had more aspirations for her kids than she ever had for herself. I saw that she really recognized the fact that the world is different than it was when she was a girl and that kids today need all the education they can get in order to cope. I saw, finally, that she could give herself permission, not to attend to my needs that our daughter do well in school, since I was no longer her husband, but to attend to *our daughter's* need to do all right in the world." If Stanley straightened out his own behavior, his ex-wife then could easily give herself permission to be an attentive mother.

After that, Stanley began to center all discussions on the daughter's problems, "not my problems concerning her problems. I would start conversations by saying to my ex-wife, 'Here's what's happening with our daughter over here . . . just got her report card and she got a D in science. She likes science and we both know she's a smart kid, but she doesn't get her reports in on time. Where do you think we should go from here?' I didn't blame or accuse; I just told her what was happening."

When Stanley stopped blaming his former wife for not getting their daughter to study more, she felt free to show her concern about the situation, too. Stanley admits he had to "resist the temptation to ask her to be concerned about *me,* since I was the parent witnessing the tears and frustration our daughter showed Sunday nights when she attempted to cram all her homework into the evening hours of the waning weekend. My ex and I began to talk about what we could do." Stanley made some suggestions about setting up specific times for their daughter to study and creating a quiet place in both homes where the girl could actually sit down and do her homework. "I told my ex about my rules for watching TV, which she adopted. I offered to be sure our daughter had the right books when she set off for her mother's house."

Stanley and his ex-wife eventually were able to agree that their daughter would have exactly the same rules and standards imposed in both houses. "Actually, I was saying the same things I'd been saying before, but in a different *language.*

Before, I was a lousy negotiator, blaming her and always using the phrase 'Don't you think you should be doing . . .' and acting angry. Once I changed my behavior and centered everything on our daughter, my ex-wife's behavior changed, too. I got in the habit of using 'I' statements and simple declarative sentences like 'Over here I've found it helps to . . .' " He stuck to concentrating on what bad study habits were doing to his daughter, not to him. "I only described what I saw happening to my daughter, and I didn't blame anyone for that. The language and my new style of negotiating were crucial to working through this problem."

After this breakthrough in communication, the parents let their daughter know that they *both* agreed that she was to do her homework at both houses at a steadily paced schedule. At the beginning, the girl was still reluctant to work hard at her mother's house. "My ex-wife called me one day and moaned, 'How do you get her to do it?' I gave her a lot of support, agreeing that it was hard for me, too, to get her to settle down sometimes. I'd say to her, 'I've found such-and-such works,' and she seemed grateful for the suggestions. Before long, our daughter realized that it was now important to her mother, too, that the homework be done properly and on time. She and I both realized that we had to guard against shared custody becoming a way for our daughter to get away with not doing what was good for her to do."

Stanley says that his former wife did not radically change her personality or much of her philosophy. "I'm still the more serious one. She didn't change overnight and become exactly like me; but she did agree that our daughter needed to do what was assigned her in school, and I became satisfied with that."

By the end of the term, the parents finally were able to enlist their daughter's cooperation in the plan. Stanley explains, "Now both parents ask, 'What books do you have to take with you to the other house?' She knows her mother and I consult about her school progress. We don't have long conversations and we're very businesslike, but we both feel it has helped her enormously not to be able to manipulate the two of us. That kind of power is addictive for kids."

The daughter's grades came up to a B-plus average within a year. "She doesn't feel overwhelmed with work anymore," Stanley says happily. "She doesn't cry like she used to or whine as much, and now she's been put in enriched classes in English, math, and history."

Basic Principles of Negotiating

Simone Katz-Savlov believes that parents who share custody of their children can teach themselves to become Straight-Shooter Spouses if they remember the basic principles of negotiating:

1. Take your anger about a problem involving shared custody somewhere *safe*—yell, scream, kick a pillow, or talk to a sympathetic friend. Try not to direct the anger at the child or the other parent.

2. When you're calm, plan time to discuss the issue with the other parent.

3. Stay focused on the needs of the child and not merely your own needs. For example, *you* don't need your child to do well in school; *your child* needs to do well in school for *his or her own sake.*

4. Elicit suggestions from the other parent about the problem, but don't sound patronizing. Use the kind of language that sounds normal for you. Avoid left-handed encouragement such as "I don't suppose *you'd* have any suggestions?"

5. Don't be a know-it-all. Recognize that the other parent may have some valid ideas regarding your children. Remember that the other parent has some good things to offer your youngster, too.

6. Try to stay flexible and receptive to possible solutions. Offer several choices you'd be willing to live with. Present your

preferred alternatives and have a fall-back position ready—or be prepared to adjourn until another time. Also, know your own bottom line.

7. When you speak in the language of partnership, acknowledge that you have a *mutual* problem needing a mutually satisfactory solution. The basic premise is "What can we do to fix things?"

8. Monitor your own behavior carefully so that you won't slip back into an old, unsatisfactory style of negotiating. Suspend negotiations for a time if old buttons start to get pushed.

9. Once a resolution to a conflict is found, be sure you follow through on your end as to what you agreed to do.

10. Schedule a short period of time to test your solution. Agree that you both will keep tabs on the situation and will report to each other on how things are actually working out.

11. Offer support to the other parent whenever you can. Give positive information as well as detailing the remaining problems, and acknowledge to each other that it isn't always easy to accomplish what you're attempting to do.

Learning to negotiate on what you think is best for your children takes preparation—and practice. Start by negotiating the simplest issues first. Before you launch into negotiation, review the communication skills you'll need and make a determined effort to stay focused on the specific goal you're after. Pick a likely time and location for the negotiation and rehearse first (perhaps with a friend or in front of a mirror) what you want and what plan of action you propose. Keep in mind a "beginning, middle, and end" to your negotiating session. Prepare a "let's put this on hold for a while" line in case emotions start to heat up.

Even a Straight-Shooter must realize that his or her behavior won't cause the other parent to change miraculously, but *you* will change and things will have to be different because of that. As you hone your negotiating skills through frequent contact with your child's other parent, and as you slowly learn the new language of shared custody, you'll begin to develop techniques that transform you into a genuine Straight-Shooter Spouse. Your newly acquired savvy will be of enormous help when you deal with another important group of people involved in cooperative parenting: the Supporting Players.

Chapter 14

Shared Custody's Supporting Players

How to Fit Stepparents, Relatives, Lovers, Friends, Acquaintances, and People You Meet on the Street into the Coparenting Picture

Reports from the front lines. Defining the Blended/Extended Family. The tangled web of family constellations. Identifying "Interested Parties" in your child's life. The Shared Custody Bull's-eye. Beware the Saboteur. The role of grandparents in shared custody. Enlisting the support of extended-family members in your shared custody plan. New spouses and old issues. The "Ten Pounds of Love" Theory. The differences between mothers and fathers—and parents. Accepting the permanence of the parent-child bond. Friends, functionaries, and acquaintances—a matter of education. Reeducating the educators. Keeping tabs on your child's custody network.

I have a file in my drawer labeled "Reports from the Front Lines." Over the years I have thrown in odd scraps of paper with quotes from people I've met in my travels who were pioneering a new social structure called the Shared Custody Family. Some of their comments make me cry; some make me laugh.

On Lovers and New Spouses:

"This is a romance? I've never been so exhausted in my life! Instead of breakfast in bed served by the new man in my life, now I get up earlier than ever three mornings a week to pack the lunch of a strange five-year-old before I dash to work. How do people *do* this?"

On Grandparents:

"My son's grandmother told him that I must not love him very much, since I allowed him to live last year with his father. After she said that, he ran out of her house, sobbing, and we couldn't find him for four hours."

On Being a Grandparent:

"I just want to say how grateful I am that my son and former daughter-in-law are doing joint custody. She lives in Oregon and we live in California, and without this arrangement I doubt that I would ever have been able to enjoy my granddaughters the way I do since the divorce."

On Stepparenting:

"Being a stepparent can be a pretty thankless job, especially with joint custody. You have all of the problems of being a parent with few of the payoffs. After all, the kid has a *real* dad a mile and a half away, and he casts a very long shadow."

On Stepsiblings:

"It's hard being the youngest. My stepbrother used to be the youngest, but now he's in the middle, and all he wants to do is punch me and tell me to get out of his room. It's my room, *too*—at least when I'm at my dad's house."

On the Shared Custody Routine:

"Just when I think I can't take his kids and my kids another minute, it's time to ship them off to the other parents', and then my husband and I can have some time to ourselves ... and boy, do we need it!"

On Former In-laws:

"When my former husband and I were married, his parents and I were very close. Now that we are separated and trying to share custody, his parents refuse to speak to me. My children's grandparents are *therapists,* mind you!"

On Blending Families:

"My stepchildren almost wrecked my second marriage. My own teenage daughter and my new husband's teenagers despised each other on sight. Those first years with them were truly horrible."

On Relatives:

"My entire family—the aunts, uncles, cousins—think my sharing custody with my ex-wife is crazy. They call her a slut and can't understand how I can allow my daughter to be with her and her live-in boyfriend, but they don't say a word about me and my live-in girlfriend. It's wild!"

On Friends:

"My friends think we have the most peculiar setup they've ever seen. Often they'll say to me, 'Doesn't this joint custody business confuse your kid? Aren't you afraid all this shuttling back and forth will make him a schizophrenic?' "

On Acquaintances:

"I mentioned to a woman I met recently at a committee meeting that my child's father and I share custody, and she looked at me as if I must be a streetwalker not to have gotten sole custody."

On School Personnel:

"I had to put up a real fight to get my telephone number *and* my former husband's number printed in the school roster. The woman in charge snapped at me, 'Well, what if *every* divorced parent insisted we print both numbers; the roster would be thick as a regular telephone book!' "

It can be upsetting to outsiders when divorced families in general, and families sharing custody in particular, don't mirror commonly held notions of what the American Family is supposed to be. Even Ronald Reagan, who was the first divorced candidate ever to be elected President, felt it necessary to campaign for the preservation of the nuclear family. However, with two children from his first marriage, to Jane Wyman, he brought the first *blended* family to the White House.

The Reagans are not unusual. One out of every seven households has at least one remarried parent or one child from a previous union. About 750,000 children each year see a parent remarry and create a blended family. Regardless of the custody arrangements divorced parents eventually work out, children link families that have been formed and re-formed through marriage and divorce. All the links forge a new type of special network, a *constellation* of families.

A gigantic system with two major subsystems is created: one consists of the original family of Mom, Dad, the kids, and blood relatives; the other includes all the new people who enter the system when someone remarries or enters a long-lasting relationship. "It's absolutely incredible how complicated the relationships within this huge family system can get," says Nancy Weston, codirector of the Divorcing Family Clinic in Santa Monica, California. "To understand where trouble may come from, you need to diagram the Extended and/or Blended Family and see the tangled web of all those relationships," she notes. "Somebody quite removed from the child can get sick, change jobs, file for divorce, move, or remarry, and boom! Everything blows up!"

To see graphically the "tangled web" Weston was talking about, I have outlined my own son's Supporting Players' Network. After studying the various constellations, map out *your* children's Extended/Blended Family connections.

JAMIE'S EXTENDED FAMILY (1982)
("Interested Parties" in Family He Was Born to)

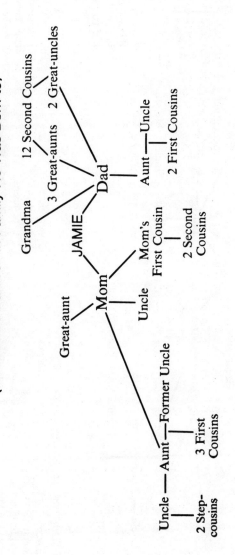

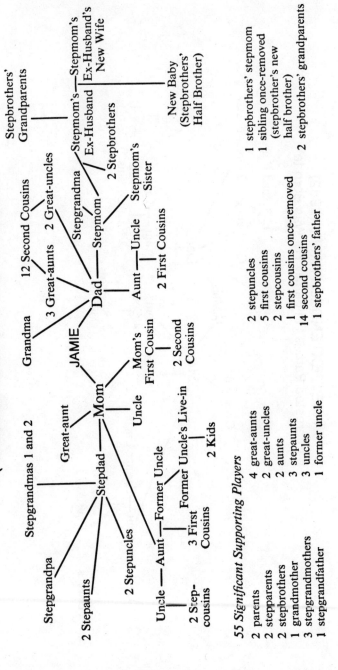

JAMIE'S BLENDED/EXTENDED FAMILY (1982)
("Interested Parties" in Combined Families)

55 Significant Supporting Players

2 parents	4 great-aunts
2 stepparents	2 great-uncles
3 stepbrothers	2 aunts
1 grandmother	3 stepaunts
3 stepgrandmothers	3 uncles
1 stepgrandfather	1 former uncle

2 stepuncles	1 stepbrothers' stepmom
5 first cousins	1 sibling once-removed
2 stepcousins	(stepbrother's new
1 first cousins once-removed	half brother)
14 second cousins	2 stepbrothers' grandparents
1 stepbrothers' father	

The Supporting Players must be identified and analyzed, especially in shared custody situations where there is frequent and continuing contact. Even if you can't stand your wife's surly first husband or your former husband's disagreeable mother, their relationship to the Blended/Extended Family cannot be ignored if those people have any kind of significant relationship with your child.

Hugh McIsaac, director of the Los Angeles Conciliation Court, which mediates thousands of disputed custody cases every year, warns, "It's been our experience that anyone important within that family system who is *not* a party to the shared custody agreement will often attempt to sabotage that agreement. Sometimes there is a relative who has a stake in keeping the conflict between the parents alive. Very often," he notes, "we've found in our Conciliation Court work that you have to *involve in the mediation process itself those people who have an interest in the outcome of the joint custody negotiations between the parents* [emphasis is mine]." This can mean grandparents, stepparents, stepbrothers and -sisters, and even housekeepers—anyone who is close to the center of what can be called the Shared Custody Bull's-eye. Think of your child as the focal point for these spheres of influence.

It becomes easier to understand the web of relationships surrounding your child and to see how they affect your youngster once you map out in black and white how all these people literally run rings around your immediate family. Not only is your child the center of a complicated family network; he or she is also part of various subsystems comprising schoolmates and teachers, neighbors, friends, and people involved in the child's extracurricular activities. Any one of these Supporting Players intent on causing trouble—depending on how close that person stands in relation to your child—could be a Saboteur. Sometimes, involving the *potential* Saboteur in the process of arranging the shared custody routine means you must actually hold a conference so that each person affected by the arrangement can voice opinions and preferences. This doesn't mean

SHARED CUSTODY BULL'S-EYE

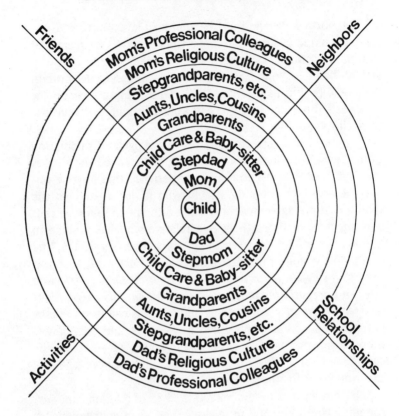

granting everybody special powers in the outcome, but merely finding out what their concerns are. At other times it may simply mean that you take the time to explain to a friend or relative or baby-sitter *why* you feel coparenting will benefit your child. You can acknowledge how difficult it may be to coordinate two households, but you might also tell interested parties that *any* divorce is difficult and that sharing custody, in your view, is the best way for you and your former spouse to provide for the needs of your children. Without attempting to get their approval, tell them how important you feel they are to the youngsters and that you believe they could greatly contribute to the success of your coparenting plan.

Enlisting the Support of Extended-Family Members

Grandparents, especially, need reassurances that the divorce will not mean they will lose contact with their grandchildren and that, in fact, they have a better chance of remaining part of the child's life through a shared custody arrangement. Perhaps more than other members of a family, grandparents are not prepared for divorce. In their day, most couples stuck with their marriages, regardless of how unhappy they might have been. It becomes especially difficult for some older family members who may have no prior experience in dealing with the aftermath of divorce to cope with the divorce of their children if they foresee the loss of their grandchildren in the process.

If talking to former in-laws is difficult or impractical, a thoughtfully written letter outlining your reasons for establishing a shared custody arrangement could be a welcome substitute. You can reassure your former relatives of the important part they play in the lives of your children, an action that may help construct bridges to the new relationships you are defining with extended-family members in both directions.

However, it isn't merely immediate biological family members who can sabotage shared custody plans. A jealous stepsibling, a disgruntled new spouse, an unhappy housekeeper, or a nosy neighbor could cause trouble, too. The best antidote is simply to call them on it and pointedly explain why you feel shared custody is in everyone's best interests. Confronting the issue may at least reduce its impact upon your child.

But what if the problem comes from your ex-spouse's new spouse or even your own new spouse? Many books have been written on the problems of being a stepparent or of marrying someone who becomes your child's stepparent, and you may want to refer to the Suggested Readings in Appendix D. A friend once told me, "If there is any advice I would give to a parent who is about to remarry or to an adult who is about to become a stepparent, it's to realize there is no such thing as the Brady Bunch. No one lives that way!" What the Brady Bunch never acknowledged is that stepfamilies are created out of *loss*. (In fact, the prefix "step" is derived from an Old English word that means "deprive" or "bereave.") Every stepfamily has members who have sustained the loss of a primary relationship. They've lost a spouse, a child, or a parent—unless they have avoided part of that loss through a shared custody arrangement. When parents remarry, the "Myth of the Instant Family" still persists. Parents choosing new mates think, "I love you and you love me and we'll love each other's kids and they'll love us." The disappointments can be devastating.

Most of the trouble seems to come from the mistaken notion that *there are only ten pounds of love*! The Ten Pounds of Love Theory goes like this: If a child gives five pounds of love to Mom and three pounds to Stepdad, then Real Dad gets only two pounds of love. But the only limits on a child's capacity for love are put there by those who are afraid they somehow won't get their share. As successful joint custody parents can testify, a child with permission to love all the meaningful adults and children in his or her life has more than enough love to go around. It is when a youngster gets the message that "if you love your stepparent you won't have enough love to give to me (or vice versa)," that he or she comes up short. A natural parent doesn't *lose* love if a stepparent gains the love of a child. Often the mere fact that one side has given a child permission to love freely will help everyone. Social worker Sue K. Simring, in a study reviewing the research literature on the effect of remarriage on children, found that when children are allowed to maintain continuous relationships with both parents, they tend to form *stronger*, not weaker, attachments to their stepparents.

In shared custody situations in which the children spend significant time with *both* their biological parents, stepparents must realize they are *not* replacements for the originals. Stepparents need recognition and thanks from all sides for their tremendous contributions to the welfare of the youngsters, but there is no biological bond. As one parent in an extended family explained frankly to a *New York Times* reporter, "If one of my kids and one of her kids were about to be hit by a car and I could save only one of them, I'd save my own kid." Biological parents don't have to be ashamed of this reality, and stepparents needn't be afraid of it.

In my own Extended/Blended Family, the adults learned about that special bond between biological parents and their children in the months following my former husband's remarriage to a woman with two sons of her own. Soon after the ceremony Jamie began acting angry or indifferent whenever his father picked him up at my house. He began crying over his homework at our house and didn't want to play with friends who dropped over. When I asked what was bothering him, I got the wan reply "I . . . dunno . . ." Finally one day he blurted out that he hated his older stepbrother because "he's so mean to me and only likes hamburgers," and that when the three boys got into fights, his dad and stepmother "don't care who gets hurt." It took persistent digging, but clearly—for whatever reasons—Jamie was feeling *lonely* in the face of what he saw as the hostility of the Supporting Players at his father's house and felt "nobody's ever on my side."

It was difficult to raise the subject with my former husband because the problem had started in *his* household. But after all, whatever *was* going on over there was impacting on my current husband and me, since we were left with the tears and tantrums. So, with some trepidation, I called Jamie's father on the phone and, trying to use the Language of Joint Custody, I tentatively started with "Just wanted to let you know what's been going on here . . ." I tried to describe what I saw happening, with no judgments as to *why* it was happening. Since I had told Jamie I was going to speak to his father, I said, "Jamie says he feels you treat him differently now; that you treat him the *same* as the other two boys. What do you think he means?"

His father was somewhat defensive at first. "Jamie is just going to have to learn to be a sibling instead of an only child," he said. I agreed he would have to adjust to having two brothers, adding how hard it must be suddenly to be the parent of three children instead of just one. And, I commented, the other two children must have their own problems adjusting to having someone new in their lives. "I try to be fair to all three," my former husband said. "But it does seem like there's less time. Everything's so much more complicated now."

I rang off, telling him that I thought it was all right if his special relationship as Jamie's father was out in the open and that it didn't seem like favoritism to me. "The two boys have the very same thing with *their* father," I said, adding that I thought things would probably work out over time.

Two days later the phone rang and Jamie's father asked to speak to him. My son picked up the phone listlessly and said hello. Soon, however, his eyes brightened and his old familiar enthusiasm returned. "Great, Dad!" he said, beaming. "Let's have *fish* and play backgammon after dinner ... Okay ... Great! See ya tomorrow night!" He turned to me after he'd hung up the receiver. "Guess what, Mom! Dad says that tomorrow night is Jamie Night, when the other kids are going to be at their dad's. I get to decide what's for dinner and what games we play after I finish my homework!" He turned and ran next door to play with a neighbor.

It was such a simple solution, it astounded all of us. Apparently, my son merely needed to be reassured that his special bond with his own father had not been broken; that there was room for him in the new family constellation. He would certainly have to become accustomed to having siblings as Supporting Players in his life, but he had regained the security of knowing he still had a real mom and a real dad. As soon as Jamie was out the door, I called my former husband and said, "You and your new bride are brilliant."

Friends and Functionaries

Outside the immediate Extended/Blended Family, the Supporting Players most often encountered are friends, acquaintances, bureaucrats, and teachers.

Friends, like family, may need to hear your ideas regarding the shared custody plan you've designed: why you have chosen it over sole custody and why you hope they will help you create a new kind of family and social network for your child.

Functionaries such as insurance company clerks, tax preparers, and school personnel may have to be "educated" by you as to how a shared custody arrangement relates to their particular bailiwick. For example, once the typist for the school telephone roster hears that "my child's father and I want the friends of our youngster to feel comfortable about calling either home," knee-jerk resistance to doing something out of the ordinary usually subsides.

Schoolteachers and administrators may require "postgraduate" education in shared custody. Many are shockingly out of touch with the needs of children from divorced families. A poll of more than twelve hundred parents from forty-seven states, published by *Principal* magazine in 1979, revealed that one child in five had experienced divorce and that at some schools children from divorced homes comprised as large a part of the enrollment as *90 percent*. Yet these parents, whether in shared or sole custody situations, told the pollsters that their children's schools most often assumed there were two natural parents at home; and when the educators were aware there were not, 66 percent of the parents said they often heard school personnel refer to family styles other than the two-natural-parents model as "abnormal."

The poll also found that the sensitivity of teachers and school administrators varied widely and that many parents were concerned about the educators' preconceived negative ideas regarding divorced families. The parents worried that speaking frankly about their situation might expose their children to "labeling" and low expectations from school personnel. A full 35 percent of the parents polled said they had heard people at their children's school making disparaging comments about the homes of divorced parents.

Parents sharing custody are in the unique position of communicating to school authorities that their children still have *two* parents (and sometimes more) involved in raising the children. Of course, they must also deal with the prejudice against "shuttling" children between two homes. However, the only way the school system will become more attuned to what is happening in the real world of divorce is if parents sharing custody speak up and enlist the cooperation of those who guide and care for their youngsters so many hours a week.

An important part of educating the educators is to have the facts in hand and to point out politely that:

1. Each year in the United States, new divorces involve one million children.

2. The age of children of divorce is dropping: most are between five and twelve years old—and that means they're of elementary-school age.

3. Ten percent of fathers head single-parent homes, and a growing number of fathers are cocustodians of their children along with their ex-wives.

4. The majority of single parents—including parents sharing custody—work. In the United States, 68.1 percent of all divorced women whose youngest children have reached school age are in the work force. The scheduling of parent-teacher conference hours should reflect this fact.

5. By 1990, 50 percent of all children of school age will have lived with parents who are separated or divorced. Teachers must therefore be more sensitive to these children's needs.

The poll by *Principal* magazine also revealed the tactless language teachers use regarding children of divorce. Nearly

50 percent of those questioned heard school personnel use such terms as "broken home." Parents sharing custody can let school officials know that, in their view, such language stereotypes children unfairly and needs changing. Your child's teacher should know of your concern that the divorce experience can isolate youngsters. Supportive teachers, the poll found, are of enormous help to divorced parents and their children during the initial period of stress and change. The poll also showed, however, that some teachers needed to be reminded that not every child has a father who is physically available for the Father-Son Banquet or a mother able to attend the Mother-Daughter Luncheon.

Parents sharing custody will, no doubt, have to request specifically that both mother and father be sent grade reports, school calendars, and notices of parent-teacher conferences, as required by the Family Educational Rights and Privacy Act of 1974. If a school refuses to do this, that refusal must be backed by a court order or a legally binding document.

As the nation's educators are being asked to adjust to the prevalence of divorce among the families of school-age children, some parents who share custody have joined committees to review the way in which families are presented in school texts. They have urged school administrations and textbook publishers to adopt curriculum materials that show varied family styles, or, at the very least, to include books in school libraries that show something other than the two-natural-parents-in-one-house model. They are also urging curriculum writers to take note of the fact that by 1980 only 14 percent of all American families—whether or not they were affected by divorce—had a dad who was the sole breadwinner and a mom who stayed at home with the children.

Divorced parents, and especially parents sharing custody, "are in a unique position to help and strengthen the American Family . . . not only as an 'ideal,' but as it really is," says Phyllis L. Clay of the National Committee for Citizens in Education, the organization that paid for the poll published in

Principal magazine. "I make a plea [to the nation's educators] to recognize a wide variety of family configurations as potentially healthy . . . and ask them to support children in the situations in which they find themselves. Children are the ones who ultimately benefit from increased sensitivity on the part of teachers and decreased tension on the part of parents," she says. Parents sharing custody can join in that plea to urge the Supporting Players in the education field to help, not hurt, the children with whom they have such intense daily contact.

Effects of Conflict on Children

What struck me so forcefully from my own experience in learning to deal with my child's Supporting Players—and what I heard from other parents time and again—is that a problem for *one* person in the complicated network of the Extended/Blended Family is often a problem for *all*. Regardless of who in a child's environment circulates nasty, insensitive remarks or insinuations, it is the child who is at the center of the network, and the child is often torn by a sense of loyalty to all sides. Often such a conflict will intensify the child's own sadness about the divorce and will have an impact on the way he or she responds to family and friends, teachers and schoolmates, and even the neighbor down the block. The ripple effect of *nonsupportive* Supporting Players undulates back and forth across the Shared Custody Bull's-eye, affecting many different people up and down the line.

A basic approach to dealing with uncooperative Supporting Players is, first, to analyze the *source* of the conflict, pinpointing where the trouble lies on your Extended/Blended Family chart. Then try to involve in the solution those most immediately affected. This may require getting these people into a small room just to talk. If tempers are really hot, you may want to think about asking a family therapist trained in family-systems work to act as a neutral third-party mediator until a resolution to the problem can be developed by those involved.

Says therapist Nancy Weston, "People are often reluctant to do this kind of thing, but when you have a gigantic system like this, anybody important who is left out of it is going to make trouble. The more the conflict between the adults, especially, can be reduced, the more we can provide an environment for these children where they have appropriate access to all the supporting adults in their lives."

Weston, the mother of three daughters whom she raised as a single parent, and now the grandmother of a little boy, admits that the thought of not being able to see her grandson, should her daughter ever divorce, "is simply unbearable." She urges divorced parents to foster positive Extended/Blended Family relationships whenever possible. "We can't give children of divorce the old kind of life in a little-bitty nuclear family, but we *can* offer them a life in a great big 'family' where there are a lot of people who care for that child, and love and want to help him or her grow up to be an emotionally healthy adult."

Shared custody can provide the best structure through which an Extended/Blended Family can give your youngster that gift of health.

Chapter 15
Starting Over

Changing from Sole to Shared Custody

Grandpa Vert. It's never too late to try sharing custody. The Vergons' experiment. Starting from scratch. When shared custody won't work. Official and unofficial joint custody. Petitioning the court for a new custody order: forms and facts. Parents who share custody: the silent (but growing) minority.

Vert Vergon was instructing his strapping sixteen-year-old-son, Vance, on the fine art of grilling a steak. The teenager and his father wanted to finish their Memorial Day cookout in time to get to Los Angeles Airport by five o'clock to pick up Vert's daughter, Vivian, her husband, and their new baby girl.

"I'm a grandpa now," Vert told me, laughing. "It's just great!"

Vert told me his former wife, whom I hadn't seen in more than two years, was presently in Indiana. "She's back there trying to sell her mother's place before she starts working for her state counseling license. She's a Ph.D. in psychology now, you know," he said. His pride was startling to anyone who was aquainted with Vert and Phyllis Vergon's tumultous family history.

After a divorce that ended seventeen years of marriage, the Vergons had made thirteen trips in four years to Los Angeles Superior Court over disagreements about the care of their two children, who were ten and twelve when papers were filed for the divorce. The Vergons' custody order was a typical one: sole custody to the mother, alternate weekends to the father. But for four years the couple's anger regarding the circumstances of their breakup resulted in screaming battles, calls to the police, Christmas presents unaccepted, furniture impounded, and a degree of escalating warfare that horrifies both Vergons when they look back on it.

"I was furious, he was furious, and the kids were in the middle," Phyllis told me with tears in her eyes when I first interviewed her, in 1978. In the years following their court fight, *both* Vergons had heart attacks. And the kids, Vivian and Vance, developed serious problems at school and in their relations with both their parents.

During the highest fevers of their battles, Vert, a printing salesman and author of a book on theoretical physics, established a group called Fathers Demanding Equal Justice. With four thousand members in the Los Angeles area by 1980 and affiliations with some eighty-five fathers' rights and parents' rights groups around the country, Vert's organization has protested the lack of enforcement of custody visitation orders, has lobbied to make joint custody a presumption under the law, and has assembled the latest scientific data on the problems of children who lack access to both parents following divorce. Following his biggest battles with Phyllis, Vert sent a heavy packet of information to every family judge in Southern California. "Some of 'em actually read it," he says, smiling.

At that same time, Phyllis, a former home economics teacher and travel agent, realized her children were manipulating both parents. "I finally talked to Vert one night and we began to compare notes about the problems each of us was having with the children. We agreed to check with each other about certain things the kids said and did. It was our first cooperative move."

At Christmastime in 1976, the Vergons agreed to split the cost of a set of drums for Vance and went together to buy them. "It was a big step," Phyllis told me two years later, "and it got easier and easier to call each other and decide what we should do about the kids."

Neither parent remarried, and while both children were in high school, "we'd talk every day," said Phyllis. "We were friendly, but separate." Slowly, despite years of court battles and bitterness, Vert and Phyllis began to trust each other again as parents.

Both Vergons acknowledge that the children seemed much more secure once the couple switched from sole custody to shared responsibility for their care. "But they suffered with us," said Phyllis, "and you can't remove that pain." She began to cry. "I'm just so sorry we put them through those four years. . . . It was agony for the kids. You can't go back . . . they know you can't go back, but at least we finally started to work with them whenever we saw a problem developing."

The new cooperative efforts paid off. Vivian graduated from high school and soon married. Vance's infatuation with drums led him to join a small band while continuing his schooling. "The kid realizes how competitive the music business is," Vert notes proudly, "but he's hardworking and I think he might make it."

Vert's health has improved since a bypass operation, and so has Phyllis's. "At least I'm still here," Vert jokes. He is busy trying to persuade the scientists at Cal Tech that he has a compatible theory of physics regarding speeds greater than light, and he is still active in Fathers Demanding Equal Justice. "I've solved *my* problem, but there are still a lot of terrible injustices."

Phyllis, who intends to use her psychology doctorate in a career as a family therapist, shares Vert's views. In fact, she helps her former husband stuff envelopes for fund raisers for the fathers' organization. She admits she was against joint custody before she began to live it, but now she thinks divorcing couples with children should be required to take twelve weeks of instruction "to learn what divorce means to children and how the absence of a parent is like a death to them."

As supportive as Phyllis and Vert Vergon are of sharing custody as a concept, they agree that there are some parents for whom coparenting simply will not work. Alcoholics who are abusive toward their children and former spouses do not make reliable cocustodians; nor do drug addicts or parents with severe mental illnesses; nor do parents who are, at bottom, children themselves, unable to consider anything but their own needs and desires. But for many others—even for parents with as difficult a history as Vert and Phyllis Vergon's—it's rarely too late to work out a shared custody program, regardless of how much time has elapsed since the divorce or how much bitterness it engendered.

The Vergons decided they would simply *live* joint custody, and never officially altered the court documents in their case. Some parents, however, may wish to mark their shift to joint custody legally. If you are among them, once you have decided on a shared custody parenting plan, you must petition the court to change the custody arrangements that are on file. Forms and legal language vary from state to state, but the accompanying sample agreement to modify an existing custody order may help you and/or your attorney in framing a request to the court.

APPROVED AS TO FORM AND CONTENT

_____

TOM SMITH
Attorney for Petitioner

_____

MARY BROWN
Attorney for Respondent

ORDER

IT IS ORDERED that the Final Judgment of Dissolution of Marriage entered on May 22, 1978, and all subsequent orders, in the matter of Marriage of Doe, Case No. _____, is modified to order joint custody of the minor child JOHN DOE, JR., with physical custody to be shared by the parents in such a way as to assure the child of frequent and continuing contact with both parents.

Dated: _____

_____
Judge of the Superior
Court

In cases where only one parent desires to shift from sole custody to joint custody, the forms and steps are more complicated and the outcome is far from certain. An excellent primer on contested modification orders can be found in a book by Joseph L. Matthews called *After the Divorce* (see Appendix D).

But if you and your former spouse do agree on sharing custody, even if you live in a state that does not sanction legal and/or physical joint custody, and even if a judge turns down your petition to change from single parenting to coparenting, you still can, of course, both agree to go forward with de facto shared custody. Vert and Phyllis Vergon's de facto coparenting agreement worked and serves to show that regardless of how far you may have traveled since your divorce, there is still time to switch. The Vergons were able to join a groundswell of parents who eventually "get well"—parents who rid themselves of the rancor brought about by their divorce and who learn, in time, to work together for the benefit of their mutual offspring.

Vert Vergon probably speaks for thousands of other parents who have learned from their failures as well as from their successes when he says, "Let sole custody be the exception, not the rule." Children, he believes, belong with, not to, their parents.

The message that families such as his are sending across the nation is this: Shared custody is working. Psssst! Pass it on.

Appendix A

Divorce Mediation Sources

General Sources

American Arbitration Association
Family Dispute Services
140 W. 51st St.
New York, NY 10020
212-484-4000

Publishes a pamphlet of AAA rules, with addresses of 24 regional offices, many of which provide family dispute resolution services.

American Bar Association Dispute Resolution Center
1800 M St. N.W.
Washington, DC 20036
202-331-2258

Publishes a $9 directory of ongoing mediation programs and resource agencies throughout the U.S.

Association of Family Conciliation Courts
NOVA Law Center
3100 S.W. Ninth Ave.
Fort Lauderdale, FL 33315
305-522-2300

Lists conciliation courts throughout the U.S.; refers counselors who are Association members.

Family Mediation Association
9308 Bulls Run Pkwy
Bethesda, MD 20817
301-530-6930
Provides a directory of mediators throughout the U.S.
certified by the FMA.

Family Service Associations of America
44 E. 23rd St.
New York, NY 10010
212-674-6100
Provides information about many agencies throughout
the U.S. that offer divorce counseling.

The Joint Custody Association
c/o James Cook
10606 Wilkins Ave.
Los Angeles, CA 90024
213-475-5352
213-474-4859
James Cook acts as a clearinghouse for information relating to joint custody, including lists of mediators and
lawyers who support the joint custody concept.

Parents Sharing Custody, Inc.
18401 Burbank Blvd.
Suite 229
Tarzana, CA 91356
213-345-4715
An association of divorced parents who endorse sharing
custody and have practical knowledge of mediators.

Single Dad's Lifestyle
P.O. Box 4842
Scottsdale, AZ 85258
602-998-0980 (24-hour hotline)
This magazine also provides an updated list of local fathers' rights organizations that, in turn, have access to
local attorneys/mediators with experience in joint custody.

State Mediation Sources

Arizona

Conciliation Court of Maricopa County
Superior Court Bldg.
Third Floor
201 W. Jefferson St.
Phoenix, AZ 85003
602-262-3296

Conciliation Court of Pima County
Superior Court Bldg.
111 W. Congress
Tucson, AZ 85701
602-792-8468

California

Child and Family Divorce Counseling Service
Children's Hospital
3801 Sacramento St.
San Francisco, CA 94119
415-752-1935

The Conciliation Court
Sonoma County Superior Court
Room 107J
Hall of Justice
600 Administration Dr.
Santa Rosa, CA 95401
707-527-2765

Dept. of Domestic Relations and Conciliation
1221 Oak St.
Oakland, CA 94612
415-874-6284

Divorce Mediation
Room 370
San Joaquin Superior Court
222 E. Weber St.
Stockton, CA 95202
209-944-3511

Divorcing Family Clinic
2424 Wilshire Blvd.
Santa Monica, CA 90403
213-829-9764

Family Court Services
1558 West St.
Suite 1
Reading, CA 96001
916-246-5707

Family Court Services
San Bernardino Superior Court
351 N. Arrowhead Ave.
Room 200
San Bernardino, CA 92415
714-383-1406

Family Court Services
San Francisco Superior Court
City Hall
400 Van Ness St.
Room 463
San Francisco, CA 94102
415-558-4186

Family Court Services
Old Superior Court Bldg.
161 N. First St.
San Jose, CA 95113
408-299-3741

Family Court Services
Government Center
San Luis Obispo, CA 93408
805-549-5473

Family Law Counseling Service
1600 Shattuck Ave.
Suite 200
Berkeley, CA 94709
415-548-5551

Family Mediation Center of Marin County
610 D St.
San Rafael, CA 94901
415-459-1628

Family Mediation Service
285 Hamilton Ave.
Palo Alto, CA 94301
415-328-7000

Jewish Family and Children Services
1600 Scott St.
San Francisco, CA 94115
415-567-8860

Simone Katz-Savlov, M.F.C.C., Divorce Mediator
300 S. Beverly Dr.
Suite 106
Beverly Hills, CA 90210
213-479-6711

The Law Centers of Mosten and Associates
8620 S. Sepulveda Blvd.
Los Angeles, CA 90045
213-641-9151

Los Angeles County Conciliation Court
Room 241
111 N. Hill St.
Los Angeles, CA 90012
213-974-5524

Marriage, Family, and Divorce Counselors
Suite 300
3704 Mount Diablo Blvd.
LaFayette, CA 94549
415-284-2811

Mediation Institute of California
1798 Technology Dr.
San Jose, CA 95110
408-298-5353

National Institute for Professional Training in Divorce
Counseling
17542 Briarwood St.
Fountain Valley, CA 92708
714-962-9921

Bonnie Neuman, Attorney/Mediator
169 Pier Ave.
Santa Monica, CA 90405
213-392-3088

Elizabeth O'Neill, Attorney
Former Conciliation Counselor
554 Grand Ave.
Oakland, CA 94610
415-839-4050

Simon/Chosak and Associates, Divorce Mediation
1101 S. Robertson Blvd.
Suite 202
Los Angeles, CA 90035
213-275-0797

Colorado

Center for Dispute Resolution
430 W. Ninth Ave.
Denver, Co 80204
303-629-1204

Christian Conciliation Services
7790 E. Arapahoe Rd.
Suite 200
Englewood, CO 80112
303-770-9521

Divorce and Custody Mediators, Inc.
1720 Emerson St.
Denver, CO 80218
303-837-1555

Family Dispute Resolution Inc.
Suite 302
United Bank of Littleton Bldg.
5601 S. Broadway
Littleton, CO 80121
303-798-3288

Family Mediation Center
P.O. Box 1978
Boulder, CO 80306
303-444-4790

Connecticut

Family Division, Superior Court
80 S. Main St.
West Hartford, CT 06107
203-566-8012

Joseph Steinberg, Attorney/Mediator
Steinberg and Louden
99 Pratt St.
Hartford, CT 06103
203-246-7200

Delaware

Family Court of Delaware
Mediation/Arbitration Units
P.O. Box 2359
900 King St.
Wilmington, DE 19899
302-571-2215

Florida

Dade County Conciliation Unit
3300 N.W. 27th Ave.
Room 219
Miami, FL 33142
305-638-6865

Family Conciliation Unit
1 River Plaza
Suite 210
305 S. Andrews Ave.
Fort Lauderdale, FL 33301
305-765-4012

Georgia

Edward Henning, Lawyer/Mediator
Henning, Chambers and Mabry
Suite 825
2200 Century Pkwy N.E.
Atlanta, GA 30345
404-325-4800

Resolve Mediation Center
2959 Piedmont Rd. N.E.
Atlanta, GA 30305
404-237-5588

Hawaii

The Divorce Clinic
Marybeth Webster, Director
Room 211
217 S. King St.
Honolulu, HI 96813
808-521-3803

The Neighborhood Justice Center
1538 Makiki St.
Honolulu, HI 96822
808-949-1017

Illinois

Marriage and Family Counseling Service
Daley Center
Suite 1901
Chicago, IL 60602
312-443-7914

Indiana

Divorce Mediation Associates
Suite 314
8801 N. Meridian St.
Indianapolis, IN 46260
317-846-4937

Domestic Relations Counseling Bureau
City-County Bldg.
Room 742
Indianapolis, IN 46204
317-236-3858

Family Mediation Services, Inc.
808 Maple Ave.
LaPorte, IN 46350
219-326-7774

Family Service of Bartholomew County
712 Washington St.
Columbus, IN 47201
812-372-3745

Iowa

Iowa Children's and Family Services
1101 Walnut St.
Des Moines, IA 50309
515-288-1981

Maryland

Divorce and Marital Stress Clinic
Green Spring Station
Suite 317
2360 W. Joppa Rd.
Lutherville, MD 21093
301-825-0977

Divorce Mediation and Counseling Services, Inc.
Fidelity Bldg.
Suite 1423
210 N. Charles St.
Baltimore, MD 21201
301-685-6152

Mediation Services of Annapolis
2083 West St.
Suite 3C
Annapolis, MD 21401
301-224-3322

Massachusetts

Divorce Resource and Mediation Center, Inc.
2464 Massachusetts Ave.
Cambridge, MA 02140
617-492-3533

Children's Judicial Resource Council
34 Royal Ave.
Cambridge, MA 02138
617-876-8036

John A. Fiske, Lawyer/Mediator
Healy, Lund, and Fiske
189 Cambridge St.
Cambridge, MA 02141
617-354-7133

Probation and Family Service Dept.
Probate Court for Bristol County
441 County St.
New Bedford, MA 02740
617-996-5669

Minnesota

Family Dispute Service Mediations
511 Eleventh Ave. S.
Suite 265
Minneapolis, MN 55415
612-333-1264

Hennepin County Family Court Services
500A Government Center
300 S. Sixth St.
Minneapolis, MN 55487
612-348-7556

Mediation/Domestic Relations Division
Ramsey County Dept. of Corrections
1745 Courthouse
St. Paul, MN 55102
612-298-4379

Nebraska

The Conciliation Court
Hall of Justice
17th and Farnam Sts.
Omaha, NE 68183
402-444-7168

New Jersey

Dr. Kenneth Kressel, Divorce Mediation
Dept. of Psychology
University College
Rutgers University
360 High St.
Newark, NJ 07102
201-648-5819
or
120 S. Second Ave.
Highland Park, NJ 08904
201-247-5986

New York

Family Mediation Service of New York, Inc.
111 Fourth Ave.
New York, NY 10003
212-674-7508

Family Service Association of Nassau County, Inc.
129 Jackson St.
Hempstead, NY 11550
516-485-4600

Family Studies Center, Inc.
John Haynes, Director of Divorce Mediation
Huntington Bay Professional Bldg.
161 E. Main St.
Huntington, NY 11743
516-423-3377

North Carolina

Divorce Mediation Center of Charlotte
Suite 11
723 S. Sharon Amity Rd.
Charlotte, NC 28211
704-365-1979

Family Service Mediation Center
610 Coliseum Dr.
Winston-Salem, NC 27106
919-761-1410

Ohio

Divorce and Family Mediation Services
Randy Mullins, M.S.
270 Regency Ridge
Suite 212
Dayton, OH 45459
513-435-2078

Oregon

Family Services
Dept. of Domestic Relations
Room 350
Multnomah County Courthouse
1021 S.W. Fourth Ave.
Portland, OR 97204
503-248-3189

Family Mediation Center
3434 S.W. Kelly St.
Portland, OR 97201
503-248-9684

Pennsylvania

Individual and Family Consultation Center of
Pennsylvania State University
Catherine Beecher House
University Park, PA 16802
814-865-1751

Andrew Vogelson, Ph.D.
509 Woodbrook Lane
Philadelphia, PA 19119
215-247-5533

Texas

Family Court Services
Dallas County Juvenile Dept.
Third Floor
Old Court House
Dallas, TX 75202
214-749-8674

Family Mediation
P.O. Box 8126
San Antonio, TX 78208
512-222-9358

Virginia

Center for Separation and Divorce Mediation
3705 S. George Mason Dr.
Falls Church, VA 22041
703-998-5552

Divorce and Marital Stress Clinic
1925 N. Lynn St.
Arlington, VA 22209
703-528-3900

Divorce Mediation Service
4121 Meadowdale Blvd.
Richmond, VA 23214
804-359-1513

Family Mediation Service
6823 Sorrell St.
McLean, VA 22101
703-442-9090/9066

Washington Mediation Service
Box 103
Great Falls, VA 22066
703-442-9090

Washington

Neutral Ground
P.O. Box 1222
717½ N. Main St.
Walla Walla, WA 99362
509-522-0399

Northwest Mediation Service
Nancy Kaplan, M.S.W., Executive Director
27-100 N.E.
Bellevue, WA 98004
206-455-3989

Wisconsin

Family/Divorce Counseling and Mediation Services
Ann L. Milne, A.C.S.W.
314 E. Mifflin St.
Madison, WI 53703
608-251-0604

Dane County Family Court Counseling Service
210 Monona Ave.
311A City-County Bldg.
Madison, WI 53709
608-266-4607

For future editions, the author would appreciate receiving information on divorce mediation sources for the
following states: Alabama, Alaska, Arkansas, Idaho,
Kansas, Kentucky, Louisiana, Maine, Michigan, Missis-
sippi, Missouri, Montana, Nevada, New Hampshire,
New Mexico, North Dakota, Oklahoma, Rhode Island,
South Carolina, South Dakota, Tennessee, Utah, Ver-
mont, West Virginia, and Wyoming.

Appendix B

Shared Custody Laws in the United States

What follows is a breakdown of states whose legislatures have passed (as of 1981) some kind of statute allowing for joint custody. New York attorney Doris Jonas Freed, chair of the Custody Committee of the American Bar Association, Family Law Section, has kindly made her yearly update available. She warns that nearly all fifty states have bills concerning joint custody in the hopper and that the current status of legislation in a particular state can change. Most states (with a few notable exceptions) allow the judiciary to decide in favor of joint custody on a case-by-case basis.

States with Some Form of Shared Custody on the Books:

California, Connecticut, Hawaii, Iowa, Kansas, Kentucky, Massachusetts, Michigan, Minnesota, Montana, Nevada, New Hampshire, New Mexico, North Carolina, Ohio, Oregon, Texas, and Wisconsin.

States Whose *Courts* Have Been Generally Supportive of Shared Custody (this list includes some states with no official shared custody legislative policy):

Alaska, Arizona, California, Hawaii, Michigan, Nevada, New Hampshire, New Jersey, North Dakota, Wisconsin, and Utah.

States That in the Past Have Generally Expressed Hostility Toward the Concept of Shared Custody in Child Custody Decisions:

Alabama, Florida, Georgia, and Louisiana.

Appendix C

Sample Shared Custody and Property Settlement Agreement

What follows is an actual shared custody and property settlement agreement filed by Los Angeles divorce attorney Donald S. Eisenberg for his clients. Names and identifying details have been deleted to protect the couple's privacy. As filed with the court, it was a sixteen-page document describing the distribution of property and the custody arrangements for the couple's three children.

As with many middle-class parents, their material possessions consisted of two vehicles, a small house, some furniture, and a small business; they were encumbered by a mortgage and about $1,800 in credit-card debts. Wealthier parents would, of course, require a more complicated agreement, but this sample offers parents and their attorneys suggestions on how both property and the care of children can be divided equitably—and in the best interests of all concerned.

MARITAL TERMINATION AGREEMENT

THIS AGREEMENT is made and entered into this _____ day of _____, by and between _____ (hereinafter referred to as "Husband"), and _____ (hereinafter referred to as "Wife").

This Agreement is made with reference to the following facts:

1. The parties were married at _____ on _____ and ever since have been and now are Husband and Wife.

2. Irreconciliable differences have arisen between the parties, as a result of which they have separated and ceased to live together as Husband and Wife as of _____, which is _____ years, _____ days from the date of their marriage. They are now agreed and intend to live apart permanently.

3. Husband's social security number is _____ and Wife's social security number is _____ .

4. The parties desire by this Agreement to effect a complete and final division of their property, and to resolve all rights and obligations relating to spousal support or maintenance. The parties, in effecting this Agreement, have endeavored to divide their property equally so that such a division would result in no taxable transfer by either party. The parties further intend to relinquish any and all past, present, or future claims that each may have against the property or estate of the other party and his or her executors, administrators, representatives, successors, and assigns, except as otherwise provided herein.

5. An action for the dissolution of marriage of the parties is currently pending in the Superior Court of the State of _____ in and for the County of _____ bearing Case No. _____ wherein Husband is the Petitioner and Wife is the Respondent. Wife has not appeared in the action as of the date of this Agreement.

NOW, THEREFORE, in consideration of each and all of the promises, covenants, agreements, waivers, and transfers hereto, each such provision being given in consideration for each other provision, it is mutually agreed as follows:

I. GENERAL PROVISIONS

It is the intention of the parties hereto that this Agreement shall specifically settle for all time each and all of the rights, duties, and obligations of each party with respect to the other, and determine, divide, sell, or otherwise transfer, as set forth herein, all of the rights in and to or with respect to the property which each party now owns, possesses an interest in, or may own or possess an interest in in the future. This Agreement may be submitted by either party for approval by the Court or merger by the Court in the judgment in the action now pending for dissolution of their marriage, but this Agreement shall not in any way depend for its effectiveness upon such approval or merger.

In consideration for the execution of this Agreement by each of the parties hereto, each party waives, releases, and forever discharges the other party, his or her heirs, executors, administrators, assigns, property, and estate, from any and all rights, claims, demands, and obligations of every kind and nature for community property, homestead, inheritance, family allowance, letters of administration, dissent, and distribution; and each party is and shall be forever barred from having or asserting any such right, claim, demand, or obligation at any time hereafter for any purpose, except as may be provided by Will or Codicil executed after the date of this Agreement. Except as may be herein provided to the contrary, the parties hereto shall and do mutually waive, release, and forever discharge the other from any and all actions, suits, debts, claims, demands, and obligations whatsoever both in law and in equity, which either of them has had, now has, or may at any time in the future have against the other upon or by reason of any matter, cause, or thing, prior to the execution of this Agreement.

Each of the parties hereto does hereby waive with respect to the other the provisions of Section _____ of the _____ Civil Code relating to claims reflected by a General Release, and, except as aforesaid, this Agreement is intended to and does release all claims, whether known or unknown, which either of the parties may have against the other.

This Agreement is entered into freely and voluntarily by each of the parties, free from any duress, constraint, or influence of any kind or nature, on the part of either.

Each party represents that he/she has, at all material times prior to this Agreement, had the opportunity to consult with and to be represented by an independent attorney, selected by such party. Wife acknowledges that this Agreement has been prepared by _____ , attorney for Husband.

INTERLOCUTORY JUDGMENT OF DISSOLUTION OF MARRIAGE

I. DIVISION OF COMMUNITY PROPERTY
A. *Nature and Extent of Property:*

The parties acknowledge and agree that each has had an ample opportunity to investigate the nature, extent, and value of each and every item of property which either party now owns, possesses an interest in, or claims to own or possess an interest in. Each party has determined that except as otherwise herein expressly set forth, all of the community property of the parties, including furniture and furnishings, clothing, jewelry, and personal effects, has previously been distributed by and between the parties.

Neither party has made any representation to the other as to the value of the community property or other property or with respect to any property, and each party has relied on his or her own investigation and judgment with respect to all property and all matters herein contained. Further, the parties agree that the community property hereinafter set forth for each party represents, in each party's estimation, a fair and equal division of the community property of the parties.

B. *Community Personal Property to Respondent:*

Respondent is awarded as her sole and separate property the following items of personalty:

1. All of the furniture and furnishings, personal effects, jewelry, and all other items of personalty now in the possession of Respondent at _____ .

2. The 1980 _____ automobile, bearing license number _____ .

C. *Community Personal Property to Petitioner:*

Petitioner is awarded as his sole and separate property the following items of personalty:

1. All of the furniture and furnishings currently in his possession.

2. The 1979 _____ automobile, bearing license number _____ .

3. All of the right, title, and interest in and to Petitioner's business, and any goodwill which may be attached thereto, together with all of the personal physical assets of said business, to wit:

a. The 1978 _____ pickup, bearing license number _____ .

b. Tools and equipment.

D. *Community Debts:*

The debts of the parties shall be apportioned in the following manner:

1. Petitioner shall pay the debt to _____ in the principal balance of approximately _____ which Petitioner has incurred on behalf of his business. With respect to said debt, Petitioner does hereby indemnify and hold Respondent harmless from any and all claims, liabilities, and obligations arising out of the payment of such debt; and further covenants and agrees that if any claim, action, or proceeding is hereafter brought seeking to hold the Respondent liable on account of such debt, the Petitioner will, at his sole expense, defend Respondent against any such claim, action, or proceeding, whether or not well founded.

2. Respondent shall pay the following obligations, as her sole and separate responsibility:

a. J. C. Penney   Approximately $300.00
b. Sears   "   300.00
c. BankAmericard/Visa   " $1,000.00

Respondent does hereby indemnify and hold Petitioner harmless from any and all claims, liabilities, and obligations arising out of the payment of such debts; and further covenants and agrees that if any claim, action, or proceeding is hereafter brought seeking to hold the Petitioner liable on account of such debt, the Respondent will, at her sole expense, defend Petitioner against any such claim, action, or proceeding, whether or not well founded.

II. DIVISION OF FAMILY RESIDENCE
A. *Ownership:*

The residence of the parties located at _____ shall be divided equally in kind so that each party will have an undivided one-half interest as Tenant in Common. Concurrently with the execution of this Agreement, the parties agree to execute a Deed to the property to themselves as Tenants in Common and to have the same recorded immediately thereafter.

B. *Occupancy:*

Respondent is awarded the exclusive occupancy of the family residence until the occurrence of the earliest of the following events:

1. All of the minor children of the parties have attained the age of eighteen (18) years.

2. Respondent moves from or abandons the residence.

3. The sale of the residence by mutual agreement of Petitioner and Respondent.

4. Respondent resides with or cohabits with another Adult for a period in excess of 30 continuous days without the express consent of Petitioner.

5. The death or remarriage of Respondent.

C. *Maintenance and Repairs:*

1. During the term of Respondent's occupancy of the family residence Respondent shall maintain the family residence in good repair and shall be solely responsible for all normal expenses associated with the maintenance and operation of the home. In the event a major repair or improvement becomes necessary, i.e., such as a new roof, Respondent shall consult with and obtain the consent of Petitioner before making any such repair or improvement.

2. In the event of the condemnation of the property or its destruction, the proceeds remaining after payment of all liens, encumbrances, and reasonable necessary costs of sale shall be divided in accordance with Subparagraph F hereof. In the event of the partial destruction of the family residence covered by insurance, any insurance proceeds shall be used for the repair and/or restoration of such residence to its former condition, and any remaining funds shall be used to reduce the amount of any existing encumbrances in accordance with the applicable terms of any outstanding notes and deeds of trust.

D. *Mortgage Payments:*

Until the family residence is sold in accordance with the terms of this Order, Respondent shall be responsible to make all required monthly mortgage payments and shall pay all property taxes and assessments against the property. It is acknowledged by the parties that Petitioner's obligations to pay child support, as set forth in Paragraph IIIB below, reflect a contribution by Petitioner to the mortgage payment on the family residence. In addition, Respondent acknowledges that her obligation with respect to the mortgage payments on the family residence reflects the fair rental value of her use and occupancy of said residence, and therefore no reimbursement shall lie on account of any payments with respect to the petitioner's one-half ownership in the property.

E. *Sale of Residence:*

On the first of any of the events described in Paragraph IIB to occur (other than the death of Respondent), either party shall have the option to purchase the other party's interest in the residence by giving written notice to the other within thirty (30) days of such occurrence. In the event the parties are unable to agree on a purchase price or on which party is to purchase the residence, then the residence shall be immediately offered for sale to a third party and the proceeds from such sale shall be divided in accordance with Subparagraph F below. In the event of the death of Respondent, Petitioner shall have the right to purchase the residence from the estate of Respondent.

F. *Division of Proceeds:*

Upon the sale or other disposition of the family residence as a result of the occurrence of any of the conditions set forth in this Order, the proceeds from such sale or distribution shall be divided as follows:

1. All liens, encumbrances, taxes, and charges (including escrow fees and costs of sale, if any) shall be deducted from the gross proceeds.

2. The net proceeds remaining shall be divided in two equal portions representing one-half of said proceeds, and each half shall be allocated to the account of Petitioner and Respondent respectively.

3. In addition, Petitioner shall be credited with the following sums:

    a. Four Thousand Dollars ($4,000.00) on account of the current value of one-half the furniture and furnishings awarded to Respondent.

    b. Eight Hundred Dollars ($800.00) on account of sums withdrawn from the Trust Account held for the benefit of the minor children.

    c. Seven Hundred Seventy-five Dollars ($775.00) on account of sums advanced by Petitioner following separation on account of debts incurred by Respondent. Respondent's account shall be debited in the sum of Five Thousand Five Hundred Seventy-five Dollars ($5,575.00) on account of the foregoing items. Petitioner shall receive no interest on the forbearance from receipt of these sums, such forbearance being given in consideration for the repayment from the proceeds of the sale of the family residence.

G. *Obligations Respecting the Family Residence:*

Although Respondent shall be solely liable for the payments due on the family residence, which such payments include at the present time payments on a note secured by First Deed of Trust to _____ and payments on a note secured by Second Deed of Trust to _____ , Petitioner and Respondent shall both remain liable on said obligation. Consequently, in the event Respondent is unable or unwilling to make any required mortgage or property tax payment, Petitioner shall have the right to make such payment directly to the creditor and shall be entitled to reimbursement from Respondent for each such payment.

III. SUPPORT AND MAINTENANCE
A. *Spousal Support:*

1. Each party has therefore waived, now and forever, any and all rights to spousal support both temporary and permanent, and the court orders that neither party shall take any sum from the other on account of spousal support.

B. *Child Support:*

1. The parties have three children of their marriage whose names, ages, and dates of birth are set forth as follows:

_____ , age six years, born 1973;

_____ , age four years, born 1975;

_____ , age two years, born 1977.

These above-named children are the only issue of said marriage; there are no other children living or dead.

2. Petitioner shall pay directly to Respondent as and for the support and maintenance of the minor children the following amounts:

a. From March 30, 1980, until the date on which the obligation owed to _____ (set forth in Paragraph IIG hereinabove) is paid in full, Petitioner shall pay the sum of Four Hundred Thirteen Dollars ($413.00) per month.

b. From and after the date of the extinguishment of the joint obligation to _____ , Petitioner shall pay directly to Respondent, as and for child support of the minor children, the sum of Three Hundred Dollars ($300.00) per month, payable monthly on the first day of each month and continuing unabated until the last such child of the marriage shall have passed his/her eighteenth (18th) birthday.

3. The parties understand that all obligations for child support are by statute subject to modification by order of the court. Notwithstanding this fact, however, the court makes the above Order for child support in view of the age, income, earning capacity, and obligations of each respective party and the needs of the children. If, at any time, either party shall deem it necessary, for whatever reason, to seek a reduction or increase in the child support obligation set forth herein, then, in that event, the court shall be referred to the provisions of this paragraph so that such court may know the intention of the parties and the court in setting the above support order, the relationship which the support set forth herein bears to mortgage on the joint family residence, as well as the needs and requirements of Respondent and the minor children for the foreseeable future.

a. All obligations to pay child support shall continue until there are no children of the marriage alive, unmarried, or under the age of eighteen (18), at which time all obligations shall cease.

IV. PARENTING RESPONSIBILITIES

The parties herein have three children of their marriage: _____ age 6, _____ age 4, and _____ age 2. Each parent believes himself/herself and the other to be fit parents and recognizes the unique contribution which each has to offer the children. The court therefore orders that each party shall continue to share the responsibility for the care of our children and each fully participate in all of the major decisions affecting their health, education, and welfare, while disrupting their life pattern as little as possible. The parties shall share the joint custody of the children with only the most minimal necessary formality in scheduling time with them, subject to consideration of schedules and the necessity of reasonable notice, in order to retain a flexible opportunity for each of them to be with the children and help raise them.

In consideration of the Agreement of the parties, the court further orders as follows:

A. *Custody and Residence:*

1. Petitioner, _____, and Respondent, _____, shall share the joint physical and legal custody of their children.

2. The children shall principally reside with Respondent as further set forth below.

3. Should any change of circumstance occur which materially affects the care of the children or Petitioner's access to them, the residence of the children shall be reconsidered in light of the then existing circumstances. Should either Petitioner or Respondent move from the _____ area, or change jobs, every effort shall be made to facilitate the continued exercise of joint custody so that the children continue to enjoy the benefits of both parents. In considering future living arrangements for the children, Petitioner and Respondent shall have due regard for the children's preference and the environment and care which each can provide.

4. It is anticipated that Petitioner, as well as Respondent, shall spend regular and considerable time with the children. Petitioner shall be with the children and responsible for their care at least two weekends (Friday night, Saturday, Saturday night, and Sunday) per month, the time and arrangements for which shall be agreed upon no later than the 25th day of the preceding month. Petitioner shall be responsible for the children at least one entire week during the months of June, July, and August, the time and arrangements of which shall be agreed upon by the 25th day of the preceding month. Peti-

tioner shall also spend time with the children, whenever possible, on their birthdays and on major holidays.

5. It is expressly understood and agreed by the parties that the above enumerated times that Petitioner shall be with the children and responsible for their immediate care are minimums, and shall be a standard. Petitioner's employment as self-employed requires flexibility in child-care responsibilities and parental involvement. Each of the parties has acknowledged that, as currently constituted, Petitioner leaves for work prior to the children's appointed school and day-care activities and that he is required to work on Saturdays in order to meet the needs and responsibilities for himself and the children. Therefore, the terms of this order are to be liberally interpreted to allow the children the maximum of benefit to be derived from the love, concern, and care of both Petitioner and Respondent. Neither parent shall assume that the other parent is required to care for the children unless agreed. Nor shall either parent abdicate responsibility to parent the children based on the inconvenience or difficulty which such care may require of that parent.

B. *Dependency Exemptions:*

1. So long as Petitioner shall be paying the support which is set forth in Paragraph IIIB hereinabove, he shall be entitled to claim the dependency exemption for each child on his federal and state income tax returns. If at any time Petitioner shall, by agreement of the parties, cease to provide the support set forth herein, or such support shall not be required of Petitioner, then Respondent shall be entitled to the dependency exemption for each such child for whom support is no longer continuing by their agreement.

C. *Medical and Life Insurance:*

Both Petitioner and Respondent shall keep and maintain such life insurance, insuring their lives as they can reasonably afford, naming the children as the beneficiaries on each such policy, so that neither parent shall unreasonably burden the other in the event of the untimely death of one of the parents. Petitioner and Respondent shall mutually determine what, if any, health insurance is appropriate for the care of the minor children and shall divide the cost of such insurance equally between them.

D. *Emergencies:*

1. Both parties shall mutually make major decisions affecting the children, including but not exclusively to authorize major medical, dental, institutional, psychiatric, or other care, and schooling and educational placements; to inspect and receive school records; to inspect and receive medical records; to withhold or give consent to marry; and to permit enlistment in the armed forces.

2. Notwithstanding the above, the parent in whose actual physical custody any child subject to this Order is at any particular time shall have sole responsibility for meeting any medical or dental emergency which may arise, and in such emergency, the permission of both parents is not and shall not be necessary.

E. *Disputes:*

In the event any dispute or disagreement arises regarding the terms and conditions of custody as set forth herein, the parties mutually agree to jointly seek the advice of a mutually agreed-upon mediator or the office of the Family Court Conciliation Service for the resolution of the conflict. Neither party shall seek or institute proceedings for the modification of this custody arrangement by litigation without first having so sought and attempted to resolve their conflicts through mediation.

V. MISCELLANEOUS

A. *Community Debts:*

Except as otherwise provided in this Agreement, each party therefore releases the other from any and all liabilities, debts, or obligations that have been or will be incurred by that party, and each party shall indemnify and hold the other harmless from such debts, liabilities, and obligations. Furthermore, each party agrees that if any claim, action, or proceeding is hereafter brought seeking to hold the other liable on account of any such liability or obligation, then the party who incurred that obligation will at his or her sole expense defend the other party against any claim, demand, or threat thereof, whether or not well founded, and will hold the other party harmless therefrom. That defense, if any, shall include the payment of reasonable attorney's fees and costs incurred in connection with the action.

Dated: _____   _____

SUPERIOR COURT

Appendix D

Shared Custody Suggested Readings

For General Information About Shared Custody:

Galper, Miriam. *Joint Custody and Co-Parenting Handbook.*
Philadelphia: Running Press, 1980.
A series of reports from the trenches by parents who opted for
joint custody arrangements in the 1970s.

Ilfeld, Frederic W., Jr.; Holly Zingale Ilfeld; and John R. Alexander. "Does Joint Custody Work? A First Look at Outcome Data
of Relitigation." *American Journal of Psychiatry* 139:1 (January
1982): 62–66.

Ricci, Isolina, *Mom's House, Dad's House: Making Shared Custody Work.* New York: Macmillan, 1980. A therapist gives prescriptions for coparenting based on her years of clinical work.

Roman, Mel, et al. *The Disposable Parent: The Case for Joint Custody.* New York: Holt, Rinehart & Winston, 1978.
The authors throw down the gauntlet, challenging the opinions of
armies of "either/or" custody experts who claim sole custody best
serves the interests of children after their parents' divorce. The
studies presented directly contradict this notion.

Steinman, Susan. "The Experience of Children in a Joint Custody
Arrangement." *American Journal of Orthopsychiatry* 51 (1981):
403–14.

Woolley, Persia. *The Custody Handbook.* New York: Summit Books, 1979.
This book surveys many types of child custody arrangements, with special emphasis on sharing responsibility for children after their parents' divorce.

About Children of Divorce:

Briggs, Dorothy Corkille. *Your Child's Self-esteem.* New York: Dolphin Books, 1975.
This book is not about divorce per se, but offers sensible and specific information on child behavior and development. It is especially helpful for divorced parents to use as a yardstick for measuring normal childhood behavior at various ages. This is basic reading for parents—period—and a must for divorced mothers and fathers.

List, Julie. *The Day the Loving Stopped.* New York: Seaview Books, 1980.
A devastating account of the "typical" divorce and its effect on children.

Wallerstein, Judith S., and Joan Berlin Kelly. *Surviving the Breakup.* New York: Basic Books, 1980.
This book has the best information available to date on the impact of divorce on children. A must for parents who want to learn what not to do in the aftermath of their separation.

For Children of Divorce:

Bienenfeld, Florence. *My Mom and Dad Are Getting a Divorce.* By mail from EMC Corp., 180 E. 60th St., St. Paul, MN 55101. Price of $5.20 includes postage.
This book is illustrated with cartoon characters and helps both children and their parents cope with the emotional impact of divorce, offering positive ways of getting important issues out in the open.

Gardner, Richard A. *Children's Book About Divorce.* New York: Jason Aronson, 1970.
This book has become a semiclassic. It is written for children but will help parents anticipate questions and problems.

Grollman, Earl A. *Talking About Divorce and Separation.* Boston: Beacon Press, 1975.
This book is illustrated for children but has topic-by-topic explanations and guidelines for parents in the back section.

Richards, Arlene, and Irene Willis. *How to Get It Together When Your Parents Are Coming Apart.* New York: David McKay, 1976.
This book is aimed at helping teenagers deal with their parents' divorce.

For Divorced Mothers:

Singleton, Mary Ann. *Life After Marriage.* New York: Stein & Day, 1974.
A how-to guide for reorganizing life after divorce, with practical information on most subjects relating to single women and single mothers.

Women in Transition: A Feminist Handbook on Separation and Divorce. New York: Scribner's, 1975.
A practical approach to the many aspects of divorce; full of resource listings and addresses.

For Divorced Fathers:

Biller, Henry, and Dennis Meredith. *Father Power.* New York: David McKay, 1974.
Proof positive of the value—and necessity—of fathers' sharing significant roles with mothers in raising children. The book offers advice on the art of effective fathering. One chapter is devoted to divorced fathers, stepfathers, and single fathers.

Levine, James A. *Who Will Raise the Children? New Options for Fathers (and Mothers)*. Philadelphia and New York: Lippincott, 1976.
This is a general book about parenting and the need for fathers to participate in the lives of their children. Levine focuses one chapter on fathers and the issue of custody.

Silver, Gerald A., and Myrna Silver. *Weekend Fathers*. Los Angeles, Calif.: Stratford Press, 1981.
This book was generated by the authors' anger at a family-law system that favors mothers over fathers. The Silvers call for a presumption of joint custody and for a major overhaul of the adversary legal system.

About Divorce:

How to Do Your Own Divorce (editions for various states)
Many states are represented in the series by Nolo Press. These how-to books do not recommend that you divorce without legal representation. However, they give basic legal grounding regarding the law in your area—which can be crucial for child custody. To see if there is an edition for your state, check with Nolo Press, 950 Parker St., Berkeley, CA 94710. Tel.: 415-549-1976.

Hunt, Morton, and Bernice Hunt. *The Divorce Experience*. New York: Signet Books, 1979.
A good guide to understanding the emotional process of divorce.

Krantzler, Mel. *Creative Divorce*. New York: New American Library, 1975.
This best-selling classic gives first aid for the newly divorced.

Matthews, Joseph L. *After the Divorce*. Berkeley, Calif.: Nolo Press, 1981.
Similar in format to *How to Do Your Own Divorce,* this guide explains to laypeople how to change child-support orders, custody/visitation matters, and spousal support. The original edition was intended for California. Nolo Press, 950 Parker St., Berkeley, CA 94710. Tel.: 415-549-1976.

About Divorce Mediation and the Art of Negotiating:

Cohen, Herb. *You Can Negotiate Anything.* New York: Lyle Stuart, 1980.
This book is breezy and anecdotal, but has some useful pointers.

Coogler, O. J. *Structured Mediation in Divorce Settlement.* Lexington, Mass.: Lexington Books, 1978.
This book was written for marital mediators but appeals to a much wider audience of people interested in the nuts and bolts of resolving conflict through third-party intervention.

Haynes, John M. *Divorce Mediation: A Practical Guide for Therapists and Counselors.* New York: Springer Publishing, 1981.
Written primarily for the health professional, this book is useful to the layperson not only to familiarize him or her with the process of mediation but to offer comparison by which private mediators can be judged.

Irving, Howard H. *Divorce Mediation: The Rational Alternative.* Toronto: Personal Library Publishers, 1980.
This book presents a system of mediation that is being used in North America. It is written both for laypeople and for professionals in the divorce field.

Karrass, Chester L. *Give and Take.* New York: Thomas Y. Crowell, 1974.
———. *The Negotiating Game.* New York: Thomas Y. Crowell, 1970.
These two books focus on negotiating in the business arena but offer numerous negotiating strategies and tactics that can be used in settling domestic disputes.

Nierenberg, Gerard I. *Fundamentals of Negotiating.* New York: Hawthorn Books, 1973.
This book offers psychological skills and practical strategies for bargaining in business and personal negotiations.

About Stepparenting:

Baer, Jean. *The Second Wife.* New York: Doubleday, 1972.
A practical guide for dealing with the stressful situations in second marriages, including stepparenting and coping with former wives.

Maddox, Brenda. *The Half Parent.* New York: M. Evans, 1975.
This book focuses on legal questions of stepparenting and stepparent-stepchild relationships.

Simon, Ann. *Stepchild in the Family.* Indianapolis: Odyssey Press, 1964.
This book deals with what it is like to be a stepchild, including fears of relating to stepsiblings and stepparents.

Visher, Emily, and John Visher. *Stepfamilies: Myths and Realities.* New York: Lyle Stuart, 1980.
A husband-and-wife team warns against the myth of the "instant family" and other fairy tales of extended/blended families, and offers some prescriptions for making blended-family relationships more harmonious.

About Single Parenting:

Atkin, Edith, and Estelle Rubin. *Part-time Father.* New York: Vanguard Press, 1976.
A portion of this book discusses shared custody arrangements, but much of it focuses on how fathers can best cope when they do not live with their children.

Forman, Lynn. *The Divorced Mother's Guide.* New York: Berkeley Publishing, 1974.
A chatty book about pulling things together after divorce—specifically regarding children, self, career, dating, and friendships.

Knight, Brian M. *Enjoying Single Parenthood.* New York: Van Nostrand Rcinhold, 1980.
This paperback discusses a wide variety of single-parent situa-

tions, including parents who share the rights and responsibilities of parenthood after divorce.

Woolley, Persia. *Creative Survival for Single Mothers.* Milbrea, Calif.: Celestial Arts, 1975.
This book explores the experiences of single mothers with a refreshing lack of self-pity, and offers numerous coping strategies.

Index